IT'S LIKE THE LEGEND

IT'S LIKE THE LEGEND

Innu Women's Voices

Edited by

Nympha Byrne & Camille Fouillard

gynergy books

Technical editing: Jane Billinghurst
Cover illustration (detail): © Mary Ann Penashue
Cover & inside graphic: based on traditional designs created by Innu women, hand-painted on caribou-skin coats
Printed and bound in Canada

Gynergy books acknowledges financial support for our publishing activities from the Government of Canada through the Book Publishing Industry Development Program (BPIDP), and the Canada Council for the Arts.

Published by:
Women's Press
180 Bloor St. W. #1202
Toronto, Ontario, M5S 2V6 Canada
Managing Editor: Ruth Bradley-St-Cyr

The following contributions have been previously published and are reprinted by permission: Marie Pokue's "To the People I Lost" in MCC *Women's Concerns Report* (Winnipeg, MB: Mennonite Central Committee, May-June 1992), p. 5; Shanut Rich's "Mishtapeu" (under the title "Mistapeu") in *Innu Tipatshimun* (Sheshatshu, Lab.: Innu Resource Centre, June 1973); and Mary Jane Pasteen's "Women Speared the Caribou" & Mary Madeline Nuna's "Shaking Tents and *Anik-napeu*" can be found on the Innu Nation Web site at www.innu.ca.

Canadian Cataloguing in Publication Data
Main entry under title:
It's like the legend
    ISBN 0-921881-56-8
1. Naskapi women. 2. Naskapi Indians — Social conditions. I. Byrne, Nympha, 1962- II. Fouillard, Camille.
E99.N18I88 2000   306'.089'973   C00-950035-9

for the elders whose teachings we will pass on

and for our children,

Shunee, Roy, Shane, Kimberly

and Esmée

with love

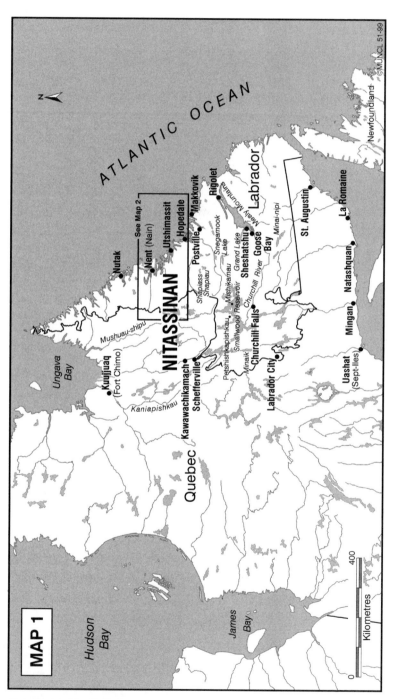

MAP 1

Cartographer: Charlie Conway

©MUNCL 51·99

Newfoundland

ATLANTIC OCEAN

Labrador

Nutak

See Map 2

Nent (Nain)

Utshimassit

Makkovik

Rigolet

Hopedale

Postville

La Romaine

St. Augustin

Natashquan

Mingan

Uashat (Sept-Iles)

NITASSINAN

Snegamook Lake

Shapiass Shapiau

Mealy Mountains

Minai-nipi

Grand Lake

Sheshatshiu

Goose Bay

Mishikamau Lake

Churchill River

Smallwood Reservoir

Petshishkapishkau

Minaik

Churchill Falls

Labrador City

Mushuau-shipu

Ungava Bay

Kuujjuaq (Fort Chimo)

Kawawachikamach

Schefferville

Kaniapishkau

Quebec

Hudson Bay

James Bay

400

Kilometres

0

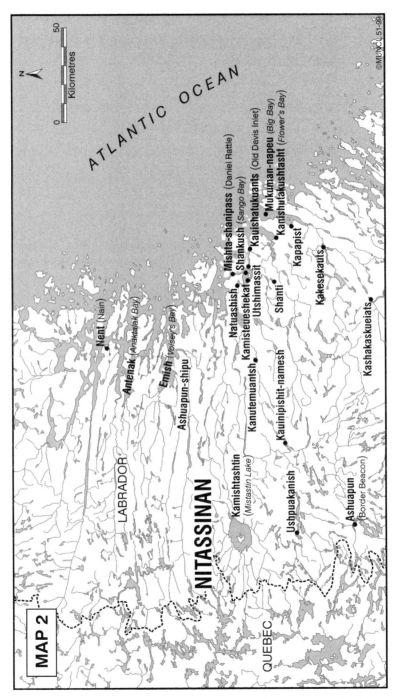

MAP 2

ATLANTIC OCEAN

LABRADOR

NITASSINAN

QUEBEC

Nent (Nain)

Antenak (Anaktalak Bay)

Emish (Voisey's Bay)

Ashuapun-shipu

Natuashish

Kamisteushekat

Kanutemuantsh

Mishta-shanipass (Daniel Rattle)

Shankush (Sango Bay)

Utshimassit

Kauishatukuants (Old Davis Inlet)

Mukuman-napeu (Big Bay)

Kanishtuifakushtasht (Flower's Bay)

Kapapist

Kakesekauts

Shanti

Kauinipishit-namesh

Kashakaskueiats

Kamishtashtin (Mistastin Lake)

Ushpuakanish

Ashuapun (Border Beacon)

Kilometres

0   50

N

©MUNCL 51-99

Cartographer: Charlie Conway

Acknowledgements

We are grateful to all the women who gave their stories. We are deeply honoured by the trust they placed in us to carry their words gently to the published page.

Many people helped us see this project come to life step by step. Innu Nation presidents Katie Rich and Peter Penashue, as well as the executive director of the Innu Nation, Germaine Benuen, provided moral and financial support.

Joy Scheifele and the Mennonite Central Committee office in Goose Bay provided computer and fax assistance. Joyce Marshall and Innushare donated a computer to the project. Laurie Tretina served as a cyberspace liaison person, a patient go-between for too many e-mail messages. Grace Bavington and Roberta Buchanan encouraged us from the very beginning and provided us with the gift of Winnifred Mellor, who entered much of the material from Sheshatshu women on the computer. Marguerite Mackenzie gave us advice on how to standardize Innu-aimun spellings. Julie Brittain helped serendipitously to bring us together to work on the final manuscript. Our gratitude goes out to Peter Armitage for all his computer advice and for his work on the maps and toponyms.

Thanks go out to many people for their help in compiling the photographs of all the contributors: Tom Green for his photos of Mary Jane Nui, Mary Georgette Mistenapeo and Charlotte Gregoire; Theresa Penashue and Jose Mailhot for the picture of Shanut Rich; and Joel Rich for the pictures of Cecile Rich and Elizabeth Rich.

We are grateful to Harold Hiscock and the Department of Canadian Heritage for providing funding for the projet.

Finally, we are thankful to the spirit of our friendship for her guidance along this journey.

Contents

Introduction

Nympha Byrne & Camille Fouillard

The Innu are a people who inhabit Nitassinan, the Innu word for "our homeland," which encompasses a large portion of the Quebec-Labrador peninsula. Until recently, the Innu were known as the Montagnais and Naskapi people. Today the Innu number approximately 15,000. The majority live in 11 communities in Quebec, mostly along the North Shore of the St. Lawrence River; about 1,500 live in two communities in Labrador. Utshimassits (*Oots-shee-mah-seets*), or Place of the Boss, is the Innu name for the community of Davis Inlet, on the northeastern coast of Labrador. Sheshatshu (*Shay-shah-joo*) is located in central Labrador, at the western end of Atatshuinipek^u (Lake Melville).

Before settlement became a way of life in the 1960s, the Labrador Innu lived a nomadic life for nine months of the year. During the summer, they would gather at various meeting places, including Old Davis Inlet (Kauishatukuants), North West River (across the river from Sheshatshu) and Sept Iles (Uashat). The more northerly barrens of Labrador are the traditional territory of the Mushuau Innu, or People of the Barrens. About half the Mushuau Innu settled in Utshimassits. The other half settled in Kawawashikamach, near Schefferville. A few Mushuau Innu families also live in Sheshatshu.

This book came to life to give a voice to Innu women. Sometimes we count on just one person to tell the stories, but everyone has a story and too often there is no one to listen. Even those people who seem so quiet have a lot of stories to tell. As well, since the nomadic way of life of the Labrador Innu came to an end, it seems that only the men have told stories. Only the men have had a voice. We wanted to hear the stories of the women. Innu storytelling is rich and creative — full of heart. We felt that the women were unaware of the power of their words. We wanted to help them discover this strength.

This is the first book of Innu stories by Innu women from Labrador. We want to pass these stories on to our children — including Innu, other First Nations and Canadian children. We want them to know the history of the Innu. Previous books on the Innu have resulted from the work of non-Innu people who came to research the Innu and to write our stories, often from a non-Innu point of view. These visitors have published a number of books, which are interesting but have mostly focused on the lives of men. They have largely left out the stories of Innu women.

Some of the things these visitors wrote have left many Innu baffled. They don't understand what has been written about them. Have the visitors really understood the Innu and their culture? As well, some of these books were based on research from the writings of missionaries. These Christians were not interested in our culture. They wanted only to destroy the soul of our culture, such as the sacred rituals of the drum dance and the shaking tent.

In the fall of 1994, Nympha invited Camille to work with her to produce a book by Innu women. Nympha is a Mushuau Innu from Utshimassits, now living in Goose Bay. Camille, a French-Canadian woman who makes her home in St. John's, Newfoundland, has lived and worked with the Labrador Innu for over 15 years. Both of us had worked on the 1992 People's Inquiry, a self-examination by the people of Utshimassits after a house fire killed six children. This inquiry revealed to us and to many others the power of using words, of telling the personal story.

We both had dreams of what we wanted to include in our book. Nympha wanted to collect stories from the elders before they passed away. Camille had a file of transcripts and writings from Sheshatshu women during the Innu campaign to stop the establishment of a NATO military flight-training base on their land in the late 1980s and early 1990s. The memories of the elders are priceless resources that might otherwise be lost; the stories of Innu protests documented a turning point in Innu history and cried out for publication.

We set out to produce a book that would honour and build on the Innu storytelling tradition. We wanted to hear whatever the women had to share. We did not set boundaries or restrictions about form or content. Our aim was to listen and learn. We wanted to be as inclusive as possible, that is, to include words from all the women who shared stories and writings with us. At the same time, we wanted to produce an anthology that would appeal to a wide audience. This dual goal presented us with many challenges.

In February 1995, aided by a small grant from the Department of Canadian Heritage, we sent letters to 60 women in Sheshatshu and Utshimassits, outlining the project and inviting them to share their stories with us. In the spring we visited both communities to promote the project, to gather women's input and to encourage women of all ages to contribute. Public, kitchen and tent meetings were held. We posted announcements on community radio and television channels, and distributed posters and flyers in public buildings and to each household in both communities. Women told us they loved the idea of a women's book.

Women immediately began to submit writing or to request that Nympha sit with them to record their words. Over the next couple of years, we nagged many others to contribute to the book. We approached Sheshatshu women to submit their protest stories from the 1980s and to provide us with updates. We received some written submissions in Innu-aimun, the language of the Innu. Others were in English and some came in both languages. We also borrowed writing from other sources: a poem from a Mennonite Central Committee newsletter, a legend from an Innu Resource Centre newsletter and memoirs from the Innu Nation home page on the Internet. Some of these helped us to reach further back in time to fill some obvious gaps in our collection. We also hoped that their inclusion in the anthology would provide these stories with a larger audience.

Our contributors include elders and girls, single and lesbian women, wives, partners, mothers, grandmothers and great-grandmothers. They include a receptionist, hunters, a chief, informal leaders, a peacekeeper, teachers, addictions counsel-lors, social workers, students and homemakers.

Nympha carried out the laborious task of transcribing the stories she collected on tape in Innu-aimun. She wrote down word for word what the women said. Sometimes the women introduced many different people into their stories. It was not always clear who they were and what their relationships were to the storytellers. Nympha had to return to the women to check these and other details. Nympha had been reluctant to stop the women as they spoke, because she did not want to break the flow of their stories, or to send the storytellers off into other tales. Once the transcriptions were completed, Nympha translated the stories into English. Many times she ran into Innu words that did not translate into English. Sometimes she had to explain the word in sentences. Sometimes she had to pick the closest English equivalent. As she translated, Nympha also began the process of editing.

The editing process was a long, arduous task. Both of us worked on the stories separately and compared notes by phone, e-mail or snail mail. Finally, in September 1998, we decided to put aside two weeks to focus on the editing without interruption. Early on in the process, we made a decision to try to leave the stories alone as much as possible as we edited. We wanted to keep the rhythm and the flow of the women's storylines intact. We removed repetition when we felt it served no purpose on the written page. When the storyteller digressed too much, we took out the tangents we felt distracted the reader from the real story. In terms of content, it was often clearer to Nympha what to edit, what to keep in or take out, because she knew the people, the language, the culture and the communities intimately. In cases where we made any substantial changes to the original stories, we asked the contributors to review them and asked for their approval. Camille's editing involved standardizing grammar and punctuation. We had thought to leave the English grammar alone, that it would lend a more authentic tone to the stories if we left them told the way many Innu use English as a second language. In the end, we were concerned that the storytellers might appear at a disadvantage in English.

Distracted by our lives, we found the project dragged on for three years. Nympha returned to school to obtain high-school and college diplomas, while Camille earned a living and gave birth to a baby girl. As well, during one visit to Utshimassits to work on the project, Nympha was arrested and jailed. Fortunately, this was not a total loss for the book, as the time and the experience served as inspiration for writings by Nympha, which are included in this collection.

This compilation includes a variety of genres, although the majority would be categorized as memoirs. Also included are legends that have been told for as long as our people have been on this land. Others are excerpts from personal journals, as well as poetry, essays, speeches and testimonies. A few of these writings have been previously published; other stories have been told at various gatherings both within the communities and to the outside world.

The memoirs tell the tale of life for the Innu both before and after community settlement, when Innu land became coveted for large-scale industrial developments and the Innu lost access to some of their territories. The stories told in the memoirs range in subject, from early childhood memories of living off the land to, among other things, first loves, first encounters with Euro-Canadians, being evacuated to hospital as unilingual children, going to a foreign school, a priest grabbing a drum from an elder during a sacred dance, surviving a violent marriage, taking care of the animal spirits, carrying fire before matches, being educated as an Innu, coming out as a lesbian.

A number of writings stem from the late 1980s, when the Innu made a name for themselves in Canada and across the world for their spectacular acts of civil disobedience. These actions continued into the 1990s and have forced governments in both Canada and Europe to pay attention more than once. What is not known by many is the significant role the women played in these acts of rebellion and in the assertion of Innu authority over their land. The women had been silent for decades. They began to speak out and act.

The first protest occurred in 1987, when a group of Innu hunters, women, children and elders headed for Akamiuapishku (the Mealy Mountains) to shoot caribou where their ancestors had always shot caribou, but where the Newfoundland government insisted the hunting was illegal. It was the women and children who sat on the caribou to prevent the wildlife officers from confiscating them as evidence of illegal hunting.

The following year, the Canadian and Newfoundland governments decided to invite their European allies to set up a NATO superbase, to conduct up to 40,000 military test flights and to practise aerial combat and bombings on Innu land. The Innu decided to confront NATO's military might head on. For years they had been the brunt of 6,500 low-level test flights at speeds of up to 900 kilometres an hour and as low as 30 metres above the ground. The noise of the killer planes startled hunters, terrified children, frightened the animals and polluted the waterways. Canada's plans for a massive NATO training centre in their midst was the last straw for the Innu. Hundreds camped on the grounds of the air base at Goose Bay. On more than 15 occasions, they marched onto the runways to halt the killer jets during their takeoffs. Repeatedly, they also invaded the forbidden bombing range near Minai-nipi (Burbot Lake).

Sanctioned by the elders, it was the women, with a couple of youth, who initiated these actions. Elderly woman sang hymns as they marched onto the runways, while younger women carried placards and babies, held the hands of their children and grand-children, walked side by side with the men. When the media cameras arrived, the official male leadership stepped into the spotlight. Innu women were arrested and spent time in jail for these actions. In court they succeeded, along with the men, in embarrassing the legal system. For example, at one trial, they refused to speak English in court and ensured that no Innu interpreter could be found to provide translation. Through their actions, they attracted worldwide attention. Plans for the NATO base were cancelled and the federal government was forced to put the Innu on the shortlist for land-claims negotiations.

The actions against NATO military flight training became part of a far-reaching Innu campaign for public support. The actions stirred a wave of unity among the Innu people on both sides of the Quebec-Labrador border, and spurred a solidarity movement of pacifist, environmental, women's, aboriginal-support, human-rights and church groups across North America and Europe. For the first time, Innu women were sent out to speak at events, and they quickly gained a reputation as articulate spokespersons for the Innu cause. Court testimonies, speeches, essays and journal writings by Innu women of these times are included in this book.

Innu women took another decisive action in December 1993, when a group of Mushuau Innu women evicted a judge and his court from Utshimassits. The previous year, two young Innu, one of them a woman, had taken the initiative to travel to the First Nations Tribal Police Institute in British Columbia to train as peacekeepers. Upon their return, the Mushuau Innu Band Council approached the provincial government for recognition of the two peacekeepers and to coordinate six weeks of on-the-job training for them, an arrangement made with the RCMP in other places in Canada. Instead of celebrating the accomplishments of the two Innu, the province refused to recognize them and threatened to charge them with impersonating police officers. Chief Katie Rich hired them anyway to work as peacekeepers for the band council.

In the summer of 1994, Newfoundland justice minister Ed Roberts attempted to bring the court back to Utshimassits. On two occasions, he ordered RCMP officers in full riot gear to escort a judge back into the community to hold court. The federal government also cooperated by providing National Defence helicopters to bring in the 100 police officers and court personnel. The minister of National Defence also issued an order to close the airstrip in Utshimassits and to stop all traffic within 10 kilometres of the community to keep the media and their cameras out. The Innu resisted this invasion and prevented all military aircraft from landing. Roberts abandoned his plans, but travelled to Ottawa and convinced the federal government to suspend all talks with the Innu, including negotiations for land rights, devolution and relocation of the Utshimassiu Innu to Natuashish (Sango Pond). However, the province was embarrassed into negotiating a justice agreement with the Mushuau Innu. Signed the following spring, that agreement finally recognized the Innu peacekeepers as legitimate police officers. An arrangement was worked out for them to police the community along with the RCMP. The community celebrated the agreement with a drum dance, where they forced Roberts to dance.

Around that same time, three women, including Nympha, were arrested in Utshimassits for their role in evicting the judge. Nympha's writings in jail about this experience are included in this anthology, as are excerpts from the testimonies of the three women in court.

These direct actions gave many Innu the courage and the strength to begin to fight their inner demons as well. A healing movement began in the early 1990s and swept through both Sheshatshu and Utshimassits. In Utshimassits, the 1992 tragedy of the house fire and ensuing People's Inquiry also spurred many to stop drinking and begin to put their lives in order. Many Innu from both communities — men, women, children and occasionally all of them together as whole families — availed themselves of addiction-treatment services and programs outside the province, within the communities and in *nutshimit* (the country).

Dozens of community workers were trained in addictions counselling. They began to organize healing programs that involved the elders and their knowledge of traditional Innu spirituality and values. Women began to create safe spaces for the cries of anguish of so many, particularly as stories of sexual abuse surfaced. Women brought the issue of sexual abuse out of the closet, by telling their own stories, confronting their abusers and supporting each other through the pain. While the struggle with addictions continues in both Sheshatshu and Utshimassits, a number of people have learned to live more healthy lives and now serve as role models, providing hope for the future. Many of these are women who have come to see their healing as a lifelong journey through which they must continue to help themselves and support each other. A number of personal stories and poems about healing are included in this anthology.

In the meantime, external threats to the Innu and their culture continue. The federal government has approved an increase in low-level flights to 18,000 per year. Construction of a nickel mine at Emish (Voisey's Bay) is scheduled to begin as this book goes to press. Premiers Brian Tobin and Lucien Bouchard are discussing a Lower Churchill hydro-electric development on a number of Innu rivers. Forestry companies such as Abitibi-Price and Kruger are eager to begin clear-cutting Innu forests. The Newfoundland government plans to plough a trans-Labrador highway through southeastern Nitassinan to provide access to coastal communities and to open the area to industry. A national park is planned for the Akamiuapishk^u area. Sports fishing and hunting camps continue to multiply each year. All this is happening on Innu land, or at least on disputed land, and all the while the Innu are in active land-claims negotiations with both Canada and Newfoundland. Nitassinan is considered Crown land by governments, and Newfoundland has refused to legislate any interim protection of disputed lands while negotiations are ongoing.

Innu respect for the sanctity of the land is at the heart of Innu culture. The struggle for the land is a struggle for the survival of

Innu culture and identity. These recurring themes of threat to, struggle for and love of the land are echoed throughout this anthology.

We believe this book is also part of the struggle. We hope it will serve as a bridge between the Innu and the outside world. As the readers travel through these stories, they will sit close with Innu women. Perhaps they can imagine themselves perched comfortably on a bed of aromatic fir boughs, with a fire crackling from a small sheet-metal stove as soft moonlight shines through the canvas of the Innu tent. Or perhaps readers can invite these Innu women into their own homes and offer them a cup of strong tea. We hope readers will connect with the humanity of these stories. The door will be open for the reader to enter the world of the Innu. Readers will join the women in a place where experiences of love, pain, fear, laughter, sorrow, joy and hope cut across our differences.

We could say much more about the women's words that follow, but we will stop now and let them speak for themselves. Our work is not complete. As we write this introduction, we are scheming to find further funding to enable us to produce this book in its original language, Innu-aimun.

Tshishue neskamanants iskueuts katipatshimuts ke essi minuantshi utipatshimunu-uaua. Tshinaskumitinan!

Nympha Byrne & Camille Fouillard

Spring 2000

IT'S LIKE THE LEGEND

Grandfather Eagle

Nympha Byrne

I could feel your strength
brushing my pain
You've given me courage
to stand up for the People
I am proud,
proud to be Innu,
proud that I'm a woman.

I have cried for so long
watching weakness
from our community.

We have to stand up now
and walk through
this heavy path.
We will struggle
I know
But we will make it through.

I see the brightness
from your wings
and the warmth
from your blessings.
You've touched my heart

to be able
   to free my spirit to our People
      to free my spirit to the land
         to free my spirit to the animals

      Thank you Grandfather Eagle
   for the touch
from your soft wings.
Thank you for your visit.

This poem was written in jail in March 1995.

Mishtapeu

Shanut Rich

Once there was a boy who had lice. He had so many lice that his father couldn't sleep at night.

"When we leave here, let's leave our son behind, because how can we sleep when he has so many lice?" the man told his wife.

"All right," the woman replied. The next morning, she didn't give any clothes to her son.

"Mommy, put on my clothes," said the boy.

"I will do it after I have finished loading my sled," his mother answered. Everyone left except the woman and her son.

"Put on my socks and clothes," said the boy. "We are going to be left behind."

"Just a moment," his mother replied. "When I am good and ready, then I'll put on your clothes for you."

"Hurry up," ordered the boy.

After the woman had put on her snowshoes, she said, "Son, I am going to haul my sled a little way, just to try it out. Then I will come back for you." She went over to the sled, hauled it to the soft snow and off she went. The boy saw his mother going away.

"Mother, you are leaving me," he cried out. He tried to run after her, but he didn't have snowshoes. "Mother, I am cold."

"I am leaving you here because you have so many lice," his mother answered. "That's what your father told me to do."

The boy turned back to the camp. He wrapped himself in a caribou skin that had been left behind and he began to cry. The spirit Mishtapeu heard the crying and went over to see who it was. When the boy saw him, he was frightened.

"Mommy, Mommy, someone is coming after me," he cried out. "It's awful. It's awful," he screamed.

"Grandson, your mother is the one who left you behind," the spirit said to the boy. "Why did she do it? What's wrong?"

"They told me I had too many lice," the boy said.

"That's nothing," said the spirit. "Nothing is wrong with you. I can kill your lice right now." So the spirit began to warm the boy with his hairy body. He held the boy and started to kill the lice.

"I will save only one lady louse and one man louse so that, when the people come on earth, they will have something to do when they can't go hunting and have to stay home out of the snowstorm," the spirit told the boy.

When the spirit was finished, he told the boy they would go and find his mother. The next day they came to the camp. There were many people there, but the spirit knew where to go.

"That's your mother's teepee right there," he said to the boy. "Go to your mother."

They entered the teepee and his mother was surprised to see him.

"Who brought you here?" she asked him.

"My grandfather," replied her son. "He is sitting outside."

The mother opened the door of the teepee with a stick and she saw the spirit sitting there. He was great and he was big and she said, "This monster has brought our son back."

"You are the monster for leaving your son in the old camp," the spirit replied. "Why did you do it?"

The woman didn't say anything. She was afraid. The boy went back to his grandfather because he loved him and he invited him into the teepee.

"Tell your mother to make a soft place at the side of the teepee, where I can stay," the spirit told the boy.

When the boy asked his mother to do this, she said, "How do you expect to bring in your grandfather? He is too big."

"I won't be so big when I come inside," said the spirit.

When the woman had finished, the spirit entered and began to shrink. He never went out after that but stayed in the teepee with his grandson. Every night the spirit blew on the boy and the youngster began to grow very fast. Soon the boy was big enough to go hunting with his father. The spirit always put a magic spell on his grandson so that they would always kill caribou. The boy always brought home caribou loins and liver for his grandfather. But the spirit grew tired of staying in the teepee all the time.

"Am I always going to live with the people?" he thought. So he left, but before he went he gave the boy's mother some advice.

"Try to stop my grandson from crying when he sees that I am gone," he told her.

The boy returned from the hunt and ran into the teepee with his meat.

"Grandfather, the caribou is killed and I have brought you a loin and the liver," he called out.

"He is gone," his mother told him.

The boy did not like it. He searched for his grandfather's tracks and he followed them out of the camp. The spirit knew that his grandson was following him. He heard him calling, "Grandfather, Grandfather, wait for me." When the spirit heard this, he waited. He didn't have the courage to go on because he loved his grandson very much.

"Grandfather, let's go home," said the boy.

"No, I cannot live with the people," said the spirit. "But you go back, and when you want to remember me, make a small tent inside the teepee and go inside that small tent. I will come to you there and you will see me." The spirit tried to leave but the boy insisted, "No, let's go home."

"I will not go home," replied the spirit. "It is not right for me to live with you all the time. Never before have I lived with the people. This was the first time and now I must be separated from the people."

"No," said the boy. "Let's go home."

"No, I will not be going home," the spirit said firmly. The spirit picked up his grandson. They flew through the air and the boy was dropped into the camp, but he stood up and started to run after the spirit again. The people in the camp tried to grab him, but he caught up with the spirit.

"Grandfather, I will live with you," he told the spirit.

"No," said the spirit. "You can't do that. You eat and I don't eat at all. You wouldn't be able to survive."

"All right," said the boy, "then let's go home."

"No," said the spirit. And he picked up the boy and flew him back to the camp again. But the boy left right away and started to run after his grandfather.

"What can I do with my grandson?" the spirit wondered. "How can I stop him from chasing me?" He picked up a rock and put it across his track and the rock grew into a mountain with a cliff on each side. When the boy came to this mountain, he couldn't climb it. He went back to the camp, but he never stopped crying, day or night. The people tried to speak to him, but he was always crying. He never stopped.

The old people came to the boy and asked him, "If we are all ready to do something for you, what would you like?" The boy wouldn't stop crying, but he asked them to make him a shaking tent so he could see the spirit. The old people misunderstood him and thought he was saying, "I would like to shoot at summer birds with my bow and arrows."

"Look for the summer birds," the elders said to the other people. There were no summer birds where they lived. It was always winter. But the people agreed to look for the summer birds. They called everyone, the people and the animals, together. The caribou and the wolf were the leaders because they were the fastest.

"Are you going to come with us?" they asked the otter.

"Yes, because I love children," replied the otter.

"Are you going to come?" they asked the porcupine.

"Yes," said the porcupine. And the skunk and woodchuck also agreed. They all went on their way to look for the summer birds. They didn't have anything for grub.

"There is a beaver living near here," said one of the pack. "He has some fat, so let's stop by there to get some of it for grub." Before they reached the beaver's dam, they told the otter not to laugh at the beaver. Every time the beaver moved, he farted.

"You always laugh," they said to the otter. "It will be better to tickle you first so that you won't make the beaver angry." So they tickled the otter until he couldn't stop laughing. He laughed and laughed until he couldn't laugh any more.

"That's enough," pleaded the otter. "I'm pissing." The people left him alone and went to the beaver's house. They asked him to spare some fat for grub. The beaver took out his fat and broke it into pieces for them, but while he was doing this, he farted and farted. The otter tried to stop laughing but he couldn't. The beaver wrapped his fat up again and packed it away. But before he could hide it, the people grabbed it from him and ran away.

After a while, they saw a muskrat swimming in the water, and the people said to themselves that he probably knew where to find the summer birds.

"Muskrat, muskrat," they called out. The muskrat dove underwater and reappeared.

"I heard the people, I heard the people," he said. "I will tell the people who have the summer birds." The muskrat started to swim away with his tail sticking out of the water, but the people called out to him.

"Muskrat, do you like fat? Would you like some?" they shouted.

"Yes, I like fat," replied the muskrat.

"Come over here and we will give you some."

After the muskrat had eaten, he gave the people the information.

"Every night they have a dance," he said. "They dance where the birds hang in large bags on the walls of their camp."

"And what do they do in the morning?" the people asked.

"You see over there — that's where the moose swim across to the other side of the river," replied the muskrat. "When the people see a moose swimming in the morning, all the men run to their canoes and after him. Everyone in the camp goes after him. The only things they leave behind in the camp are the summer birds."

They gave more fat to the muskrat and one of the people said, "Will you try to do something for us? Will you put holes in their canoes and chew their paddles halfway through — not completely, just enough? And in the morning, will you take a stump and swim across the river with it?"

So the muskrat ate the fat and swam back to his home near the people who had the summer birds. The people smelled the fat on him.

"I wonder what the muskrat has eaten?" they thought. "It smells like fat."

"I found some weeds and they were very fresh," the muskrat replied. "That's why I smell so greasy."

When everyone was asleep, the muskrat chewed down the paddles and made holes in the canoes. When it was almost daylight, he picked up the stump and swam with it. When daylight came, two old women saw something moving across the river where the moose usually swam.

"The moose are swimming across," they called out. The people ran from the camp and pushed their canoes into the river. Some of them sank. Others were breaking their paddles. While they were in the water, the other people came and ran away with the bags of summer birds.

"People are taking away our summer birds," the two old women called out. Some people swam to shore and chased the thieves. First they caught up with the porcupine. They began to kick him around. They kicked him until he was as round as a ball, and then they left him and said, "Now the people will call him 'porcupine.' "

The chase went on again. They caught up with the otter and ran over him until he was almost flat. They found the woodchuck on top of a tree. The whitefish hit the woodchuck's tail with an arrow and the woodchuck jumped into the air and hung there in space. "We will call him the northern star," the people said.

So they chased the people with the summer birds. Wherever the birds passed, the snow melted and it was like the beginning of spring. When they came to lakes after the birds had passed, the ice was already melted and the snow was almost completely gone.

"Let's give this up," one of the people said. "Let's leave them alone if they agree that the summer shall go back and forth." So they called out to the people who took the summer.

"It's all right," they said. "We will not bother you. We will not chase you. But from now on, the summer shall go back and forth."

"All right," said the wolf and the caribou.

So the people turned back and the others went on their way. When they arrived at the camp where the boy was, they opened the bags and let the summer birds fly into the forest. The people made a bow and arrow for the boy. He went shooting birds and he stopped crying. He killed a bird with a white crown. He cut it open, took off its skin and put the skin on himself. Then he flew away.

The people wondered what had happened to the boy. They saw his clothes on a branch and, near his clothes, they saw a summer bird with a white crown.

"He must be the bird," the people said. "I suppose that is what he wanted to be."

And the old people decided, "We shall name the bird *Kautu-uasekunisku-uenisht*."

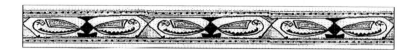

Women Speared the Caribou

Mary Jane Pasteen

In 1976, the year Miste Mani-Shan (Mary Jane Pasteen)
died, George Gregoire interviewed her about the old days.
She told him her story in Innu-aimun. Over 100 years old
at the time, Miste Mani-Shan recounted memories of a
nomadic life when contact between the Mushuau Innu
and White people was rare. This story hints at the rough-
and-ready division of labour between men and women
that existed in traditional Innu society. The men did most
of the large-game hunting and the women prepared the
food; made clothing, tools and tents; and tended small
children. But it was not unusual for women to help with
the hunting, and if a woman was busy elsewhere, a man
would readily look after the children. Women could also
be heads of families and handle their own traps. Miste
Mani-Shan's son Tshenish remembers when he was a
child and his mother speared caribou with ease, and how
she would carry a whole caribou on her back. For a spear,
he said, his mother would sometimes just tie a knife on the
end of a stick.

The last time I went to *nutshimit* (the country) was about 12 or
13 years ago. It was around 1963 or '64. We went to Emish, where
we stayed for a while, and then we moved almost to the
Mushuau-shipu (George River). At that time there were a lot of

caribou. My late husband, Miste Ueapeu, was still alive. When a person went out to hunt for caribou, he did not have to go far away.

My late mother told me there were lots of marten around the place where I was born. In the old days, people say my mother used to get a lot of marten. When we went to Pakutapin (Tasialuk Lake), the Hudson's Bay traders would be there and she would sell her furs.

I heard when I was young that there were lots of Uaskaikan (Fort Chimo or Kuujjuaq) Indians who died from starvation. Some of them were frozen to death because they did not have enough clothes to wear. They dressed like we dressed when we were inside the tent. Mushuau Innu must have left some meat somewhere along the Mushuau-shipu, but the people who died of starvation did not make it to the cache of caribou meat in time. Probably they were already too weak to move. Only one family made it to the caribou meat.

My late father's name was Netuapeu, or Waiting for Morning to Come. My mother was Nenitshitau. Those were just the nicknames we used before the missionaries came. After my parents passed away, I was adopted by Ussenitshu, or Young Man.

I know we are related to the Cree Indians from James Bay in some way. Maybe my great-great-grandfather was related to them, or my great-grandfather. That was probably before the White people came to Labrador and Quebec.

⚜ ⚜ ⚜

In my early days, there were no matches. The only way we could make a fire was by using a kind of rock that was just like flint. When we wanted to make a fire, we had to get real dry, rotten wood and two pieces of rock to rub together. Then the fire would start easily.

Not very long ago people used to make teepees out of caribou skins. First they would take the fur off the skins and make them soft. Then they smoked them. It took 10 caribou skins to make a teepee. At one time there were no sewing needles. They used bones to make needles. Axes were made of bones too. A *mitshikun* (scraper) made of wood and metal could also be used to clean the skin.

I used to kill caribou when I was young. Whenever the caribou crossed the Mushuau-shipu and there were no men around, we women had to chase caribou by canoe. I would be in the front of the canoe with a spear. It was no problem to kill a caribou. A lot of women killed caribou in the water with spears or guns.

People used wood to make pots. You couldn't cook with them, but you could get water. When you wanted to cook something, you had to use a caribou stomach. First you dried the stomach real good, and then you boiled some water. Then you hung the caribou stomach over, but not too close to, the fire. When the water boiled, you could cook with it. They say that a caribou stomach would never break as long as you took care of it.

I also remember in *nutshimit* when there was no food at all. The only way to survive was to eat rock moss. Before you cooked the rock moss, you had to wash it real good. Then you could cook it. It tasted like cereal, but it was kind of black. Sometimes when we were in *nutshimit* and there was nothing to eat, pregnant women would have new babies and their breasts couldn't give any milk. We would go out and catch a fish, any kind of fish, and boil it. The pregnant woman had to drink the water so her breasts could give milk.

The caribou breed and calve around the Mushuau-shipu. If you look to those mountains, you can see thousands of caribou and calves. I remember the times the caribou had to cross the river. Their young calves also had to cross. When the young ones made it to the other side of the river, they couldn't walk. The people who didn't have canoes would throw rocks at the calves and kill them.

This story is about 90 years old.

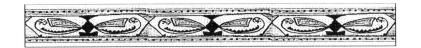

Shaking Tents and Anik-napeu, The Toadman

Mary Madeline Nuna

In this story you will meet the Toadman and experience a shaking tent firsthand. The shaking tent ceremony, or kushapatshikan, was one of the most important rituals in traditional Innu society. The shaking tent was a small, conical structure with a framework of poles covered with caribou hides. In the summer, it was erected in the open air. During winter, it was set up inside another tent on a floor of fir boughs. The shaking tent ceremony was performed by a shaman known as the kamanitushit. In the shaking tent, the shaman would communicate with the animal spirits, contact people living in other groups to bring their souls into the tent and even wage terrible battles with other shamans in faraway places. The shaking tent was a powerful device that could be dangerous when misused. Seventeenth-century accounts of Jesuit contact with the Innu indicate there were women shamans at that time. Women and men were equals. Both could be utshimau (leaders). Women seemed to relinquish these roles almost exclusively to men as Christianity took hold, although elders in Sheshatshu remember a woman shaman called Uenuitamishkuen. A woman could acquire spiritual power by butchering,

*cooking and preparing hides of the animals that were
killed by her husband.*

When I moved here to Sheshatshu, I saw shaking tents. I saw a
shaman, the late Uashau-Innu (Antuan Ashini), do the shaking
tent all the time only in *nutshimit*, never in the community. We
always went up Kamikuakamiu-shipu (the Red Wine River) far
into *nutshimit*. The shaking tent is really good to witness or be
a part of. It is the same as the television, that shaking tent. If
you could witness it, you would really like it. You would have a
great time. It's very entertaining. It certainly made me laugh.
We could hear singing inside the shaking tent sometimes. Like
anyone, the way they are, they could be brought into the shaking
tent from far away. And when someone was brought in there,
they sounded so close and so clear.

Anyone could be brought in there from any place. Like the
late Mani (Mary Michel) told us once that our father, Pien
Gregoire Sr., was brought in there, but we weren't there at the
time. Uashau-Innu was the late Mary's father. She said that
one time when a shaking tent was being performed by her
father, my father was brought in there. She said that he was
singing, and he sounded so clear and close. It was only his spirit
that was brought in there, not all of his physical being, only
his spirit.

It's like the way someone speaks to you. That's the way it
sounded from the shaking tent. It was very good fun. It is a great
time and, when stories are being told, it's like listening to a radio.
When spirits speak from inside the tent, they might guide us
where to hunt for the animals. For example, if you wanted to
kill caribou, the spirits would tell you exactly where the caribou
are. You could talk to the spirits, the ones who you heard from
inside there. Like, for example, the one who is called Mishtapeu
— the One Who Owns the Animals. This spirit is heard
through the shaking tent. And when the Mishtapeut (more
than one spirit) sing, it is really good to listen to them, to the
songs of the shaman. The Mishtapeut are really loud singers.

When the late Uashau-Innu was doing the shaking tent, sometimes he brought Anik-napeu (the Toadman) into the tent. Anik-napeu sounds like an Innu when he speaks. All the animals speak like Innu. If you want to ask Anik-napeu for something or if you want to find out about something, he will tell you. The animals can all speak from the shaking tent, including the one who owns the marten, Uapishtan-napeu (Marten spirit), and the one who owns the porcupine, Uhuapeu (Owl spirit).

It is said that the Toadman is very good and handsome. He looks like a White man. He is the one who took an Innu woman a long time ago. It is said that he talks about his wife and claims that she will never die as long as he lives. He lives under the ground, under the mud. It is said that he grabbed this Innu woman from the mud when he took her at Petshishkapishkau. She was an old man's daughter. The woman must have been picking bakeapples in the marshes. The Toadman lives in the mud, and she was stuck and sinking in the mud. He grabbed her feet and it is said that she described his hand as being very white or pale. If you were going to chop the Toadman's hand off, you couldn't even hurt him with a chopping axe. The axe would just bounce off his arm and you wouldn't be able to cut through it. Anik-napeu has strong hands. He should never be disrespected.

Anik-napeu lives at Petshishkapishkau these days, at the place where he stole the woman. But it is said he is also everywhere in this world. He could be anywhere, because he must own or control the frogs. All the frogs must listen to him and be very good. I heard that not very long ago, over on the beach where the new houses are, the kids were playing with a frog. They were drinking at the cove over by the last house on the beach, where that brook is. Those young men were playing with a frog. It is said that you cannot be disrespectful toward the frog. They were making it drink hard liquor. And it is said they heard someone singing and they ran away. It must have been Anik-napeu they were playing with, and who they were disrespectful of. It is not good to be disrespectful of Anik-napeu.

Tshenut, the Elders

Mary Martha Hurley

I want to learn more about our History.
   I am seeking help from you.
   Please, do not ignore my plea
It is important at least you share
   Some of the old ways of your life.

Turn around and face me
   and we should speak our minds.
It could take years, months or many hours
   Until I will understand.

   I am sorry for what had happened
I forgive you for not being able to teach me.
   It will take time, I know
But at least it is a beginning.

   Don't be ashamed of our History.
   You know we are so Rich
With all the Love and Resources we have.
   Let's get off from the chair
and sit on the boughs while we chat.

An Orphan Grows Up

Cecile Rich

As a small child, Cecile found herself an orphan at the mercy of a harsh aunt. This early misfortune was remedied when she was adopted by a kind and generous family. The mistreatment of children within the Innu culture was rare before the recent cultural breakdown that has led people to lose touch with their spirits. Seventeenth-century missionaries and 19th-century anthropologists have all written of the loving attitude of the Innu toward their children. One cannot pick out an orphan or adopted child by the way he or she is treated. Such children are in no way set apart from the life of the group, but are taken in and cherished by their new family. Children and adults will often call several people nikau *(mother), whether they have biological ties or not. This also applies to* nutau *(father),* nukum *(grandmother),* numushum *(grandfather),* natesh *(brother) and* namesh *(sister).*

From this story, one might think Innu dogs are brutal, but generally they are highly intelligent, tough and hard-working little dogs. They are good hunters who know who the master is. They are not known to snap at or bite people without good cause, although children are warned to not get too close, especially with food in their hands.

I remember some of the places we used to go in *nutshimit* (the country). One time we were travelling and we passed Kauishatukuants (Old Davis Inlet) and ended up at a lake called Kamitishanikants. The late Matshieu (Matthew Ben Andrew), who was a Sheshatshu Innu, used to hunt there. He would go hunting in the daytime and come home late in the evening. I was living with Matshieu at the time because I was an orphan. My mother and father had died when I was only small. I lived with my uncle Shushepiss and aunt Akat (Joseph and Agathe Rich) for a while. Later I was taken to Sheshatshu and placed with Matshieu's family, and that is where I spent a lot of my growing-up years. We were always in *nutshimit* and we would see a lot of the country. Every spring we went back to Sheshatshu.

One day when Matshieu returned from his hunt, I heard him calling out to me when he took off his snowshoes.

"Shishin, I found *manteuts* (visitors), Mushuau Innu, your people, and you can go tomorrow and meet them," he yelled out to me one day. "You can stay overnight down there. We'll go tomorrow. Just get lots of boughs for the tent floor."

"Okay," I said. I was very excited. The next day I left to meet them. Many people from Kauishatukuants came to see me, including all my relatives. I visited everyone in their tents. My uncle Shushepiss was very happy to see me.

"My niece is back," he said and he hugged me. I told him that I was going back to Sheshatshu and he said that I should.

One little girl was always following me around. I felt very sorry for her. Her name was Kautashet (Lucy Piwas) and she was young — she must have been the same age as Cheryl, my granddaughter, about five years old. Kautashet was always crying for me. Everywhere I went she would follow me and all the while she cried.

"Why is she crying like that when she is around me?" I asked Pukue (Charlie Pokue). "Are you crazy? She knows that you are related to her and she wants to be around you. That's why she is crying," he said. I was tired and tried to sleep, but Kautashet was in and out of our tent. Finally she went home to bed.

We camped at Kamitishanikants for a long time. That's when I knew that Manishish, Matshieu's mom, was sick because she was complaining about her pains. I also knew the old woman was dying because I had seen a *uiskatshai* (a whisky-jack) as we had travelled to the camp. The *uiskatshai* had fallen next to me and died right there. I asked Matshieu's mother if this had happened before. She said no and maybe that was the sign of her death.

My godfather was also at this camp. His name was Napeu (Sam Napeo) and he was my aunt Akat's son. Napeu is my cousin. Our fathers were brothers.

"Come here, my godchild," he said when he saw me. I couldn't go to him right away because I was uncomfortable. I was shocked when I looked at him. He had scars all over his face. He looked so pitiful, like an old man, and I felt sorry for him. Finally I went to him and I was told the story about how the dogs attacked him and almost killed him.

When we got ready to go back to Sheshatshu, I felt I would really miss the people from Kauishatukuants. I cried as we left, but I had received a gift from my godfather. He had given me snowshoes that he had made. My tears fell and I felt very lonely for my people, the Mushuau Innu.

"Why don't you stop crying?" Mani-Katinin (Kathleen Nuna) said to me. She was also living with Matshieu's family and we were like sisters. She was picking on me! As we walked along, she was sinking into the soft snow because she had no snowshoes. When we stopped for a break, she told me to take my snowshoes off. She said she wanted to try them on, but after I took them off she wouldn't give them back to me. Now I didn't have any snowshoes. I was the one doing all the work pulling out gear on the *utatshinakeaskut* (komatik, or sled) and sinking into the snow, and she was the one with the snowshoes! We stopped to camp long after we passed Kauishatukuants. I wondered how far we had travelled.

It took us a long time to reach Sheshatshu. When we arrived, Matshieu's mother got very ill right away. She lost weight very fast. I often wonder what kind of sickness she had. When she was dying, she asked for her son, Matshieu. She wanted to talk to him.

"The child you are looking after is very nice. Don't ever let her go. Don't ever place her with anyone else," she said to him about me. "Always take care of her. I am going to die. I can see the child you are caring for is remarkable. I can see a brightness around her that is not around anyone else. It is a sign of love."

This is what the old woman saw in me. She said she would really miss me after she died. She told Matshieu that I would go directly to the spirit world when I died. There would be nothing in my way on that journey. I was very honoured to hear that, and I still believe that I'll go to heaven when I die.

The old woman was sick for a long time. She invited me to be with her when she was ready to die. I stayed and cared for her all night. There were also a lot of other children staying up with me. She kissed me and kept telling me not to leave her son. She told me I could go only when I was ready to get married.

"Will you ever get married?" she asked me.

"I am not sure. I don't know if I will get married," I told her.

After she died in the spring that year, we went back to *nutshimit*. We camped with Stakeaskushimun (the late Simon Gregoire). We went to Uashat (Sept Iles), and then back to *nutshimit*. That is where I almost died. A cross was laid on my chest. I was really dead. I was told I had no pulse and I was not breathing at all. A bad tooth infection almost took my life. When I woke up, Matshieu was crying.

"What's wrong?" I asked him.

"You were dead and now you've come back to life again!" he replied. I told him I didn't remember anything that had happened to me. I guess I had a really bad infection. After I got a little better, Stakeaskushimun built a *mitishantshuap* (sweat lodge) inside the tent for me. He then blew the hot air from inside the lodge onto my bad tooth. I stuck only my head inside the sweat lodge. There was a lot of infection draining from my tooth. It just kept flowing really bad. It looked very ugly and it smelled. It made me cough. The next day I felt better. It was my own crucifix that

Matshieu had placed on my chest as I lay dead. He told me that he had prayed for me. He was sure I had no pulse. I must have come back from the dead. I have never had a toothache since.

After I felt better, I started working at my chores again. I was back to my normal self and I would walk long distances by myself. After I finished my work each day, I would walk around the woods to find porcupines. One time I was checking the traps and found a live lynx. I tried to get it, but it was too big and scary! It tried to attack me! I hadn't brought anything with me to kill it. I was wondering what would happen if I tried to shove a stick into its mouth. I couldn't get near it because it was growling at me. It was too dangerous. Sometimes I wonder why I wasn't smart enough to spike it with something. I could have killed it, but I returned home from checking all the traps without the lynx.

"There is a lynx in your trap, but I couldn't do anything with it," I told Matshieu. "It was trying to bite me. I couldn't go near it." Matshieu went to check his trap and he carried the lynx home on his back. I asked him if the lynx could be eaten and he said yes. After it was skinned and cleaned, we roasted the shoulder blade and ate it. The meat was good and it tasted like partridge. Lynx eat partridge, mice and rabbits, so that is why it tasted like small game.

♙ ♙ ♙

One time when I was still living with my uncle Shushepiss, my aunt Akat didn't want to feed me. We were travelling a long way by foot and I was pulling the *utatshinakeaskut* (komatik). We stopped to take a break and they started a fire for tea, while I sat on my komatik. I didn't want to bother to go to the campfire to get any tea. My aunt Akat cooked lots of food. She put whole partridges in the pot. My uncle Shushepiss told them to give me something to eat once it was cooked.

"We will not give her any food, because she won't do any work," I heard my aunt Akat say. I sat on my komatik and laughed to myself. I was afraid I would make her mad. I didn't want her to hear me laugh.

"At least give her some tea," my uncle said.

"She doesn't need to drink tea," my aunt replied. "She doesn't need any, because she never makes it." I didn't pay any attention to them while they argued. I was just sitting there, wondering what they would do. After everyone was finished eating and ready to go, I went over to the campfire. There was a little bit of tea left in the pot, so I drank it, but the food was all gone and I didn't get anything to eat.

They started to walk again around noon. It was dark when we stopped to set up the tents. I was pulling a lot of gear for them on my komatik. It was very heavy. I was trailing behind. When I got there, it was dark and the tents were already up.

"Is this how fast you travel?" my aunt Akat asked me.

"I am very tired," I replied. I went inside the tent. She had just left me to fend for myself.

When I travelled with Matshieu's family, he would ask me how fast I could travel. He was never mean to me. I would let him know when I was hungry or when my feet were tired without any fear. I was always so happy when I was travelling with him and his wife, Mani-Aten (Mary Adele Andrew). We were always on the go. We worked hard. Sometimes Matshieu and Mani-Aten would go ahead without us and I would tag along behind with Mani-Katinin. Sometimes they would have the tent all set up when we got there.

Other times, I would be the one who would go ahead of everyone to break the trail. They would send me up front with my komatik loaded with stuff. When we stopped for a break and started the fire, I always had something to eat. I would just take the food I needed.

My aunt Akat and uncle Shushepiss always tried to get me to live with them again. They didn't want me to stay with Matshieu, but I always said no. I told Matshieu how she had treated me. He said not to listen to them. My uncle Shushepiss really wanted me back to live with them. It was only my aunt who didn't want to feed me.

My sister Matinin (Madeline Katshinak) told me a story about how we were once left on this island. It was at Kamashkushiut, near Kauishatukuants, a place where we used to camp. I was very small. Matinin said I was already walking, but my younger brother, Nisikutshash (Raphael Rich), wasn't. Our uncle Shushepiss wanted us to get in the canoe to go to a place nearby called Shanut, where he was camped. But my aunt Akat didn't want us in the boat. Matinin kept walking along the shore to see if anybody was paddling by in their canoe. She didn't see anyone, so we stayed there on the island. Early in the morning Matinin started walking again, while I was still asleep. People came along in their canoes. It was our other uncle Utshishemushish (George Rich). I was awake by then and I waved to him as he approached. He took us off the island to bring us to Kauishatukuants. Later on our uncle Shushepiss came with my aunt.

"I'm here to pick up my nieces and my nephew. I want to take them back to my camp," he said. "You left us on the island and you don't care about us," Matinin replied. They took my brother and sisters in the canoe, and I got in too. Our aunt was arguing with Matinin. They wanted to split us up. They didn't want to take Matinin. She said they took me away in the canoe. Matinin went berry picking and, when she came back, I was gone. Someone told her that our aunt Akat took me away to their camp at Shanut.

I wondered what our aunt did to me after she took me away, so I asked Matinin. She said there were a lot of people camping there. Utshishemushish was also camped there. They were always drinking in that camp. I wonder what I was up to, such a small girl in the midst of all that drinking? Maybe I was always playing outside and the only one I hung around with was Nishapet (Elizabeth Rich). I guess we went through the same thing together. I don't remember what they did to me, but I was told my aunt didn't want to give me any food. She was so mean.

✿ ✿ ✿

One time I remember everybody in Sheshatshu was scared, but I didn't know why. It was in the spring, almost summer, and people were camped near the river. They were in the woods and not by the shore. One night someone came to our tent when we were already asleep. We were told to get up. It was pitch dark. There was someone the people were afraid of, but I was not scared myself. I put on my clothes and went to the tent where the people had gathered. They were talking about how this person was not leaving the camps alone. They made plans to set up a shaking tent. When the tent was up, we could hear the ones who wouldn't leave the camps alone. They came into the shaking tent, made a popping sound and then the spirits spoke. They said it was the old shamans who were fighting against each other. They were using their powers against each other.

✿ ✿ ✿

There were elders who were camping with us in Sheshatshu. I was very close to the elders and worked hard for them. I would cut wood and fetch water for them. I also picked boughs for their tents. I would lay the clean boughs on the floor of their tents. I would stay overnight in their tents. I was always around and when I was ready to go home, I would give them a kiss. I missed them when I left. I missed the many stories they told me to help me go to sleep. They were very old, but they cooked their own meals, mostly roasting meat by the stove. Later when I visited them in the evenings, they taught me about religion.

There was one elderly woman, Pinamen Mackenzie, who taught religion. She told me to come and pray with her in the evenings. I went and we prayed together. She showed me how. The school in Sheshatshu — Peenamin Mackenzie School — is named after her. Every year she taught me more religion, but it took me a long time to learn. I got very tired of it. I told her I couldn't learn, but when I heard the bishop was coming, I asked Pinamen to tell him that I wanted to learn religion. She did and he said he would pray for me, so that I would be able to learn. I learned how to read that year and I was very happy.

My husband-to-be, Tami (Tommy Rich), was also taught how to read, but he didn't learn because he was not listening. He would not pay attention. He was too busy always picking on me. One time I was kneeling down, praying. He ran inside and hit me on the head. I didn't see him either coming in or running out. My grandmother Pinamen told him to leave the women alone.

"You don't pray and you don't know anything about prayers," she told him. "Stop flirting with the girls. Can't you see we are praying hard!" She made me laugh. But my husband-to-be didn't want to leave us alone. They sent him away, but he kept coming back. We prayed and sang for a very long time, possibly for hours. When we got very tired, I would go home. Matshieu would ask me where I had been. I told him I was practising how to read and learning all about religion. I was also keeping the tent warm for the women by fetching wood, bringing it inside the tent and keeping the fire burning in the stove.

I missed *nukum* (my grandmother) Pinamen when she died. I saw her spirit when she died. She came in the room where I was sleeping in my old house. I saw a shadow on the wall. Her shadow was walking and then she just stood there and I saw her head. She did not have much hair; it was shoulder length. I asked her what she wanted. I thought she was my daughter Akat. She never replied, so I went back to sleep again. I never saw her again. Later I heard she had died on that day. I guess she had just come to visit me for one last time. I was so upset because she couldn't teach me any more religion. I was very tired and restless, but I was still always praying. Now my eyes are bad and I can't see very well.

♠   ♠   ♠

Before Mani-Aten married Matshieu, they were living together, but she was always trying to go back to Uashat. It did not seem like she wanted to marry him. One time while we were travelling, she disappeared all by herself. She started a fire and we could see the smoke where she had stopped. I tried to walk in front instead of behind her, because I would get very cold when I had to stand around and wait for her. She didn't pull much on her *utatshi-nakeaskut* (komatik), only her blankets. Now she had gone off on her own. I told Matshieu's mother, Manishish, that I was going to look for her. I followed the smoke from her fire in the woods and went to meet her. When I got there, I asked her what was wrong.

She said she was melting snow for water to drink. I told her to hurry up because it was getting dark. We couldn't see the others. They had gone on ahead. She was making me tired. I was already weary from walking and I had had to walk back again to look for her. She drank the water and I put the fire out for her. I took her komatik, left it by the trail, took my komatik and went off again. I told her not to run away again. I told her she would never make it back to Uashat because it was getting dark and we had come a long way. So she came with me and we caught up with the rest. Then she walked behind Matshieu, who was breaking trail. Manishish was mad at her.

"Don't start walking back again while we are travelling. You won't be able to make it to Uashat. It is a long way from here," said Manishish to Mani-Aten. "If you have your man up there, try not to miss him too much." She scolded her, but Mani-Aten never said anything. Manishish made me laugh the way she talked to Mani-Aten. The next day when we were taking the tent down, Manishish also had some advice for her son.

"We are getting ready to go now. You can tie her on the komatik. She is slowing you down. Tie her really tight on the komatik!" Manishish said to Matshieu. Mani-Aten was pregnant and slowing everyone down. I told Manishish that we should not do that because it might hurt Mani-Aten in her condition and she might get sick.

Matshieu never took her on the komatik, but halfway across the lake, we saw them heading back to where they had come from. Manishish saw they had gone back, so she followed them.

She was an old woman, but surprisingly she caught up with them. She was gone for a long time. I had told her I would go on, because I would get cold if I waited around. But I stopped and watched her as she crossed the big lake toward the shore, and I waited to see her catch up with them. In the meantime, the people who were travelling with us must have gone far ahead. I started walking again. The lake was very big and it took me a long time to make it to the shore. Mani-Katinin walked with me, pushing my komatik, which held a lot of stuff, including my clothes and our food. Finally we made it to the camp. Miste Penute Ashini, my late husband's old friend, called me over to help set up the tent. It was getting dark.

"She slows us down because she always tries to turn back," I complained to Miste Penute.

"Tie her on to your komatik tomorrow morning and go off with her," he said to me. "I'll go first and you follow." I told him I couldn't do that because I already had too much stuff on my komatik.

When Manishish arrived at our camp with Matshieu and Mani-Aten, I had the boughs ready, but I had not yet cut the small trees to use for the frame of the tent. Matshieu cut these, but Mani-Aten never helped us. She just sat outside. We never said anything to her. I think she was upset. I was worried about her because of the way she was acting, always trying to go back to Uashat.

The next morning Matshieu told his father-in-law, the late Stakeaskushimun, he was going to go off for three days to check his traps. Stakeaskushimun told him he would also be gone, but he would return in three days to this camp. He was lying. Like his daughter, Stakeaskushimun wanted to see Uashat. The next morning, when Matshieu was not home, Stakeaskushimun took Mani-Aten and headed for Uashat. It was cold and windy. I was told to go and find Matshieu. I said I wouldn't be able to catch up with him, because he had been gone for a long time.

"Don't worry about it," said Manishish. "Matshieu will be back tonight and he'll go and look for them." That night

Matshieu returned with muskrat and fox from his traps. He inquired about Mani-Aten. Where was she? I told him Stakeaskushimun had come and taken his daughter and all her belongings. Matshieu drank only water and left to look for her with his komatik. He probably thought he needed it for her belongings. He made it to their camp that night. Mani-Aten heard him coming and ran out of the tent to hide away from him. Matshieu went to the door of the tent.

"What is going on here and where do you think you're going?" he asked his father-in-law.

"We are going to Uashat," replied Stakeaskushimun.

"You cannot take Mani-Aten with you," Matshieu told him. "And I want the rifle I gave you. We will wait for you at our camp, but only for three days."

They did return to the camp after three days, and the people got ready to break camp. The *utshimau* (leader) in that camp was Miste Penute. He was the one to say that we were to move the camp that morning. He had told Matshieu they would be leaving early. It was still dark when Miste Penute came to our tent.

"Get up and get dressed," he said. "We are going back to Sheshatshu. I'm ready to go now and my komatik is packed." Stakeaskushimun and his wife had a lot of children to pull their komatiks. Everyone was helping. We all left and there were so many of us walking. We made it to Sheshatshu. We had travelled a long way. I don't remember how many times we had set up camp along the long way.

Stakeaskushimun arrived after us. He was also Shuash's (George Gregoire's) father. When he arrived, he started arguing with his wife. We never said anything to them. She sat by the door crying and arguing. A while after we got to Sheshatshu, Shanime (Germaine) was born to Matshieu and Mani-Aten.

♠ ♠ ♠

There was this old man and his wife who always asked me to visit and help out, so I would go to their tent. When they were getting ready to leave for Uashat, they wanted to take me with them. I took off into the woods, because I didn't want to go with them. I stayed there a long time until I was sure they had left, but they were still waiting for me when I returned home. They told me to go and get Matshieu. They asked him if they could take me along with them. They wanted me to stay with them. The old woman joked with me. Her name was Shishin (Cecile) Uashau-Innu.

"Shishin, we both have the same name," she said to me. "Look at my son-in-law. He is very handsome."

"You are only making fun of your son-in-law," I told her. He was not handsome and she was just laughing at him.

She asked me whether I would marry her son when I got older. She said I could be her daughter-in-law. I was afraid of her, and her husband was very old.

"Come 'my wife' and visit again," Shishin's husband said to me. "I am going to play the drum for you and you can dance for me this evening. I will not put a candle on, but you can hear me sing the drum."

Later that evening, I looked outside the tent and I heard a drum beat. I went to their tent, but there were not many people. His wife was there, as well as her daughter, Niskuess (Frances), and one of her sons.

"Come right in and we will dance for my husband," Shishin said. I didn't know how to dance. I had never danced before. I told Niskuess to join us, and so we danced on the other side of the tent. We couldn't dance around in a circle because there was no room, so we had to go back and forth. Shishin was dancing on the other side by herself. One song was very long, and the old man sang on and on. I was very tired.

"When my father finishes his song, we can stop dancing," Niskuess said. I didn't know how to dance any more because I was so tired. We must have been dancing non-stop for two hours at least!

"Doesn't he get tired of singing?" I asked. Finally he stopped and called out to me. "Shishin, did you dance?"

"Yes. I danced and I am very tired. You made me very tired. Your songs are very long," I told him.

"Some of my songs are very long," he replied. "They can make you dance all night." He was very old and his beard was very white.

I remember another dance one night with drumming and singing. "Let's go to the dance," my husband-to-be said to me. "Okay," I replied. Soon after we got to the dance, the priest came in. He walked straight to the drummer and grabbed the drum off the line from which it was hung. He carried the drum right outside and took it to his house. The drummer couldn't sing for us any more. I missed the dancing. The priest was always taking the drums away from the people. He threw away our grandfather's drum. The priests had no respect for our elders.

I went to look for the drum the next morning and I found it at Matshieu's house. It was early and he was singing away with the drum. He had been drinking. The drum was now hanging in his house. He must have found the drum, which the priest had thrown away. "Do you know how to sing?" I asked him. "Why are you playing the drum?"

"I have already dreamt about the drum. You can dance and I will sing for you," he told me. He wanted to give us booze, but we wouldn't take any.

I wonder what Matshieu died from. Maybe it was alcohol that killed him. He used to go on trips a lot to work with the miners. He would travel back and forth between Sheshatshu and the mines where he worked. He made a lot of money. He would always leave us in the summertime.

I never saw Matshieu's family again. When I left to get married to Tami, Matshieu had only four children: Shanime (Germaine), Shan-Shushep (Charlie), Kenikuen (Gregory) and Aputet (Ben). I hear he had 15 children in all. He was a good man. He was good with children.

A Child Learns Respect

Elizabeth Rich

Elizabeth shares with us her memories as a small girl, trying to make sense of worlds colliding: the Innu world of survival, sharing and animal spirits, and the White world of trade, cleanliness and godliness. Now an accomplished beadworker, Elizabeth remembers the first time her family traded furs for beads in Emish (Voisey's Bay). She remembers the tyranny of a priest, who tried to snuff out their spiritual beliefs and practices, including that of the sacred drum. The animal spirits talk to the Innu through the drum to guide them on their hunt. The spirits tell them how to respect and take care of the animals, how to make offerings to the spirits, how to hang animal bones in the trees or burn them in the fire, which is also a spirit. If the hunter follows these laws, the animals will give up their lives to the hunter. If the hunters do not offend the animals and their spirit masters, they will continue to live in peace with each other and with nature.

I am only going to speak for myself and what I've seen and heard. In the early days the Innu never received food from the government. This is why they always went back to *nutshimit* (the country). There was no hope that the government would give us food. Sometimes we would run out of bannock or tea, but the men would set their traps and fish and hunt caribou. The women were good hunters too. They hunted porcupine and partridge, set snares for rabbits and put nets out to catch fish. When the women went hunting, they took their children with them.

When I was a child I was taught to respect the Utinimat-sheshu Caribou Spirit, the Giver of Food. Children were not allowed to make fun of animals or Utinimatsheshu would get angry. We were taught how to respect the spirits. I was told if I made noise outside, Utinimatsheshu would not share the animals with us. The animals were our food. We were not allowed to be negative toward our parents, like nagging at them or getting angry. The other important thing was to be careful about what we said to the hunter. We had to respect the hunter. This is what we learned. We survived by what we learned.

The Innu know that there is a Creator, and that the Creator told his own children to respect him. When I was a girl, the mother was also the one to teach her children to respect her too. She would talk to her children about Tshementun, the Creator. Tshementun is a God, the same as the Christian God. He helps people and looks after them. There is only one God.

The women taught their children that sharing and giving is very important. My mother, Akat, told us not to get upset during meals if there was not enough food to go around. Even when we had only a little bit of food, my mother shared it and gave it to the other people. As Innu, we were told that, if we were bad to the others and didn't share food with them, Tshementun and Utinimatsheshu would be upset. Parents were really happy when the children listened. Children were also happy for what they learned. We kept the things we learned.

Sometimes people were afraid when they were looking for fish. They were afraid they wouldn't be able to find any and they would starve. People would share when they caught fish. When the Innu woman cooked, she put her pot on top of the stove. I always knew right away when my mother did this that she would be sharing food with the people, the ones who were hungry. I knew the ones who were hungry. She would invite the rest of the people in our camp to eat our meal with us. We were given only a little bit to eat, or sometimes we wouldn't eat. There wouldn't be enough for the children, but the adults would eat a lot. This was hard. But I always tried to do what I was told. We wouldn't get upset while having our meals. What I would be thinking is: if only I could be made happy — because I was really unhappy with so little food. Tshementun and Utinimatsheshu's teachings were very powerful. We would hardly play because the teachings were too strong. If we were bad, our parents wouldn't get animals for food. I never learned or heard about other things.

Right after the children had eaten, my father, Shushepiss (Joseph Rich), would send us to sleep and tell us legends. When my father told me legends, his stories were similar to what he did himself. I thought that his stories and his life were almost the same. My father also used the legends. For example, he would use Kuekuatsheu's thinking. Kuekuatsheu is the wolverine. He is a trickster. My father also had a story like the one about Noah's Ark, when the whole earth was flooded a long time ago. In our legend, Kuekuatsheu is the one who made the earth again. My father didn't use the name Noah in his story.

🔖 🔖 🔖

When we were in the country, we were always travelling. In the winter, my parents would tell us we were not allowed to go on the komatik while we were going to our next camp. Only the little ones would go on the komatik. I had my little snowshoes on and my mother would take care of me. We did a lot of walking and pulled all our things along   family things like the stove, tent, clothes and food. In the summer, we carried our things on our backs. Even the little children carried things. I was never sick when I was walking like this. Life in the country was very good sometimes in the old days.

In the middle of the winter, my father would say he had to go back to the store at Kauishatukuants (Old Davis Inlet). We would start walking back. My father wouldn't let us wander off by ourselves. We would go as far as Kanishutakushtasht (Flower's Bay), and sometimes to Kapukuanipant (Jack's Brook), or to Kapapist (Big Bay) and Shankus (Sango Bay). Sometimes we travelled as far as Estinekamuk (Snegamook), not far from Sheshatshu. These are the places we would end up.

In the summertime, we would travel to Kauishatukuants by canoe made of birchbark or made of canvas from the store. We would camp across the bay from there. There were no houses for the Innu in Kauishatukuants back then, only tents. The only White people were the store clerk and his family, and sometimes the priest. My father didn't expect anything from anybody when he returned to Kauishatukuants. He knew he would not receive food from the store clerk. He had no furs, no work, no money. And sometimes we were completely out of food. The way the Innu survived, White people wouldn't survive like that alone in the country.

My father would talk about the way White people lived. "They are a proud people," he would say. He would talk about how White people had everything, how they would show off, how they survived because they didn't have Utinimatsheshu. My father would tell us he couldn't let us go to *kakeshauts'* (non-Innu people's) homes. Only my older brother could visit these homes. My father would tell us *kakeshauts* had homes that were clean and had everything, like food. They didn't ever go hungry. He said *kakeshauts* pushed people away that were not clean. This made us uncomfortable, when we were told that we would make a White woman dirty if we went to her home. I didn't go to *kakeshauts'* homes.

My father didn't like to go back to Kauishatukuants. He liked to stay where there were not very many people. That's why now I like to be where there are not very many people. My father would tell us that we couldn't find any friendliness from the store clerk. My oldest brother, Napeu, who drowned, used to ask my father, "Let's not go there. Why do you keep trading furs with those people if you have no use for them?" My father didn't listen to him. He traded furs with the clerk whenever he could. But he would tell us this was the last time, because the clerk would barely give food to the people for their furs. He would give my father some food maybe once a year — things like flour, butter, sugar, baking powder and pork. Then my father would tell us we had to go back to the country.

My father was the *utshimau* (leader), but he wasn't a leader that has money. He was the leader for the people travelling in the country, a leader in the camps. He would say when the people should camp, when they should keep going and when they should rest. Sometimes he would go hunting caribou with the other men. He would say to stay one week and then travel again.

Sometimes the priest would invite my father to the church when he was needed. My father could speak English. He was like an altar boy helping during the mass or when a baby was baptized. He would visit the people to give them the messages of the priest. The priest would never say we were not allowed to go to the church. That's the only White man's building we could go in. Everybody would sit very quietly in the church, saying prayers. Back then, the priest would stay only two weeks.

Many years ago, Mushuau Innu or Davis Inlet people never went to church. My father didn't. It was the people from Sheshat-shu who told them to go to church. Sheshatshu Innu and Mushuau Innu would meet when they were travelling in *nut-shimit*. Sheshatshu Innu would tell us to get baptized because we didn't go to church. This is what I heard when I was a child. It scared me.

Nothing was perfect in those days. The priest was in control. People showed respect for him because they were afraid of him and his control. They believed the things he said. He told them about the darkness of our drum, how we would be left in darkness after we died with only our drum, nothing else but the drum in darkness. I think this is what scared the people. We had our own beliefs, but the priest made us believe his teachings in the church. Me, I don't believe in the things the priest is teaching.

I sometimes wonder now about the things I've heard. My father told us one time there was a White man who didn't want to help his grandmother. People asked the White man to help my great-grandmother because her husband had died. This is why my father thought the White people were too proud. This happened around Sheshatshu, where her people were from. The White man told my great-grandmother to come with him and he would take her and her granddaughter away. The young girl was probably 12 years old and she was my aunt. He said he would take care of them and feed them. They would be happy and not lonely. They would live well and not go hungry. They were never seen again. Nobody knows what happened to them. My aunt and her children must be in Happy Valley now. Maybe it is only her grandchildren that are living. I often think when I see a White person that he doesn't care about the people, the Innu.

♠ ♠ ♠

I was taken away myself by a doctor because I had pneumonia. "I will take her away and she will be fine," the doctor said to my father. I had an operation in St. Anthony, but I didn't receive any abuse from this doctor. Later, when I was lonely for my family, the doctor said it would be okay even if he didn't want me to go back yet. Maybe I should have listened to him. But if I had stayed, later I would have had to look for my family like kids are doing today — those who were taken by Social Services and adopted away.

When I came back to Kauishatukuants, I was very surprised by what I saw. "Why is the government giving people money?" I thought to myself. I had not seen the Innu given social assistance before. When I was a child, I was never allowed to ask for food from other people. My parents and other parents kept an eye on us so we wouldn't do that. We were told to do something outside, but not to look for food in people's tents. I wonder now why the people don't go back to *nutshimit*. The reason must be something in the community. They are not going back because they get social assistance. This is what I think. My father didn't have any money. The government shouldn't have given me any money. I don't like it. I liked it the first time, because I didn't know the difference. The government is giving the Innu money to pay us back for our land. That's why I don't like it. Today young people don't go to *nutshimit* because no one is taking them out there. I like the old way, the way my father was treated by the government years ago. He never received social assistance. Only food was given to him. He never received any money. My father told us the stories of when they were poor and out of food. My father's stories — I still keep the things he told me in my memories.

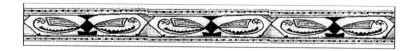

Eagle

Christine Poker

A man had a dream about an eagle. He told his wife about his dream. As he finished telling her, he heard wings flapping outside their tent. He asked his wife to look and it was an eagle. He went out to see the great bird. It was big.

"What is wrong?" he asked the eagle.

"My grandchild, I am hungry. My claws are all cracked," the eagle replied. "I was flying and I thought I saw a lot of caribou. I tried to grab them, but I grabbed an island instead. That's how I got my claws cracked."

"Don't worry, Grandfather," the man said. "I will fix your claws for you. I will make them sharp."

So the man started working on the eagle's claws. He sharpened them. When he finished, he asked his wife for a caribou hide. He asked the grandfather eagle to try his claws on the caribou hide. His claws couldn't go through the hide easily.

"A little bit more and it will do," the man told the eagle, and he worked on the eagle's claws some more. He let him try his claws on the caribou hide again. This time they went through the hide easily.

"I will go hunting and try out my claws," the eagle said and flew away. In a few minutes he returned with 10 caribou. He held five caribou in one claw and five in the other. He laid them near the tent.

"Those caribou are for you," he said to the man. "Thank you for saving my life."

Then the eagle told the man something that he needed to do from that time onward.

"Every time you cross the lake, always put some trees across the ice even if the lake is small," the eagle told the man.

The man did just that, until one night when he came home late from his hunting. He was too tired to cut some trees and he thought the lake was small.

"What can possibly happen to me?" he thought to himself. So he ran across the lake. As he tried to reach the other side, something grabbed him. He looked up and saw the eagle that his grandfather had talked to him about. This grandfather eagle had a wife who ate people. His grandfather ate animals. His grandfather had warned him about the grandmother eagle.

"If she grabs you, don't ever let go of your spears," his grandfather had told him. The grandmother eagle flew higher, carrying the man over the mountains and past the tents. He saw his tent and the light was still on. He knew that his wife was still up and waiting for him. He began to sing as they flew by the tent.

"You with the light on, the eagle has taken me," he sang. His wife heard him and started to cry. She knew that the eagle had taken her husband away and that she would never see him again.

The man was still holding his spear while the eagle took him to the mountain. He could see that the mountaintop was really sharp. The grandmother eagle took him to the sharp point of the mountain and tried to hit him hard against it, but the man held his spear up against the rock. The eagle tried again. The man's spear pierced her in the groin. She was hurt and carried the man back to her nest. There the man saw grandfather eagle looking sad. He asked the grandfather eagle to free him.

"It is not possible because grandmother eagle flies faster than me," the grandfather eagle replied. The man continued to beg for his help and the grandfather finally agreed.

"When the grandmother eagle sleeps, I will try," he told the man. They waited for the grandmother to fall asleep. Finally she did and the grandfather eagle told the man to go to the edge of the cliff. The man obeyed and the grandfather slowly moved toward the man, afraid that he would wake the grandmother. He grabbed the man and flew down to the ground, but the grandmother woke up. She flew to her husband and grabbed the man from his grasp. She took him back to the sharp rock and tried to kill him again. But the man still had his spear with him. When she tried to slam him against the rock, the same thing happened again. She hit the spear instead. She tried several times until she got tired and took the man back to her nest. The man told the grandfather that he would try to save himself from the grandmother.

"I will burn the nest tonight," the man told the grandfather eagle. "If you want to be saved, you should not return to your nest tonight."

"I will stay and be burned with my wife and children," the grandfather eagle replied. "This will be your reward for saving me from starvation."

This was the hardest thing the man had ever had to do. He loved the grandfather eagle, but he also needed to go home to his wife and child. He told him that he would burn the nest when everyone was asleep. He gathered up twigs and put them around the nest. He lit the twigs and the nest burned so fast that the grandmother had no time to escape. He stood there and watched the nest burn. When the fire was out, he took his grandfather's back and stuffed it with grass that he found nearby. He gathered more grass until the back was full.

"I'm depending on you, Grandfather, to take me safely to the ground," the man told the eagle. He knew that the grandfather was listening to him. He took the skeleton to the edge of the cliff and crawled inside. He moved back and forth to push himself off the cliff. He held on as they bumped off and fell a short ways down. He was not far from the ground. He talked to the grandfather as he dragged his back to the edge of the cliff again.

"We've almost reached the ground," he told the grandfather, as he crawled back inside. Again he moved back and forth, and with four more bumps, he had reached the ground. When he was safely down, he took the grandfather eagle and cut his back into small pieces. He threw these around in different places. Every piece turned into a small animal.

When the man returned home, he told his wife how he had killed the eagle and how his grandfather had saved him. He knew his grandfather had wanted him to save other people from the grandmother eagle.

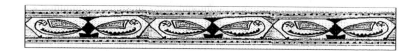

The Elders Would Never Have Allowed It

Maggie Antuan

Through Maggie's memories, we discover how the role of some elders in Innu society has changed. She remembers how her grandmother looked after her as a small child and how she learned to take care of elders in turn. In the old days, elders were respected and made the decisions. Now that she has become an elder, we learn of her pain as she experiences the changing role of elders in Innu society.

I am going to tell you my story because my grandchild told me she wanted to hear it. I will talk about the old ways. So much has changed. The old days were quite different from today.

Every year we used to go to *nutshimit* (the country) in August and camp for the fall and winter. We would prepare to go by making the things we needed, like snowshoes, moccasins and clothing. After we had everything ready, we would start to move our camp. We would camp for a while in certain areas where the caribou were killed. The hunters used to spear the caribou and the people would chase them in canoes. Sometimes the caribou were scarce. When we couldn't get any caribou, we usually went back to the place we had camped before.

We often ran out of tea in the country. We had to have tea and tobacco in those days, although we didn't really need food from the store, like chicken, canned foods or sweets. We never craved that stuff. I remember this much.

I was at Mushuau-shipu (George River) many times. My mother told me that I was born there. I believe it, because I don't remember being born. The place where I was born has another name. It is called Kashatshipet-ashinin, or The Rock That Sticks Out of the Water. The rock is big and it sticks out in the middle of this deep lake.

My grandmother Miste Mani-Shan (Mary Jane Pasteen) was always telling me stories. She looked after me whenever my mother couldn't because she was busy doing other things. Miste Mani-Shan would take over, and when she needed a break from me, she usually sent me back to my mother. My grandparents would always tell me to help my mother.

I remember when I was baptized. Father Whitehead had arrived in Kauishatukuants (Old Davis Inlet) and I went to see him. I was eight years old when I got baptized and that's why I remember.

When I was taken to *nutshimit*, I was old enough to do things myself. I first learned to do things inside the tent, but not outside. The outside skills came later. When I felt I was ready to work harder, then I started to do things outside as well. At first I was only able to carry water and wood inside the tent. I learned to work still harder and I was taught how to chop down trees.

We used to cut wood for the elders at our camp. I had a close friend who would cut wood with me. Her name is Munik (Monique Nui). She married my brother Nuke. We would also carry water for the elders and gather boughs for their tents. The elders loved it when we did things for them. They paid us back by cooking meals for us whenever they had wild meat on hand from the hunters. We received meals from them every time we cut wood.

"The wood cutters are back. Get their meals ready," I remember I would hear someone calling when we came home from cutting wood. They always had meals ready for us.

I am really surprised how our lives have changed so quickly. We have been changed by White people. We work and do things like White people. They are taking over and running our lives for us now. I don't agree with this. I often wonder how our lives would have been if the elderly leaders were still alive. They would not have allowed this to happen. They would have been very surprised if they had tried to take over our lives back then. They would have wondered about them being around us and about what kind of people they were. I think about this often. The way we are living now is not good. We will never go back to the way we were in the past. That way of life is lost. White people are in control. This is how I see it. I am very surprised about what is happening now and how things are being handled.

♣ ♣ ♣

My father died in Voisey's Bay. The Innu call Voisey's Bay "Emish" in Innu-aimun. We used to camp there, and I remember exactly where he was buried. I know I could find his grave if I went to look for it. I often think of going there to visit my father's grave. My mother was buried in Sheshatshu. I have many relatives buried in the country.

My father's name was Apenam (Abraham). His Innu name was Uitsheuake. Tshenish (Charles James Pasteen) from Utshimassits (Davis Inlet) knew my father. After my father got baptized, he married my mother. Men and women used to live together for a long time before the priests would come to marry them. Both my parents were baptized in Uashat (Sept Iles). My father was originally from Uaskaikan (Fort Chimo, or Kuujjuaq) and that is where he lived for a long time. I still remember our family leaving to go to Kauishatukuants from Uaskaikan. Then we would travel on foot from Kauishatukuants to Sheshatshu. We never travelled by plane or ski-doo. We always travelled on foot. I am still here today and I will be buried somewhere when I die.

Today the elders feel very neglected. We are getting older. I feel like no one cares about us. We feel that the people are just waiting and watching us die. We don't want to die yet. We want to live. We are not ready to go. Our time has not come yet. Eventually we will die, when our time comes.

Shushep and Me

Madeline Katshinak

*Like her sister Cecile Rich, Madeline was orphaned as
a young girl. She remembers in even more vivid detail
how it felt to be left abandoned by a heartless aunt.
Fortunately, she, too, was eventually adopted into a
more loving home, although all her brothers and sisters
were separated from each other.*

*In this story, we follow Madeline through a nomadic
life that seems at once dictated by the seasons and yet
timeless. They followed the caribou, fished and hunted,
made their clothing and tools such as snowshoes and
canoes. All the while we catch a glimpse of how they
shared everything: their wildlife, belongings, labour,
supplies, and even an occasional anthropologist. The
food would run out, the family would move on to new
hunting territories and new gatherings of people, depending on how and when paths crossed.*

I am going to start my story and tell you about a time when we
were travelling to Sheshatshu. We started from Kauishatukuants
(Old Davis Inlet) with my husband, Shushep (Joseph), my
brother Nisikutshash (Raphael Rich), and Tuminik (Dominic
Pokue) and Shushan (Suzanne). There were just the five of us.
We camped on the way and ate a meal of porcupine that we had

killed. Then we moved on and camped near Kapapist (Big Bay). We travelled very fast with our dog team.

We kept moving our camp and, one time, on the way we met Pineshikan and Nushin (Ben and Lucy Rich). We asked them to join us, but they said they could not, because they were headed back to Kauishatukuants. We tried to convince Pineshikan, but he really wanted to go back to Kauishatukuants. So we moved on to camp at a lake called Kashupaset-unipim. We did not kill any caribou on the way. Next we camped at Kashakaskueiats, where the children caught fresh fish for us to eat. The men went hunting and saw a small herd of caribou, but they did not catch any and they didn't take the time to go back to look for the caribou again.

We moved again and camped at Shapiass (near Shapio Lake). Finally Nisikutshash and Tuminik killed caribou in this area. We looked for other Innu, but there was no one else around. The day after the kill, we moved on again and camped at another place near Shapio Lake. Then we camped at Mishta-nipi (Mistinippi Lake), where we killed more caribou and had fresh meat. Again we didn't see any people there. I remember we were never hungry or sick in those days.

We travelled on and went as far as Estinekamuk (Snegamook), where we met other Innu. We could see them from afar, so late in the evening Shushep and Tuminik went for a visit. There was Ueniam (William) and the late Napesh (Joseph Toma) and Shushepin (Josephine). It was springtime and the ice was beginning to break up, so we stayed until the ice flowed out from the rivers. Once the ice broke up, Napesh killed many beavers. He shared them with everyone in the camps. I couldn't eat the beaver meat. Shushepin showed us how to cut up the beaver. We had never seen beaver before and we didn't know how to prepare it. She told us we could make a lot of money from beaver pelts. She said we would be able to sell them when we returned to Sheshatshu. She told us to watch her carefully when she prepared the skins to learn how to do it right. We watched closely as she got her skins ready for sale.

When all the ice had cleared, we used the canoe to continue on to Sheshatshu. On the way, we found supplies at a big lake called Kakatshu-utshistun, or Raven's Nest (Grand Lake). The supplies had been left for Napesh by someone from Sheshatshu. He shared them with us. Shushepin was really anxious to return to Sheshatshu. We slept outside and she never slept all night. She was too anxious. I think she couldn't wait to begin drinking. In the morning, when we left, she was very tired as she paddled the canoe. When we arrived, Shushepin's parents and a lot of other people came to meet us. I was very shy. Later when we saw Shushepin and her husband. They were drunk.

While we were in Sheshatshu, my husband, Shushep, built another canoe because we had only one. With the help of other men, he built three canoes. Then we headed back to Kauishatukuants. I was anxious to go back. When we left, Shushepin's family didn't join us. She was very tired of travelling the long distances. My brother Nisikutshash and the late Tshe-mentun (Joseph T. Rich) came along instead. They were both single men at the time. It was in the fall and we camped at one of the lakes along the way and we killed lots of caribou. We reached Kauishatukuants and in the winter we returned to Sheshatshu again. We travelled back and forth between Sheshatshu and Kauishatukuants many times.

🔱 🔱 🔱

I am going to start another story and talk about the time when we were left on an island near Kauishatukuants. My brothers and sisters were very frightened. My aunt and uncle, the people who abandoned us, left to set up camp at a nearby island called Shanut. My uncle Shushepiss (Joseph Rich) never said anything, but my aunt Akat (Agathe Rich) was mad at us. They left us behind on the island.

"Try to stay alive," my aunt yelled out to us as they were leaving. "No one will come to pick you up." She didn't frighten me, because there were other people in Kauishatukuants.

I asked Shishin (Cecile Rich) to come with me to see if anyone was canoeing by. I also took one of my brothers to check if anybody was coming. The children were all crying; they were very scared. I told them I would call out and see if someone in the other camp could hear me. We shouted out, and Uitshishemushish (George Rich) came to pick us up with his wife, Natikameum (Katie Rich). At that time they had two children, Ueuistum (Theresa) and Tshementun (Joseph T.).

I told Uitshishemushish we had been left on the island and were told to try to stay alive. He told us not to worry because he had a tent and we could stay with them. We went with him and I went berry picking with Ueshiuskueu (Theresa Asta) and Uashimemau (Caroline Rich) far into the mountains. From up on the mountain, we saw people getting on a big boat. They were moving their camps. All my brothers and sisters were taken away on this boat. Uashimemau said it looked like we were being left behind. She wasn't married then, but she was going out with my cousin.

My aunt and uncle came back for my brothers and sisters. When I returned to the camp from berry picking, I was told my aunt had come for me too. But she had said she didn't want to have me around her. She really hurt me. They took all my brothers and sisters to the camp at Shanut. My aunt made my oldest brother Anutusk (Francis) work so hard for them that he later took ill. He died while they were in *nutshimit* (the country). People have said he died from working so hard. He was very thin and had lost a lot of weight. My husband, Shushep, saw him when he had lost all the weight, but I wasn't there to see him.

I ended up with Ueshiuskueu's and Pukue's (Charlie Pokue's) family. They were the ones who came to pick us up after our berry picking and then we went out to *nutshimit*. We stayed out there for a while and then returned to Kauishatukuants. We were camping at Shankus (Sango Bay) when I heard my uncle was back in Kauishatukuants, so we went back to see them.

Later on we went to *nutshimit* and stayed there for a long time. Keseuekantsheshish, Pukue's mother, came along. Her Christian name was Manish (Mary). She was very old, but she still pulled her own gear on the komatik and she always had dried meat. She could catch up with everybody and never lagged behind. She was a very good woodcutter and would cut a lot for her son. She could still do all this work. We went as far as Kauinipishit-namesh (Black Fish) that time, and then we headed back to Kauishatukuants.

☙ ☙ ☙

Another time, there was just the two of us, Shushep and me, and we headed for *nutshimit* to a place called Kapukuanipant (Jack's Brook). We were married then, but our son Tanien (Daniel) was not born yet. There is a place where Nisikutshash (Raphael Rich) went sliding, which we now call Metshituaunapeu kashuakuet. Shushep killed some caribou there. He had left me at the camp all night while he went hunting. I was all by myself and very scared. I saw something by our platform looking at me. The dogs started barking and then I got really scared! I untied my dogs and put on my snowshoes. The dogs came with me to find out what was out there. I took my .22 rifle. I looked again and saw a round head. I shot at it. It was a raven and it flew away! That may have been what frightened me. I was not scared anymore and tied the dogs up again.

Later that night the dogs began to bark again. It was Shushep coming home. But I wasn't afraid when I heard the barking. He carried a caribou leg and all his gear into the tent. Our dogs were happy too, because there was also food for them. The next morning, we moved on to where Shushep had killed the caribou. On the way we killed porcupines and partridges. Tshenish (Charles James Pasteen) and his wife, Mineshkuesh (Theresa), later joined us at our camp. They only had two grandchildren with them, including Miste Shanin (Jeanine Pasteen).

Mineshkuesh had no snowshoes, only a really old pair that were useless. Shushep told her he had killed a large caribou and he would give it to her so she could make herself some new snowshoes. She was very happy because she desperately needed a pair. They were only visiting us, but we invited them to set up camp with us because we had a lot of caribou and we needed to share the meat. The next day they came and set up their tent. They arrived when we were out hauling the caribou back to the camp.

I had not left a note to tell them we were out, because I wasn't sure they could read. I had cooked caribou soup and a lot of boiled meat before we left. I was going to write in my note that whoever arrived should just help themselves to the cooked food. Shushep said they couldn't read, but they would probably know the food was there for them to eat. I was also going to tell them in the note to put the fire on to warm up. I had put out dried branches for them to start the fire. But when we returned, they had not put on the fire, nor had they eaten, even though they were very hungry. Mineshkuesh said she had told Tshenish the cooked meal was probably for them, but they hadn't touched the food. Maybe they thought they would be stealing.

We had been gone a long time. Shushep had killed the caribou in the mountains. We had to go up hills and down to bring back the caribou meat to the camp. It took two trips to get it all. When we returned with the first load, Tshenish and Mineshkuesh were not there yet. They were setting up their tents when we came back with the second load. We went over to see them. Shushep asked Mineshkuesh if she had eaten yet and told her that there was food all prepared for them. We headed for our tent and heated up the food for them.

We stayed at that camp for a long time. Shushep and Tshen-ish later went back to Kauishatukuants for some supplies. More people stopped by our camp on their way to pick up their supplies. There was Tuamush (Thomas Noah) and Miste Etuet (Edward Mistenapeo), the late Shanshushep (Charles Joseph Pasteen) and other people with them. We were thinking of going back to Kauishatukuants, but these people asked us to join them at their campsite. Miste Etuet told me his wife would clean my hides for me. He really wanted us to camp with them, so we finally made up our minds and agreed. Shushep left some cigarettes and tea bags behind.

Tuamush moved on to look for Napeu and Uemistikushish (Georg Henriksen). Uemistikushish was a White man who was studying the Innu. Sometimes he would camp with Tuamush and sometimes with Napeu. Sometimes they would fight over who he would camp with. Napeu would win most of the time!

We had lots of caribou at that time. We moved on to Kauishatukuants, where I cleaned and scraped all my female caribou hides. I also made dried meat. We then decided to leave again, but the people there told us not to go. They kept bringing caribou to us, which meant I had more hides to clean again! I cleaned them very quickly. Mineshkuesh was slower at it. We were very anxious to go. Spring was just around the corner. Shimunish (Simon Noah) was also in a hurry to go. I was laughing at his wife, Manian (Mary Ann). She rushed so much that she forgot her pot. I called out to her to tell her about her pot. She called out to Shimunish to wait for her, but he didn't listen. He just went on.

We followed them later and, when we arrived at the same camp we had been before, Manian pointed to all the caribou hair on the ground. I told her she was camped on the same spot where I had scraped the caribou. They had walked very fast to this camp because they didn't have much to carry. I saw their trail and the places where they had camped. Punas (Ponas Rich) was also with them and he was a very hard worker. We had a lot of gear on our return and people left us behind. It was hard travelling because it was spring and slushy, but we didn't worry when they went on ahead. Our gear fell into the water along the shoreline, but we got it out. We untied everything again. Shushep had to go into the water to get the gear and he got his feet wet. There was a lot of water on the ice.

Louisa

Christine Poker

Our little princess in Heaven
We ask God to protect you.
And he said,
"I will protect her from cold winds and sickness
for she will never suffer and
never flow tears,
but live in Happiness in Heaven."

*Louisa was Christine's niece. She died of meningitis at the
age of four.*

It's Like the Legend

Charlotte Gregoire

Charlotte shares snapshots of her life as a small girl. She also shares thoughts about what happened to her people after we were settled into village life. In the past, many Mushuau Innu would travel from nutshimit (the country) to camp for the summer near Kauishatukuants (Old Davis Inlet), a Hudson's Bay post. Here we would trade and see a visiting priest. In the 1960s, priests began to be permanently stationed at the post. One of these priests, along with some government officials, decided the Mushuau Innu should settle permanently on an island near the old post at a place we came to call Utshimassits, or Place of the Boss (Davis Inlet). The church and the government made promises of proper homes with water and sewers, paid work and a better life for the children if we went to school. On the island, people were cut off from their hunting territories on the mainland during freeze-up and break-up of the ice for up to six months of the year. For many, it was the beginning of the loss of our culture and our lives began to be run by the church, the school, Social Services, the clinic, the store and the RCMP. We began to forget Innu values, and alcohol abuse, gas sniffing, suicide and violent deaths became commonplace. In the 1990s there was no longer room to build

*new houses because of the surrounding mountains at
Utshimassits. As well, there had never been enough
fresh water around to supply houses. Many people put
alcohol aside and began to fight for relocation to a site
of their choice — Natuashish (Sango Pond) in
Shankus (Sango Bay). This place would provide them
with year-round access to their hunting territories, as
well as room for expansion and water. The federal
government agreed to fund this move in 1996 and the
move is scheduled for 2002.*

I will tell the story about what I heard of the move from
Kauishatukuants to Utshimassits here on the island, and also
what has been happening since then. The Innu way of life
changed after the move because of all the new technology
introduced in our lives, such as ski-doos, televisions and out-
board motors. There are many other things that the Innu never
used before. Before the move, we spent a lot of our time in the
Shankus area. The only time we used to move to
Kauishatukuants was when the fishing season started in the
summer.

Many promises were made to the Innu. We were told that,
after the move, we would get water and sewers in every house.
Everyone was excited. We thought that finally we were going to
live in houses with good drinking water and sewers. But we found
out that the houses were just empty shells: no chairs, no tables,
nothing. Still today, no Innu person has water and sewers in his
or her house. Only White people in the village have water and
sewers. If only we had water in our houses, it would help us to
clean our children better. Our health would be better.

I'm not saying if we got everything, we'd be like White people.
As an Innu woman, I like who I am now. I don't want to follow
another people's culture. I like the close relationship we have
with the animals and the animal spirits. I like to live in a tent.
There are so many things in a house. The tent is a small place
and I can finish all the things I need to do in one day.

It has been 28 years since the move took place, and still today nothing improves in Utshimassits. Nothing good came out of it. Instead we saw more drinking, and gas sniffing came along a few years later. The government built the airstrip, which made it easy for anyone to bring in alcohol or order liquor from Goose Bay. I'm not saying the airstrip was a bad thing. It helped to save many lives in our community. But how many young people have committed suicide since we were placed on this island? Some outsiders say the children are sniffing because the parents are drinking, but what I see is that there are many parents who don't drink and yet their children are sniffing. The children are frustrated with the poor living conditions. Our children are not the children of 30 or 40 years ago. Today's children know how the White government has mistreated the Innu. Many people have passed away without ever seeing water and sewers in their homes. Living conditions are worse here than they were in Kauishatukuants, where we lived only in tents. It is not our fault. It is the fault of the government who put us here on this island and then forgot about us.

It's like the Innu legend "Aiasheu." Aiasheu was a boy. His father took him to an island and left him there to die. But Aiasheu didn't die. He asked many sea birds to take him to the mainland, but they were all too small to carry someone his size. One night he dreamt that a dragon had come to rescue him. The next morning he saw a sea dragon with antlers. He asked the dragon to take him to the mainland. The dragon agreed. The boy used the dragon's antlers to show him where to go. This is how he survived. On the mainland he had many obstacles to conquer before he could find his mother and he had to kill his father to save his mother. He probably did this because he was sorry to see him always beating his mother, abusing her. At the end of the story, the boy's mother becomes a robin.

This is what happened to the Innu after the government moved us. Now the White people will see what is said in our Innu legend. The government put us on this island and forgot about us, but we survived. Now we want to move to the mainland. For years we have been talking about relocation to Natuashish, but nothing has happened. It is like the government wants us to die on this island. But Aiasheu stood up to survive, and we are doing the same. Like young Aiasheu, we are fighting our way to the mainland. The government is paying for what they did to us. But if there is no apology from the government, there will be no forgiveness from us.

There are times now when there are a lot of partridge and rabbits close by the village on this island. But after freeze-up, the animals move to the mainland and we cannot hunt them. About seven years ago, caribou herds migrated as far as Natuashish. For the last five years, the caribou have even come right to this island. Some walked right into the community. The caribou spirit is telling us he wants the Innu to move to the mainland.

Once the move takes place at Natuashish, I'm hoping that living conditions will improve. I'm not saying that all the problems will go away automatically. But as we continue along, some of the problems will be solved. What has been lost will reappear in front of us. Problems will be solved when our children understand more of our culture. After the move I hope we don't have too many White advisers. The elders will not be with us forever. I'm hoping our future leaders will take the right direction and follow the good path. I tell my own children to live as Innu, to learn our way of life. My husband and I take them to *nutshimit* to teach them the ways. How many times have I told them not to use English words when they speak to me? I tell them to talk to the elders as much as they can, to learn our path. We must follow one road, the Innu road. If we miss this road, we will fall apart.

♠   ♠   ♠

I will tell you about the things I remember when I was still young and lived with my parents and grandparents. These were hard times, but I really miss that way of life, especially in *nutshimit*.

Once when we were in Shankus, my father, Tshenish, left for Kauishatukuants to get relief. He brought back enough grub to last us for a few months. A few days after he returned, we all went to the country by foot. That was before we had a dog sled. I can hardly remember, but I think my grandparents Miste Mani-Shan and Miste Ueapeu (Mary Jane and John Pasteen) were with us. I was probably six or seven years old. I'm not sure whether I walked on my own or if one of my sisters hauled me. My mother, Mineshkuesh (Theresa Pasteen), was always sick, but she was still able to walk and be with us in *nutshimit*. It took us five days before we reached our destination. I don't know exactly how long we stayed, but it was a long time. There were five of us in the family — four sisters and a brother — Ketshastipineu (Mary Jane), Akat (Agathe), Shan Shushep (Charles Joseph), Shanut (Charlotte) and Atenin (Adeline). That makes seven of us altogether, counting my father and mother.

We only had one small tent and it had many holes in it. My mother couldn't do anything because she wasn't that well. Only my sisters worked and cooked for us. One day my father went caribou hunting, but he didn't kill any. The next day he went fishing, but he only got one small fish. All of us had a small piece. I don't think my father ate any. I had a very small piece, but I did not complain because I knew the fish was too small for me to have a larger piece. My father left again. This time he killed many ptarmigan (white partridge). I was very happy. Finally, I got enough to eat. My brother also killed one porcupine. I could only watch as my mother burned the quills off. It looked so easy to me. This is how I learned to do things on my own, just by watching.

During our stay in the country, I never saw any toys from the store. My sister would make a doll for me out of deerskin. She filled it with flour, tea or sugar. I would play with it until we had run out of whatever supply it was stuffed with. I didn't cry when they took it from me, because I knew Nukum (my grandmother) would make me another one. Sometimes I had to play outside, and there I would set up a small tent. It was not a real tent. It was just during the day and I only used a spare blanket. There was another girl who would play with me. We would pretend it was a real tent. We would do what our mothers did inside the real tent — look after the doll, cook and tidy up.

There were other families besides us, but I'm not sure. It is like a dream to me. A small baby died during that time, but I don't know whose child it was. I can hardly remember the incident. When we headed back to the coast, we had a dog team. Someone from Kauishatukuants must have come to visit us and lent some of his dogs to my father. I remember one day we ran out of flour. I was very hungry for bread. My father said that it was time to go back to Shankus. I was glad when I heard these words. We went there and my grandparents stayed until spring. My parents and sisters continued their journey to Kauishatukuants, because they had to take the baby's body back to the community. I stayed with my grandparents. I think it was my sister who hauled the body on her sleigh. When my father and mother returned, they brought back candies, biscuits and flour. I had never been so happy in my life as when I saw these supplies. I guess I was feeling respected.

I feel sad when I think about my past and how the Innu used to survive in *nutshimit,* how they used to help themselves. I really miss that. That is all I can remember about when I was very young.

🌲 🌲 🌲

I remember later on when I was finally old enough to help my parents in any way I could. I didn't have all the skills, but I was more than willing to help. I wasn't allowed to do any heavy work. I watched more than I helped. I wanted to learn new things from my parents. My parents taught me how a young woman would help her husband when they were in *nutshimit.* I learned how to weave and lace the insides of snowshoes and how to make moccasins. There was more woman's work to learn inside the tent. I still have those skills that I learned from my mother. If I hadn't learned these things from my parents, I would be a useless person today.

In the winter, only my father and mother would set up the tent. I was able to help and would get boughs for the floor. After the tent was set up, my father would take his gun and leave to hunt for food. He would only help set up the tent and put the stove inside. The rest was up to my mother and sisters. They would do the work. I was able to cut small sticks for firewood. My mother would put the boughs on the floor. If we had any wild food, she would cook it up for us.

By this time, my father had his own dog team. It was my job to cook for the dogs and to feed them. My mother would often help me make a fire outside to do this cooking. If there was a lot of caribou meat, I would feed them some of it mixed with seal fat. I did my best with everything. I would try to accomplish whatever task my father wanted of me.

At night, before I went to bed, I would ask my father to tell me stories, like Innu legends. My father would say to me that he was not a good legend teller, but he tried his best to tell me these Innu stories. Later I found out that he wasn't a very good legend teller, but, as I listened to him, he always sounded like he was there too, where the things he talked about happened. As he continued to tell the legends, my mother would tell him that he wasn't there. She would tell him he was lying. Then my father would laugh. At first, I really believed what he said. I thought he was there with those animals.

One day I did something wrong. I stole tobacco from my father. I used to smoke when there was no one around. When my father found out, he was angry with me. My parents used to make homebrew, but they were never drunk. Both of them would drink, but they didn't have a problem with it. They worked as hard as always.

⚓ ⚓ ⚓

Another story was the time we were in Kanutemuantsh, west of Mista-natuashu (Sango Lake), but not that far away. Early one morning I went with my sisters to get some boughs. I must have walked away from them. I didn't even know I was lost. I didn't think they would miss me either. I wasn't worried. I didn't even know that anyone was looking for me. My sisters went back to our tent to tell my mother and father. I spent all day in the woods. I wasn't afraid of anything. I guess I would have been afraid if it had been dark.

I just kept walking. I didn't know where I was headed. Finally I came across an old campsite and decided to stay for a while. I found some clothes that were all torn up. I hung them on a tree to dry. I thought I would take them home with me and use them to make a coat for my doll. After drying the clothes, I started to walk again. I came across a small brook, where I stopped to play. Suddenly I saw an animal the size of an otter. It sat on the top of a rock. Sometimes it would dive into the water and come out again, only to climb back onto the rock. It was late afternoon when I started to walk again. I wasn't worried about anything. I just kept walking. I may have thought I was going home.

It was almost dark when I heard someone calling my name, but I didn't call back. I just kept walking to where I thought I heard the person. I must have walked straight to our camp. I came out of a heavily wooded area right behind our tent. The first person I saw was old Miste Anis (Alice Katshinak) and then her husband, Katshinau (William Katshinak). Everyone had gone to look for me, except two older couples.

"Your father and mother are really worried about you," my aunt Miste Anis said to me. "They have been looking for you all day." I laughed at her and started to tell her about the animal I saw at the brook.

"Didn't you know your father was really worried about you?" she asked. She told me I must be crazy.

She wasn't paying any attention to me. I wanted to tell her about the animal and I kept arguing and insisted on telling my story. Finally she asked me what the animal looked like. I said that the animal was on top of the rock and had a red tail. Old Pukue (Charlie Pokue) took his shotgun and shot it in the air.

My father must have told him to do that as a sign that I had arrived at the camp. My father and mother came back. My father talked to me first. If they hadn't found me, he said, he would have killed himself. He gave me a hug and a kiss. My mother did the same. I felt very loved. I thought my parents would be angry with me, but they were both very happy to see me. After that my parents really kept an eye on me.

☙ ☙ ☙

I have another story. It is about my experience of being in a canoe once with my parents. It was in the middle of the summer — a beautiful day with a light wind. We were in Kamisteueshekat, near Miste-shantish (Daniel Rattle). My father told us we were going to cross the bay to Shanti (Sandy Brook). This was a long way, especially if you use a canoe. I wasn't worried because the water was so calm, but just before we reached Miste-ministuk (Big Island), the wind started to pick up. My father was shouting to my mother to paddle harder.

"Hurry. Bail out the water," he also shouted at me. I thought we were all going to die. We made it to Miste-ministuk, even though our canoe was full of water. After we landed, my father made a fire and we dried our clothes. I was really scared. We went on to Shanti that evening. I was very happy to walk on land. I thought I would never allow myself to be in a canoe again.

Even when I was only a young girl, I used to respect the land like my parents. It's only a few years ago that people started to live in a different way. Today, Innu don't go to *nutshimit* on foot anymore. The plane now takes them to the country. It is an easy way to get anywhere you want. In the winter the Innu hunt by ski-doo. It takes only a few hours and you get where you want to hunt.

Today as I watched the coastal water, it reminded me of Kauishatukuants, where my father and I used to fish for cod. Sometimes we would have a full boatload of fish. We could catch so many fish in a day, I sometimes wondered how we were going to clean them all. Today when I see my father, I wonder if he misses the work he used to do in the past.

"Don't be too anxious to get old," my father once told me. "Like my age, it doesn't do any good to me." Me and my husband, George, usually get up early in the mornings. I always remember what my father said about old age. I feel sorry for my parents. They must find it hard to live without anyone to look after them. Many times I've heard my mother saying that she can no longer cook for her husband. Whenever I have time to visit them, my mother often asks me to do the cooking for my father. Before they were old, they didn't want anyone to help them. They did all the work for themselves.

♟   ♟   ♟

Now I want to tell my story about when we were in a place called Kutshinapesh-minishtik^u (Edmund's Place), north of Utshimassits. It was summertime, and Kaniuekutat (John Poker) and his family were with us. My father and Kaniuekutat went fishing, and after we had been there for a long time, my friend Nenuskueu (Charlotte Tshakapesh), Kaniuekutat's daughter, was anxious to go back to Utshimassits. Both of us were helping our fathers. During the fishing season, we would do everything we were asked by our fathers. This time we were getting tired of fishing, but our parents wouldn't take us back to Utshimassits.

We discussed among ourselves about how we could make our parents go back to Utshimassits. We suggested that, if we kept making bread, perhaps we would run out of flour. That way our parents might want to go back for more food. Once our parents found out about our plan, they wouldn't let us use flour for bread. I guess we must have used too much flour. We did that just to run out of flour. We wanted to go back badly.

One day my father and Kaniuekutat went hunting. My friend and I took the nets out of the water and our fathers were very angry with us. They knew we were anxious to go back to Utshimassits. My father told us we were not going back until after freeze-up. Only the parents would return to get some grub. We asked if we could go with them. I was allowed, but Kaniuekutat said no to his daughter. My father then changed his mind, because Kaniuekutat wouldn't let his daughter go. My father told me he was sorry that I wouldn't be able to accompany him.

We were only young. We helped our fathers until the day we were married. I was always friends with Nenuskueu. We were still friends when she died in a boat accident. I really miss her. After she died, I often thought about her and the things we used to do together when we were in *nutshimit*.

I Am Rich

Nympha Byrne

I have the rivers to drink.
The wildlife to eat.
The tree branches for my cushion.
The firewood to make me warm.
The berries and bakeapples for my vitamins.
The roots to cure me when I'm sick.
The fir tree branches are my fragrance.
The lakes are for me my bath.
I cleanse my body in the sweat lodge.
I stay fit as I hike up into the mountains.
The elders are my singers and drummers.
My father is my storyteller. He provides me with food.
My mother is my teacher. She takes good care of me.
My grandmother is my guide. She knows the perfection of
the land and the sea.
I learn by watching and listening.
My culture is rich.
I am proud of who I am.

Before My Father Died

Catherine Poker

Catherine learned from an early age to cope with death, when she lost first her mother and then her grand-mother. Life went on for Catherine in nutshimit *and she had to depend on other women in her life to teach her the things she needed to know. She also learned many valuable lessons from her father, some of which he shared with her during his final days. She remembers special moments with her father, such as preparing for* makushan, *the feast of the caribou. This important Innu ritual is to show respect to Utinimatsheshu, Master of All the Animals. It is the celebration of a success-ful hunt and sometimes includes a dance to the drum and songs of an elder. Makushan is still often practised today.*

I never met my mother, Mata (Martha). I was just an infant when she died. I don't even remember ever seeing her. I think my older sister, Nenuskueu (Charlotte), remembers her. I was born in Nutak, an Inuit community north of Kauishatukuants (Old Davis Inlet). I don't know the midwife who helped my mother deliver me, but I heard it was a White woman.

My mother died in an accident when she went out to cut wood with my father. She was travelling with the dog team. Her dress got caught in the komatik and she was pulled along and injured. She died as a result of her injuries. She is buried in Shankus (Sango Bay). After she died, we left to go to the community of Kauishatukuants.

I barely remember when we first went to Kauishatukuants. I was not yet in school, although I was getting older. But I remember my grandmother and grandfather, Tshemish and Mani (James and Mary Poker), very well. One time my grandmother told me to go for a walk with her and she slipped off the cliff and fell into the water. I would have died too if she hadn't let go of my hand. I barely remember, but I know I was crying when I went to find my grandfather for help. I told him that my grandmother had fallen in the water and she must be dead by now. I was really crying. My grandfather knew she was missing. He had been looking all over the community for her.

Another time I remember I was sick and I had an operation. My grandfather escorted me out to the hospital in St. Anthony. When I returned home, I looked all over for my grandfather, but I couldn't find him. He had died in St. Anthony and was buried there. Nobody told me he had passed away. I don't know where exactly they buried him. I have been there, but no could tell me where his grave is. My grandparents come first in my story because they raised me.

A woman named Puamekush (the late Mary Toma) was always there for me too when I was small and when my grandfather was out drinking. She also looked after me later when my father was drinking. After my grandfather died, my father took me back into his care. By then he was married again to a woman named Anishe (the late Angela).

My father was very sad after his parents died. When his brother Shimun (the late Simon) died, he was even more lonely. Then when my sister, Nenuskueu, left him too when she drowned, he was very sad again. He lost three family members and it was too hard on him. The doctors told him that if he got depressed again, he would not get well. He knew he was going to die. He told us a lot of things before he died and he taught us important things.

♠ ♠ ♠

When we travelled in the country by dog team, we would travel long distances, as far as Kaushetinatshi (in the Border Beacon area). Once when we were headed there, we almost made it but one of our dogs got very sick. It was chasing a wolf. My father couldn't shoot it because he was afraid of getting bitten. In the morning he got up and went out to look for the dog.

"Our lost dog is back. He's sitting out here," he yelled back to the tent.

"Okay," I said.

My stepmother, Anishe, was very mean to me. When I used to ask her for some food, she would put it where they slept so I wouldn't be able to get it. She had flour, sugar and cookies — everything. When she made bannock and I was hungry, I would reach for some and she did not like that. My father would get upset with her. She did the same thing to me when we were living in Kauishatukuants and later when we moved to the new community, Utshimassits. She was always doing this to me. My father was upset with her because I couldn't spend time in the house. I spent a lot of time at my sister's house.

I was always with my father and my stepmother when they were in *nutshimit*. One time we travelled all the way to Sheshatshu. We arrived in the summer, having left in the fall before the winter came and spent the year in *nutshimit*. We were very tired of walking and our feet were hurting. When we arrived in Sheshatshu, our grandmother Matinueskueu (Monique Rich) came to meet us. We stayed there for a long time. Puamekush (Mary Toma), Napesh (the late Joseph Toma) and Tami and Shishin (Tommy and Cecile Rich) — a lot of people came to meet us. My grandmother Pinamen (Philomene) was also there. We didn't have to unload our canoe. The people did it for us.

"Where are you staying?" Tami asked us.

"I don't know," said my father.

"You can stay with me," said my grandmother Pinamen.

So we stayed there. Tami was upset because he wanted us to stay with him. He would always come to visit us. We stayed for a long time, all summer. It must have been almost fall when we went back.

We travelled with Tami and Nisikutshash (the late Raphael Rich). We also travelled with Nushin (the late Lucy Rich). What was her husband's name — Pineshikan (Ben)? Yes, that was his name, and our grandmother Matinueskueu camped with us too. One time while we were travelling, it started to snow and we didn't have a dog team. Our dogs had died. Only two survived. My sister and I pulled the komatik. We were very tired and we had to walk a long way. I wasn't that big. I had already attended school, but I hadn't yet started having my period. We didn't have a radio then. We arrived in Utshimassits before Tami. Nisikutshash, Anishenish and Nian (Angela and Leon Rich) and their little children travelled with us. When we arrived, we were very tired.

My father and the other men went to the community to get food and then went caribou hunting. They didn't stay away long because my father had an accident. He got a bad cut from a knife. He used to file his knife until it was very sharp, and then he cut himself with this same knife! My stepmother sewed up his cut. I was afraid to look. Anyone would have been scared to look at that big cut. Nisikutshash pulled him on the komatik back to the camp. We couldn't pull him ourselves because he was too heavy. We moved our camp again after the wound had healed.

Nisikutshash went back to Sheshatshu and we travelled back to Kauishatukuants with Nian's family. We arrived close to Christmas time. On our way we saw Mishen's (the late Gilbert Rich's) camp. A woman named Keseuekantsheshish was also there. We were walking because our dogs were all dead. We were very tired. As we got closer to Utshimassits, my father recognized the mountain in Kanishutakushtasht (Flower's Bay) and spotted a snowshoe trail. People were hunting in the area and soon we saw their tents. They didn't have the type of canvas tents we have today. They lived in teepees made of caribou hide. We asked our parents who the people were who lived there. Our father told us it was his brother Shimun's camp. They had bannock and butter, and Shimun made a big pot of tea. We drank up his tea and we were very hungry. Shimun told us we could use his dogs.

We set out again with his dogs on foot. We met Mishen (Gilbert Rich) in Kanishutakushtasht. He asked us if we had just come back and we said yes. We waited around for a while because it was snowing and we couldn't see. When it cleared, we headed for Kauishatukuants again. We had the loan of Shimun's dogs and Mishen had lent his dogs to Nian.

Shimun and his family walked back to Kauishatukuants without their dogs, but they arrived safely. On their way they met Peashue (Francis Piwas). He came to meet us and he brought a lot of dogs with him. Antuan (the late Antoine Tshakapesh) also came to meet us with lots of dogs. I was afraid with so many dogs around. We left our komatiks behind. They are probably still there in Kanishutakushtasht! They were very small komatiks.

We headed on through some woods and ran into people who had come to meet us. It was Peashue and Antuan who had come to meet Nian. We were so happy to see Kauishatukuants!

Later we travelled back to Sheshatshu. My father was sick so we stayed there for a long time. My sister, Nenuskueu, stayed with Napeutik's (Joseph Piwas) family in *nutshimit*. My father was depressed.

♣ ♣ ♣

My stepmother taught me how to clean hides when I was young. She showed me how to scrape the hair off and how to clean the inside of the hide. She also taught me how to tan the skins, so I know how to smoke hides now. My stepmother also showed me how to make moccasins. That's all she showed me. She never taught me how to make mitts, but Manteskueu (Mary Georgette Mistenapeo) showed me. She taught me how to cut them out. I watched her and learned how it was done. Now I can make them by myself. I don't know how to make necklaces or earrings or beaded barrettes, but my daughter Tanina (Danina) does. Sometimes I laugh at myself because of the way I do things. One time when I was tanning a caribou hide, I burned it because it was too thin. My father was also laughing at me.

I have also learned how to make tea dolls. I sometimes have some at my house that I try to sell. Manteskueu was the one who showed me how to make and sew them, how to cut them up. I dress them in parkas, with mitts and moccasins. I learned how to make the parkas from my aunt Matininish (Madeline Rich). I dress them all up and they come out really nice. Dolls filled with tea are expensive, but the ones without are less expensive. I sold one for $200. So far I have made four dolls. A White man who came to visit bought one. He was staying at the nun's house. I sold another to a woman.

When I knit socks, I sell them to people in the community. They like them. They also ask me for caribou hide. They say I tan hides very well. I don't know how to weave snowshoes. I would like to learn if someone would show me how, but I don't have anyone to show me. My stepmother tried to show me and I almost learned how to do it properly, but I don't remember. I was going to ask Utshimaskueu (Charlotte Rich) if she could show me. My son Penute has small snowshoes he hardly ever uses. They are too small for him, and my daughter has a pair too.

⚓ ⚓ ⚓

The stories I have just told you are about the kind of work I do in the country. I also used to cook meals for my late father when he came home from hunting. I did all kinds of work in the tent. I gathered clean boughs for the floor. I cooked and made sure I had meals ready for the hunters when they returned to the camp. I cleaned caribou hides and cut up caribou meat. I also took care of the caribou bones. I helped my father cut the meat off the bones and then we would crush and boil them. I looked after the bones for my father. He used to make a lot of *pimin* (pemmican) from the bone marrow and crushed bones. This was for the *makushan*, the feast of the caribou. He would scoop out a lot of grease from the broth, cut the bone marrow into chunks and mix the two together in a bowl. When it was prepared, he would freeze the mixture.

When my father went hunting he sometimes killed porcupine. One time we were camping near Kaushetinatshi (in the Border Beacon area) with Manishanut (the late Mary Charlotte Katshinak), Puamekush (the late Mary Toma), Napeu (the late Sam Napeo), Uemistikushish (Georg Henriksen) and Mitshituaunapeu (the late Raphael Rich). Uemistikushish killed porcupines too and he gave them to my stepmother and father. My stepmother showed me how to blow the porcupine up and how to use the safety pin on it so that the air wouldn't come out. This makes it easier to scrape the quills off. My stepmother told us to always do this with the porcupine and not to forget the things she was teaching us.

Puamekush taught us some things too. She told us to be good when we got older and after we were married. One time she was sitting around with my stepmother, Manishanut, my aunt Matininish and Tshipesh (Elizabeth Napeo), and they were all talking to us. They were telling us not to do certain things. They told us that, when we got older, we should never steal or lie to people. We were not allowed and we promised never to do that. We also never sniffed gas when we were younger.

My father told us so many stories about the past and the things he had done years ago. That was his way. When we were living at our old house he told me one story about when I was a child. He said I had been drinking. My grandmother had given me the alcohol. I got drunk and passed out right away.

♠ ♠ ♠

Before my father died, he told us a story that he was going to leave us. He let himself die. I knew my father was going to leave us. He told us that he was leaving his work for us to carry on. He wanted us to continue to help people the way he had in the past. "I have helped the people from Sheshatshu, and White men and women also," he said to us. "I am leaving you to continue my work. Try to continue this work. I soon must leave you. I am ready now."

Because my father was sick a lot, he would sometimes have seizures. He was given pills but many times he didn't take all the pills that were given to him. Sometimes he would be very sick and he would say he was going to die soon. Every morning when he woke up, he would talk to us about a lot of things. He told us he had seen his family's spirits coming to him and they would sit around him in the bedroom.

"They came for me and they tried to take my hand for me to go with them," he told us. "It was my father and mother, my grandfather and grandmother, and my friends."

He also saw Tami's and Mitshituaunapeu's (the late Raphael Rich's) spirits. He saw many other spirits, including the spirits of White men he knew. I cried when he told me he was going to leave us, but he wanted to go with the relatives whose spirits he had seen. He thought about it a lot and it was upsetting him. The spirits also came to him in his dreams. I heard him screaming in his dream once and my son Tomas also heard him shouting in his sleep.

Sometimes I wouldn't hear him. One time we travelled to the country to Kapukuanipant (Jack's Brook). He was already sick then but he was walking. He was all right and he was talking normally. We set up the tent. Akat (Agathe Piwas) put up the tent and I laid the boughs where my father would be sleeping. He just sat there.

"What is wrong with your father?" Munik (Monique Rich) asked me. "He is not saying anything to us. Is he always like that?"

"He is not like that," I told her. "Maybe he is not well."

Then we waited a long time for the helicopter to come and pick up my father. Akat had radioed out that he was not well. We were tired of waiting, but finally, early one Sunday morning, they came to pick him up. Tomas was coming on the boat and he almost made it to our camp just before the helicopter arrived. After they took my father, we got ready to return to the community in the boat. Miste Pinip (Phillip Rich) and Etuetish (Edward Piwas) told us not to go on the boat. They were afraid the boat would tip over, so we didn't go. They also told us Tomas would be there soon.

I knew my father was going to die, but I never passed this knowledge on to my son Tomas. He didn't know his grandfather was dying. My father asked us not to forget what he had told us.

"Don't ever leave each other, always stick together," he told us.

Sometimes now I want to leave the house since my father passed away, but Tomas doesn't want to. I feel very lonely in this house. When I went to church after he was gone, I felt like crying, because I remembered looking at his casket at the funeral service. I almost walked out of the church. I felt very emotional.

The Country Is a Healing Place

Mary Jane Nui

*This story begins with glimpses of Mary Jane as a small
girl and her close relationship with her grandparents.
Many years pass and Mary Jane, now a grandmother,
returns to the place where she was born, this time to
find healing. Here she participated in the first mobile
treatment program organized by addictions workers
from Utshimassits (Davis Inlet). This type of healing
was one of the recommendations that came out of the
1992 People's Inquiry that followed the house fire
which killed six children. Before this program, many
Innu had been travelling out to treatment programs all
over Canada. Leaders wanted to set up their own
program in nutshimit (the country), which they felt
was the best place to go for counselling and healing. In
nutshimit, the Innu can practise their way of life, cut
wood, feed their families. It is the best place to open up
and to get anger and hurt out. Participants can be a
part of nature, walk on the land, in the woods, by the
water, and talk to the Creator. Nutshimit is also a
place where the whole family can be treated, rather
than only individuals. Elders from the community, as
well as elders from away, have been involved and old
ways of healing such as the sweat lodge have been
revived. A number of programs have since been held*

for families from both Utshimassits and Sheshatshu.
The Innu front-line workers who organized this pro-
gram were trained in addictions intervention by coun-
sellors from the Nechi Training Institute of Alberta, a
First Nations-run addictions centre.

When I was growing up, we would head for nutshimit whenever my grandfather Miste Ueapeu (John Pasteen) said so. I would be very happy to go. One time my grandfather asked all of us to get into a canoe. I wondered why. The canoe was so small and there were so many of us. How were we all going to fit?

"Where are we going?" I asked my grandfather, as we set out.

"We are going to Mushuau-shipu (George River) and it is very far," he said.

I was maybe four or five years old back then. My grandfather carried me on his back while he walked. I was too young to paddle, so my grandfather did all the paddling. One time, as we were going down the river, we spotted a house covered with moss.

"What is that?" I asked my grandfather.

"It is an *esiutshiuap* (moss house)," he told me, and we headed for the shore.

People had left some of their belongings there, but there was no food. Before my grandfather got out of the canoe, he said he knew how to find out if there were people camping at Mushuau-shipu. He could tell from the freshly cut trees and footprints left behind. When he came back, he said there was no one at Mushuau-shipu. We left again and canoed down the river. There was a rock sticking up out of the water.

"What is that?" I asked him.

"It is called the Kashatshipet-ashinin (Rock That Sticks Out of the Water). People pass here all the time and see it," he explained to me.

We set up camp on the Mushuau-shipu in a place where there were no trees.

⚓ ⚓ ⚓

I don't remember everything about when I was small, but I know we didn't always run out of food. My grandmother Miste Mani-Shan (Mary Jane Pasteen) and my grandfather took good care of me. My grandfather was a good hunter and a conjurer — a person who knew a little about the animal spirits. That is why we didn't run out of food. When we were in the canoe, my grandfather would kill caribou and catch fish along the way. We did not go hungry. He was very strong in his tradition, and so was my grandmother. Sometimes we ran short of the things we needed, but other times we had plenty. I am very proud of how my grandmother raised me. I really missed my grandparents when they died, because they always took very good care of me.

When my grandfather was getting old, I looked after my grandmother. She was also old and I remembered how they had taken care of me when I was a child. The name I had for my grandmother was Kakuskuesh, or Porcupine Girl. I was very close to her. But she became very old and I couldn't take care of her any more. My grandfather was old and sick too.

⚓ ⚓ ⚓

I travelled to *nutshimit* two years ago in the spring. We ski-dooed out to the barrens. We set up camp in the place where I was born. I was very happy to be going to the country, this time on a healing program (mobile treatment program), although sometimes the weather was bad when we were out there.

I wasn't sure how I was going to make out with my healing at the time because I was a person who was always looking at the past instead of the future. I think if I had looked to the future, I would have done better. But finally I made some changes for myself after I talked with the young Innu counsellors. These people were trained in the Nechi program. I changed and now I feel better about myself. I wasn't sure if I was going to make it through the program or not. I wasn't sure about the young people because what they were doing was very hard, but I was wrong in my thinking. These young people are very powerful in what they are doing.

There were a lot of people in the camp working on their healing. I heard there wasn't enough money that time and there were more people who had wanted to come up. The mobile treatment program really worked for us. I was very happy to be around the other women. They were very good to me. We learned many things out there. The elders were there too and they taught us a lot of things. They worked very hard. When we were getting ready to leave the camp, I wanted to stay a while and canoe to see the spot where I was born. I hadn't seen that place, only from the plane. There were other women at the camp who were born there too. I was very sad when we left.

After we arrived in Utshimassits, I was very unhappy. I found the community so contaminated. A lot of things weren't going right for me. I got sick. The muscles in my legs bothered me. My family went back to our cabin in Kanishutakushtasht (Flower's Bay). I remembered how the sweat lodge had helped me during the healing program, so my husband and I built a sweat lodge at our camp and we had a sweat in this place where we raised our children. After we had the sweat, I felt better. I wasn't sick or depressed. We went back to Utshimassits and I felt a lot better again.

I like sewing and working on snowshoes. I like to work at different crafts, but sometimes it is hard because I also have a lot of grandchildren to look after. I am not comfortable having other people look after my grandchildren. I would like to have enough work stamps to receive Employment Insurance cheques, so I can have a little bit of money to feed my grandchildren.

I don't want to lose my culture and the way that we survive on wild meats and food. I don't want to lose my way of living, the things I used to carry on my back and the animals I used to eat. I don't really like to eat store food. My children still eat wild food.

* * *

One time I went to Ottawa for a protest and I kept thinking about what I was being given to eat there. Maybe it was a snake! A Native woman gave it to me and I took a bite. I was thinking I should eat it because the woman was Native too, and maybe this was part of her culture. She was also helping us. I felt bad. Next time they give me this kind of food, I will have to eat it.

I am very happy that we will have help relocating our community from Utshimassits to Shankus (Sango Bay). I want to be strong to make sure relocation takes place. Maybe we will have the strength to make the government realize we need to relocate because we are unhappy on this island. We have many problems here. I am not sure what it is going to be like when we relocate. Maybe there will be changes. When I was young and we were living on the mainland in *nutshimit*, in Estinekamuk (Snegamook), everything went well, although we were poor. We didn't have problems, only sometimes when people were sick.

The big changes happened to us when the elders died. I wonder what God was thinking when this started to happen. At first we were poor, then the elders died. I wonder what God is thinking now. We used to look after the elders, but after we settled on this island, we developed many problems. There were a lot of other deaths and some parents did not look after their children. The children started sniffing gas. The heavy drinking took over and there was a lot of violence. This is where the problems really started. Maybe if the young people had more Innu education, we might have stayed on the mainland instead of this island, and all of this would not have happened. We didn't have a school there, but the children were learning about life in the country.

Lonely for You

Aldea Rich

for Mathias

It's been two years
since you left.
To me it's only yesterday
when I screamed
and called your name.
And it still hurts
thinking of you.
It's been hard,
too hard for our kids,
too hard for me
to accept that you are gone.
Wherever I go,
your face appears in my mind.
Whatever I do,
your name keeps
repeating itself in my mind.
I loved you and always will.
All I do now is pray
and have silent tears for you.
I know that you are safe.
I feel it in my heart.
You always said that

you'll always stay with me.
Now I know what you meant.
You are always in my mind and in my heart.

Mathias died of a heart attack as a very young man,
leaving Aldea to raise their three children on her own.

I Think about These Things

Mary Georgette Mistenapeo

What does a mother say to her troubled children after one of their siblings has committed suicide? Mary Georgette sees with a chilling clarity the tragedy of alcohol abuse and gas sniffing faced by her children and grandchildren. She shares her struggles to move beyond despair and find healing for herself and her family. She talks about old ways of healing and Innu medicines, as well as new ways, such as the healing circle, a support group that meets regularly where people can talk about their problems, break the silence and discover new ways to live more healthy lives.

When I was a child, I was always in *nutshimit* (the country). I never dressed the way I dress now that I live in Utshimassits (Davis Inlet). I dress like a White person now. A long time ago, I dressed only in caribou skin. When the White man came, I changed my ways and forgot the ways of *nutshimit*. But lately it has got me thinking and I am trying to go back into *nutshimit*. Every year I go now. I want to teach my children about life in *nutshimit* and how my father used to hunt. I want my grandsons to learn these ways. My children did learn these skills when they were young, and today they are still watching and learning from their grandfather Tumish (Thomas Noah).

When I am in the community, I can't stay very long because
my grandchildren, who live with me, miss *nutshimit* and want to
go back. I can't say no to them. I go right away when they want
to leave, and we don't worry about school. They work hard and
learn more in *nutshimit* than at the school. As a child I learned
about this life. I learned to do different things. My mother,
Ueuetemiskueu, or Outdoor Woman (Alice Noah), taught me
and now I do these things without her help both in *nutshimit* and
also in the community.

I don't want to feed my children store-bought food. I am
afraid they will get to like this food too much. They always want
nutshimit food and they don't eat too much of the store food. I
buy flour to make bannock because they love bannock, but they
don't like other things too much, like sweet stuff. In the old days,
food from the land was the main thing we ate. We were strong
and healthy. People never got sick very much, but today many
Innu are sick all the time.

This sickness comes from the White man's food. Most of this
food is in tin cans. A lot of it is not fit to eat because it is full of
chemicals. White men grow their food and breed their animals
for food. They feed the animals themselves. We don't do these
things. We get our food from the wild, and these animals get their
food from nature. We are very careful not to waste any kind of
game that we catch. But for White men, they enjoy the food that
is sent in to the store.

In the past when I was in *nutshimit* and first had my children,
I never fed them canned milk. I would breast-feed them. When
I looked after other children who were given to me, I wasn't sure
what to do for milk, so I had to give them canned milk. They
would always get sick, but my children were never sick when I
was nursing them.

I nursed all my children, but today I wonder what is happening. I have almost lost the Innu way of life. Years ago, I didn't see
people drinking too much alcohol. I only saw older people
drinking, but today I see a big difference in the age of the
drinking. Now children are drinking. I never used to drink, but

things happened in our family. I lost my daughter, my grandchild and my son-in-law. Today there is still so much happening. Many people have committed suicide. I don't think it is going to stop unless people work with each other to do something about it.

♣ ♣ ♣

My children really worry me. My girls and boys drink, but some of them are not into alcohol too much. It must be 10 years since their father, Miste Etuet (Edward Mistenapeo), stopped drinking. Now three of my children still turn to alcohol and drink heavily. I can't say anything to them, but I am searching for help. I ask people for their help with this situation. I am really unhappy about my family's alcohol problems. I think these things don't come from the Innu, but from the White man.

I see a lot of things happening to our grandchildren too. They also sniff gas. I talk to my grandchildren, but they also don't listen to me. Some of them were taken away from the community one time when they were sniffing gas. They came back and the same thing happened. They were sniffing again. I don't know what to do anymore. I can only take them to *nutshimit*, but they sniff out there too. What can I do? I need to use gas when I am in *nutshimit*. Sometimes things are okay out in *nutshimit* and sometimes they are not.

A lot of people come to me for help. I am also desperate with my problems and I need their help too. When they come to me, I go right away because I know what a difference it makes to have someone to talk to. When I talk with someone, like about my children, I feel better. I am happy to ask for help from other people when I need it. I like to share things with them and to have them share with me. Sometimes I ask people if I can share more when I need to, because there is not enough time for everyone to share in the circle. Maybe some people want to go home early because they have things to do at home and at work. Sometimes I go to the women's gatherings and they really help me. I share my stories and other women also share their problems.

We have a sweat lodge, a healing place for people who are sick. The sweat lodge helps as well as the things we use inside it. I am really happy to be invited to be part of the community's healing programs. I work on the sweat lodge when people want to have sweats.

One time, when I was just a girl, my sister was put in a sweat lodge. She almost died from a tooth infection. My mother and father set up the sweat lodge for her. They blew the hot air into her mouth when she was inside the sweat lodge. After they finished with the sweat lodge, they did bloodletting on her. She got better after these treatments and the infection went away.

Another time, when my oldest daughter, Manite (Mary Theresa), was small, her throat was bad. My parents put her into the sweat lodge and did the same thing to her. Her throat was healed after they blew hot air into her throat and cut her tongue a little to make it bleed.

This also happened to me when I was very small. It was around the time when my grandmother died. I barely remember. She died in *nutshimit* and I almost died at the time too. My parents practised bloodletting on me when they saw I was very sick. I only remember that they wanted to tie me up so I couldn't move when they did the bloodletting. My grandfather was still alive then. I recovered after the bloodletting. My mother thought I was going to die.

I think about all these things now because of all the problems that are happening. Sometimes I think maybe I would have been better off dying the time I was really sick and my grandmother died. I talked to the priest about this once.

"Don't talk like that," the priest said to me. "You don't know what God is thinking." So I didn't say anything more to him, but I was still thinking I should have died that time.

When things go badly with my children, I talk to them when they are sober. I ask them what they are going to do when I die. I tell them about all the things they are doing to me. Maybe they think about what I say, and sometimes they are really angry with me. I get mad at them because I see they don't look after their

children properly. One time I was mad at one of my daughters.
I yelled at her. Right away she got mad and said she was going
to commit suicide. When I heard her threaten to commit suicide,
I thought about her sister who did commit suicide. That memory
still haunts me.

♦ ♦ ♦

Years ago Innu people would not use doctors when they were
sick. They collected plants in *nutshimit* to make their own medicines. We still use medicines from the land, and that is why we
want to protect our land from the White man's destruction. I still
collect medicines from the land.

Innu women used to have their babies in *nutshimit* years ago.
They never went to the hospital. They never used anything to
help them have their babies. Our mothers and fathers, our
grandfathers and great-grandfathers were all born in *nutshimit*. I
never used the hospital when my children were born. I have eight
children and they were all born in *nutshimit*. I was born in
nutshimit too, which is why I have respect for the land and want
to protect it from White people. I think about these times
because the Innu used to do everything for themselves. I once
saw a child born in a tent. Nothing happened to the mother.
There is no reason for doctors to make women stay in the hospital
to have their children. It is only money the doctors look for.

I remember an *eissimeskueu* (Inuit woman) had her baby at
Emish (Voisey's Bay). After the baby was born, they showed me
this little Inuk. The woman didn't need a hospital to deliver her
baby. Years ago a lot of women didn't need a hospital to deliver
their babies. Everything we needed for good medicine was on the
land. When Innu people talk about this, I think they could write
a book about their own medicines. Then other people, who don't
know about Innu medicines, could learn. All the information
would be in one book.

I was sick one time in *nutshimit*. I had pneumonia and I used
medicine from the earth. I'd seen someone use this medicine

before. I felt much better after I used it and, when I got sick again, I used other medicines from the land. When my throat is sore, I search for a medicine. I find it, use it and I am okay. My pain is gone.

One time, I had impetigo on my hands when I went to *nutshimit*. I used a medicine I found from a porcupine. You can use other animals as well, such as geese, bear or caribou. You boil the animals and use the grease for medicine. My husband came back from his hunt with the porcupine. I only use the things I have seen other people use years ago. I haven't practised blood-letting by myself. Someone could do bloodletting on me, but I can't do it to myself.

These days I take too many pills. It worries me, because that means I can't do bloodletting. The doctor said it is not good to take pills and do bloodletting at the same time. Maybe he doesn't want us to practise our own medicine. He said to stop taking pills for three days before doing bloodletting. Maybe he is telling the truth, maybe he is lying to the people, maybe he just doesn't know.

In the old days, when people had a headache, they never used Aspirin. They only used this Innu cure, which is to prick the head. I have done that to myself when I had a headache and there was no Aspirin around. I just use needles and it helps. Today the doctors have taken over and that is partly why people have so many problems.

We do not need White people. I don't think I need to ask for extra things from them such as medicines. They give me medicine when I am sick, but I think I can do without their medicine. Their medicine is not good for my system. My body is just aging. When I was sick in the past and knew something was wrong, I went to see the doctor and he told me I was just getting old. "This is what happens to people when they start aging," he said to me. He said when people are old, they have a weakening of the bones, a disease called osteoporosis. He said that is probably what I have now. But I don't think I am old and I don't want to age. Sometimes I wish I was still a young woman. Probably I don't know I am sick. Sometimes people don't know that they are sick. Maybe what the doctor is saying is true.

♠ ♠ ♠

Years ago we never used snowmobiles. We travelled by foot and pulled our things on komatiks. Later we began to use dogs for travelling. Then ski-doos came along. Now everything is easy for people. It really worries me. I think about all the animal carcasses that are no longer cared for. When the animals are killed, they are not cleaned. I see a lot of caribou bones thrown in the dump. The elders really respected these bones years ago, but now we are not taking care of them. It is like we have lost our ways, our culture. My father used to build a platform on which to lay the bones when we were in *nutshimit*. We always put everything on that platform. I remember wondering what he was doing with the bones and why he respected the animals he killed. He would hang the bones in a tree.

I think about these things today. People refer to them as remains or leftovers, but I am not sure how to properly call these things. For years I didn't take care of these things and I would just throw the bones out to the dump. Today these things really worry me. I feel I should go back to the old ways. I can take care of things now.

I went to my father to talk to him about what he thinks about the bones being dumped. He taught me how to care for the bones and to respect them and hang them in a tree. He told me when we break camp, there is a spirit that goes through the camp after we leave. This spirit cares for the animals and checks to see if there are animal bones being left in disrespect. I am learning from my father by watching him. Now I care for the bones too. I make sure I don't leave bones lying around. I clean up the camp when I am leaving and burn everything that I am throwing away. I bury my garbage in the sand.

I think about these things when I am back in the community. Maybe this is why things have gone so wrong for the people?

Maybe things have not worked out for us because we don't care about the animals and the bones? A lot of elders have died and there are very few of them around now. When they die, they will leave only us young people behind. The White people will take over when we don't have elders.

♣ ♣ ♣

A long time ago, there was a priest by the name of Father Whitehead. His real name was Edward O'Brien. He would come once in a while to pray for the people here in Kauishatukuants (Old Davis Inlet). When it was time for him to leave, he would give the Innu stuff from the government store. Then he would send the people back into *nutshimit* to hunt. We used to tell him stories about life in the country. He believed these stories.

The women used to braid their hair and tie it up. Father O'Brien really admired the women with braids in their hair. The people began to realize he was a good priest and they respected him very much. Whenever we heard he was coming to the village, we would gather and give him a welcoming party. We received him with respect. Then he would announce the time when mass would be held. Innu men and women had great respect for his religion and spirituality. The children were not allowed to come into church without their parents. The only time children were allowed to come in was when they needed to be baptized, or when they were with their parents.

Then another priest came when we were in Nutak, up the coast from Kauishatukuants. His name was Joseph. We gathered together in one group to welcome him. He told us when mass would be held. He also told our parents that we would go to confession and we would learn how to go about it. The priest had so much respect for religion that we were not allowed to make any kind of noise in church. But this priest didn't know about the braids the women used to wear. It wasn't long after he came that there were changes made by him. We started wearing clothing like shirts, pants and boots. He was also teaching us

Innu-aimun, using books. I was taught religion in Innu-aimun and I never went to school. The priest was the one who taught me.

I was also taught about how to look after the church. Father Joseph taught me everything there was to know about religion. I knew the priest well. I always listened to him about whatever it was that needed to be done for the church.

Then there was a priest by the name of Frank Peters who came to the village. I worked with him for a while before I found out what he was like. He wasn't like the other priests. He was also learning the Innu language. I taught him Innu words. He wanted to learn the words for "man" and "woman" in Innu. He used to laugh at the way the words were pronounced. I wondered why he wanted to learn what the words were for what a man and a woman look like. He was a man. He should know. I told him there were no words in Innu for the kinds of things he wanted to be taught. I wasn't too happy about it because I didn't want to teach anybody about this, especially not a priest. Finally, I told my parents what the priest wanted me to teach him.

"What kind of a priest does he think he is?" my mother asked. My father said he never heard of a priest who wanted to learn this kind of stuff about a man and a woman.

The trouble with this priest really started when the people saw he wasn't acting like a priest at all. He was controlling the people. I was very annoyed at the way he was acting. After he came and lived in our community, there was always jealousy among the women whenever they were around the priests.

There was another priest who came to our village. His name was Father Chris. I used to help him out a lot. He was a very good priest. There was also a brother who came in. It was found out that he did a sinful thing, sexual abuse. One boy told me what the brother did to him. People began to think that the priests were being taught how to do these things. We had a bishop named Peter Sutton and I knew him well. He said he wanted a church group in Utshimassits (Davis Inlet). He said he didn't want to upset any people.

♗ ♗ ♗

Long ago, the priest did the job of the social worker. In Kauishatukuants, when women were beaten up by their husbands, they would go to the priest for help and support. If a woman had trouble with her husband, the priest would let the woman stay in his house. I wondered how the priest felt about having women in his house. Women are still being battered. These days, the social worker is trying to help abused women. A lot of women end up in hospital when they are beaten up by their husbands. Even the doctors are involved. They are afraid the women might be seriously hurt. We should try to understand that the doctors, nurses, social workers and priests are doing these things for the sake of the women's lives. We must try to remember what happened before. These women used to go through these beatings with no one to turn to. The priest was the only person the woman could turn to when her husband beat her.

Nowadays the social workers and the doctors seem to be the only people who are trying to do something for battered women. Innu people are not doing anything for them. We are like those battered women of long ago. We don't seem to talk about ourselves when we were battered women. We are only looking at other women who are battered, but we used to be like them.

We also say whatever we like about battered women. Even our kids are like that. They say whatever they like to other kids, their elders or anybody who is being neglected by their families. They make fun of them. We are not allowed to hit our kids now, but in the past our parents used to hit us when we got into trouble.

We seem to be surprised about what is happening. We shouldn't be, because these things happened in the past. We seem to forget our own troubles in the past. We make fun of what is happening in other people's lives. We don't seem to care.

⚘ ⚘ ⚘

Today White people don't want to leave the land alone. They are looking for minerals. The White government never lived in our area before. The Innu cared for the land, and we never looked for any copper, nickel or cobalt. When White people found these minerals, they began destroying the land, Innu lands. The land at Emish is being destroyed. The White government is stealing the land from the Innu. He is looking for money from the land, without ever having consulted with the Innu about what he is going to do with our land.

The White government says it's his land, but I question whether there was ever a government who stepped foot on our land in the past. Was he born here? Many Innu people were born at Emish. There are also many Innu burial sites in that area. The land belongs to the people who are buried there. The Innu are buried everywhere in *nutshimit*. I would think that wherever Innu people are buried is our land.

I wonder if the White government knows where he belongs. I wonder if he ever hunted on his own land. I know many Innu hunters by name who have been hunting on our land. When I was younger, Innu hunters travelled many places. My first child was born in Emish and she grew up there. Emish is her land, but now the government is saying "This is my land." I don't think the government's babies were born there. I can say this directly to the government. If I have someone translating for me, I can say, "Were your babies born there?" I would tell the government people one of my children was born there. Then I would ask, "What about you?" I don't think the government would be able to answer me.

The government lives in luxury while we live in poverty. We know what is happening to us, but we can't do anything about it. We own our land and ourselves, but we have lost our way of living and our culture. White people and the White government are still looking young, while our young adults are looking old, men and women of all ages look old.

People say the government is only showing off because it is the big boss of the province or of Canada. We know what the government is doing to us. He is affecting our lives in a big way. People are talking about going back to our old way of life. They are saying it would be a good thing if we could also run our own community the way we see fit.

Child

Rose Gregoire

You may have sad memories
or begin to have sad memories,
but it's a great joy
to be able to feel that,
good to allow the Child to speak.
It will make us richer.

Child comes back to you crying,
but you learn
how to comfort the Child
and not to be afraid
of its tears,
that Child is not to start laughing,
that Child is going
to start playing,
but above all,
that Child is going to tell that story,
as it really should have been told.

And please listen to that story
because the Creator
is in that story,
and is telling the story
with the Child.

Go gently,
don't rush it
because the Child is knocking
on the door
asking to be let out.

So be there for the Child,
please,
no matter what she or he tells you.

The Thunder and Mosquito

Nympha Byrne

One time Thunder was craving for something to eat. He went to meet with the small insects on earth. He told them he was hungry. All the insects that could fly decided to help Thunder. He told them the only time they could fly up in the sky was when it was raining and they heard thunderstorms. Many insects said they couldn't fly up into the sky. Thunder left them to decide.

The insects got together to talk about the Thunder's request. Mosquito said that he could help Thunder. All the small insects were anxious to hear what the Mosquito was planning to give Thunder.

"I can give him blood," said Mosquito. "I can give him animal's blood or human blood."

The insects were all shocked to hear about Mosquito's plan.

"We need animals and humans on the earth," they said.

"I can lie to Thunder and tell him that I got the blood on the rocks and trees," Mosquito told them.

The other insects were hesitant to go along with Mosquito's plan, but they finally agreed. Mosquito flew up in the sky and told Thunder that he would help him, and he requested rain showers. Mosquito went back to the earth and it started to rain. He bit a human first and then an animal. It continued to rain and Thunder started to roar.

Mosquito flew up into the sky again and gave Thunder a taste of blood. Thunder said it was very good. He wanted some more.

"You have to get it yourself," Mosquito told Thunder. "You can get it on rocks and trees."

Mosquito didn't want anything to do with Thunder again. He requested that Thunder not ask him for any more favours.

"You have done a great work for me," Thunder said to Mosquito. "That's all I wanted from you. I promise that you will not hear from me again."

Mosquito left Thunder and came back to earth. The other insects were happy to hear what Mosquito had done. Thunder left to go to earth as well. He struck lightning, which hit the trees and the rock, but it did not taste anything like what Mosquito had given him. He burned the trees and cracked the rock in half. He couldn't go back to ask Mosquito, because he did not want to break his promise, and he knew that Mosquito was not coming back.

Today when there is a thunderstorm, the lightning starts to burn the forest. The mosquitoes are also thick when we have rain showers. This is how it all happened. A little white lie from Mosquito saved us. If Mosquito hadn't lied to Thunder, we could have died when lightning struck.

Early Childhood Education

Caroline Andrew

A bout of pneumonia landed Caroline in a hospital and then a boarding school in the 1950s. It was a hospital of the International Grenfell Association (IGA), which provided health services to the people of Labrador. The IGA also ran a boarding school in North West River for children from coastal communities. This was before the Catholic Church had established permanent missions and schools in Labrador for the Innu. Caroline shares the difficulties of leaving her home in Kauishatukuants (Old Davis Inlet) as a small girl to attend the boarding school. She contrasts this schooling with the Innu education she got from her parents. She shares impressions of the changes she has lived through in her life and how she sees hope in the future for the Innu by integrating the best of both worlds. For many years, Caroline worked as an Innu teacher in Peenamin Mackenzie School in Sheshatshu.

The year was 1952 and I was 10 years old. I was still living in Kauishatukuants and I had tuberculosis. The doctor told my parents I had to go to the hospital in North West River for treatment. He didn't tell them how long I would be gone. I left in February and stayed in the hospital until August, just before school started in September. I got out and they put me in the dormitory run by the International Grenfell Association, where schoolchildren from all over Labrador lived. I was still on my treatment for TB for one more year. I couldn't understand or speak English at all. I couldn't even say "yes" or "no" in English. I was very homesick for my parents. I also missed my friends back home.

When I went to school on the first day, I didn't know what they would do to me. There were two other girls from Kauishatukuants with me, but we weren't in the same grade. I didn't even understand when they asked me what grade I was in. The priest had never taught us that word. I was so scared, because I didn't understand anything about the English school. The teacher held my hand and took me wherever she wanted me. First they took me into the kindergarten classroom. The teacher did some testing on me. She asked me to count, then showed me numbers and asked me to say what they were. She also gave me a sheet of printing and I printed my name and Aa. Later they took me into the Grade One classroom. This time I did addition and subtraction, and I counted from 1 to 50 in English. I did it all because I was already learning some of the math work from the priest. The next year they put me in Grade Two and I stayed there for the full year.

After I did one year, I thought I was doing much better. I understood a few English words, and I could speak just a little too. I also wasn't homesick much because I had those two girls from home and I knew them very well. There were no phones in those days. When we wanted to hear news from home, we had to write a letter to our parents. It would take a long time for the letter to get there and to hear back from them. We weren't allowed to stay outdoors for long after school. We had to do our homework and we had to go to bed at nine o'clock. In June, when school was over, I was so happy to go back home. I thought I would never come back again. When I got home, I told my parents what I thought about the school in North West River.

When it was time to go back to school, I didn't want to go, but my parents wanted me to, so I did. They were my parents and I had to do what they wanted. This time I went with my brother Ushikuesh (Sam Nui). He was only six years old. He was in kindergarten and I was in Grade Three. We didn't like it much. When my brother was homesick, he would make me homesick too. When he cried, I would also cry. The only thing we were allowed was to go to Sheshatshu across the river on Sundays for church. After church we always had to go back straight to the dormitory. We weren't allowed to visit people. If we didn't do what the house mother told us, we would be punished. But we really were learning the English language.

After I had completed three years, I enjoyed school very much. That year was 1956. I was in Grade Four and 13 years old. That was the last year I went to school in North West River, but now that is another story.

☙ ☙ ☙

One Sunday I didn't go to church because there was nobody to come and pick us up from across the river. The ice was not safe to walk over and there was no cable car yet. Everybody in the dorm was going to their own church, even the house mother and the other women who worked there. We didn't like to stay behind. Just when they were about to leave, one of the workers asked us if we wanted to go with them. We said yes. We knew we were making a mistake by going to a non-Catholic church, but we went anyway because we were scared of getting punished by the house mother if we did not go.

The following Sunday, we went back to church on the other side of the river. This time we had no trouble getting there. Someone came for us in the canoe. As soon as the priest saw us arrive, he came to meet us. He was so angry.

"Why did you go to a non-Catholic church?" he said. "That is not your religion."

We didn't say anything because we were so scared. He told us he was going to tell the priest in Kauishatukuants. The priest would then tell our parents. He said he was also going to tell the *kamituatshet* (bishop) when he came. I didn't know what my parents were going to think when they heard this. We weren't allowed to go back to the dorm after this and there was no place to continue our schooling. The priest did not want us go to a non-Catholic school anymore and there was no school in Sheshatshu yet.

Today it still makes me angry when I remember this. I think I would have finished all the grades as far as I could. I am still angry with the priest. Now I work at a very important job at the school. That education would have helped me to do this job. I was beginning to like the school very, very much. All of a sudden, I lost everything. The two priests who were looking after Innu people in Kauishatukuants and Sheshatshu back then were Father Pierson and Father Peters.

When my family moved to Sheshatshu from Kauishatukuants, I was already 16 years old. The school here only went as far as Grade Five. I did Grade Five and that was the end of schooling for me. I never found another Catholic school I could go to. I went to work at the North West River Hospital instead.

Today I am 55 years old and I am still trying to learn more English as a second language. I haven't finished yet, but I have done so much. I am happy because I can talk to people when I want to and I don't need a translator.

My Innu education was very different. Before we moved from Kauishatukuants to Sheshatshu, I used to go to *nutshimit* (the country) with my parents, Miste Munik and Miste Nuk (Monique and Luke Nui). We would go from September to December and from February to June. This was the time for us to learn from our parents. We would watch our parents working and making things. We didn't use a pencil or paper in the country.

I was the oldest of five children in my family. I had to help my mother with her work. The first thing we had to do in the morning was gather wood for the fire, fetch water and sometimes collect boughs when it was time to change the tent floor. After we did our outdoor work, we had inside work, like cooking and sewing.

My mother taught me everything she knew about *nutshimit* jobs and about all the names for places and things like mountains, lakes, rivers, streams and different kinds of trees. She showed me how to make stockings and parkas with caribou hide, and other kinds of clothing. She taught me how to clean animals and how to cut them up. I learned how to prepare food to keep for later use. She also taught me how to dry different kinds of furs, like beaver, otter, muskrat and mink. I learned everything from her that she was taught by her own mother.

"If you don't listen and try hard, you will never learn," I remember my mother used to say to me.

This was our early Innu education in the old days. We learned by listening and watching, by practising very carefully. We learned by playing and acting like real old Innu people. We behaved like real families and this was very helpful for learning the real things, because we were doing what we saw the elders do.

My father used to go hunting every morning. He would leave our camp around five or six in the morning and he might return around seven or eight in the evening, or even later, like ten or midnight. We would stay up until he came home. We wanted to see what kind of animals he would bring back. Some children would always ask questions when they saw the animals for the first time, especially the boys. My father would tell us legend stories at night. We would listen until we fell asleep. That is the way we learned his legends. Sometimes my father was gone overnight, or even for a week at a time with other men. The women always had to stay behind to take care of their homes and children.

My mother showed me how to make and set up a tent. It is the women who have to cut up and sew the tent. All the older children have to help. The boys help their father cut down trees for the sticks to hold up the tent and for firewood to keep it warm. The girls help their mothers gather boughs for the tent floor, as well as firewood. Sometimes men have to leave for hunting before the tent has been set up, so the women and children have to do all the rest. In the old days, women sometimes even had to cut wood because the men were always busy hunting and making the things they needed, like snowshoes and sleds in the winter or canoes in the summer.

I learned about making snowshoes and how to do the weaving to fill the inside. The men look for the right kind of tree for the snowshoe frames. They work on the frames and let them dry until they are ready. Then the women take over. First they have to cut the caribou hide into strips to make the babiches to weave into the frames. These babiches have to be two different sizes and are called two different names: *atipish* and *assiminiapi*.

My mother also taught me how to tan caribou hide. First you have to put the hide up near the stove for two days. It has to be a very hot stove and we have to be careful not to get burned. We put the hide in warm water mixed with caribou brain. If there is no caribou brain, it can be any kind of animal brain. We soak the hide in this warm water and brain three or four times, take it out and let it dry. We have to keep on stretching the hide so it won't get too hard. It has to be soft as cotton before it is smoked. After the smoking, the hide is ready to be cut up and used. When we cut up the hide, we still need help there too.

"If you don't cut up the skin in the proper way, you are wasting a lot," my mother said to me. The caribou hide can be used to make moccasins, mitts, bags, caps, jackets and vests. In the old days caribou hide was used for everything, like teepees, dresses, pants for men and many other things.

Sometimes in the old days, elders taught the children how to make things, because they liked to have spares just in case they might need them later. For example, if they ran out of bullets, they had to use bows and arrows to kill small animals. Or when they didn't have any hooks or nets, they made fishhooks from animal bones.

Another important thing for families in *nutshimit* is that the women learn how to shoot, because they stay behind when the men go away to hunt. Some women are good hunters, like men. I used to go with my mother when she hunted small animals. The woman also has to hunt for the children when the man is sick. The same thing happens with the man. When the wife is sick, the man has to do the woman's work.

I learned how to clean the animals from my mother. First you remove the skin from all animals before you cut up the pieces of meat. Every animal is cut up in different ways. For example, with the beaver, we remove the skin, clean it, dry it and bring it later to trade at the store. The same goes for otter, mink, muskrat, weasel, lynx, fox, wolf and marten. The porcupine is the only one who is treated differently. Its quills are burned off. It is cut up, cooked and every part of it is eaten. As for rabbits, we set the snares and check them every day. We won't catch rabbits in the daytime. The rabbit can only be snared in the dark when he can't see where he is going.

Another important thing I learned from my mother is how to name the different kinds of trees and how to use them for making things. She taught me about Innu medicine, what kind of plants, roots or trees to use for medication. I would watch her making medicines the way she had learned from her mother.

The white birch is good for making snowshoes, arrows and frames for stretching animal furs. Sticks from the black spruce are used to set up the tent. Black spruce branches are used for the tent floor because they are warmer than other branches. The needles of the branches can be used for medicine. The branches of the balsam tree can also be used for the tent floor and for medication. The poplar tree is very useful for canoes and paddles, and its branches are also used as medications. The tamarack tree is used to make sleds, drums or snowshoes. When there is no birch tree around the camp, the tamarack can be used to make stretchers for animal furs. The trembling poplar is not used much in the country because it is not strong enough, but it is good for making toys.

Sometimes people used to run out of food, but they had this kind of medicine to keep them alive. There are certain boughs we can boil. If we drink that water, the broth will help keep us from being too hungry or weak. I have tried it and it works. We must learn these things from our elders, so we know what to do when we have that kind of trouble in our lives.

My mother also taught me how some animals provide us with medicines too. She showed me which animals and what part of each to get. There are many more things that can be used as medication, such as the sweat tent and piercing a vein with a needle. These two things can be used for almost any kind of sickness, and they're very helpful. I did try them and they work. I would like to see these taught in our community as well as in our school. Who knows? Some day we might need them.

Today when I think about the things I learned from my parents, I remember they were difficult to learn, but, if we really try hard, I know we can still do them. I am very thankful to my late mother and my grandparents. If they weren't there for me, I would never have learned these things. I don't need any help now in making these things, because I trust the first teachers I had. They were good teachers.

☖ ☖ ☖

Today I live in the community of Sheshatshu, which is near North West River. White settlers live on one side of the river and mostly Innu live on the other side. Sheshatshu has a clinic, a school, band council offices, the Innu Nation office, the Alcohol Centre and a radio station. Our community used to be called North West River, but a few years ago we changed the name on our side of the river. Our community has seen big changes these past few years.

Innu people are more involved in education now and finding more important jobs. Innu teachers have better training and they know how to help their people. In the old days Innu people didn't care about education. They did not think it was important. The important thing was their own culture. Innu people say that their culture is their education. Young people learn from elders and in turn pass this learning on to their own children. This learning happens without a pencil and paper.

Today we have a lot of new books in our school. We have a school bus. Children used to walk to school every day. This is one reason children are more interested in education than they used to be. Our school is bigger and well heated now. We teach more subjects than we did long ago. The most important subjects are physical education and music.

We want our community to grow. When houses were first built in 1963, they were much too small for large families. There were only three bedrooms, a kitchen, and a small bathroom with no running water. The houses for small families had only two bedrooms. We had electric lights, but no heaters. We just had wood stoves for heat and cooking. We used to get water from lakes and streams. It was a hard life for us. Today we have better and bigger houses. They are warmer because we have electric heaters in every room and in the basement. We also have running water so we can keep ourselves, our houses and our clothing clean. We have better roads in the community so cars and trucks can come to our houses to pick up our garbage. We now have a better standard of living, after houses were built in a proper way.

We don't have to work as hard as we used to before. For example, when we wash the clothes, all we have to do is put them into a washer, turn it on and let it do the job until it stops. We take out the clothes and hang them on the clothesline. Before we had running water, we used to get water from the lake and put it on the stove to boil, before we could begin to wash the clothes.

We never had leaders before, except for the priest, who looked after all the people and the community. He was the one who organized everything. When there were jobs, the priest had to be the first one to know, and he would pick out the person who would be hired. He was the first leader in our community.

Today we have many leaders, like the Innu Nation leaders who help fight for land claims. Second, our band council leaders help to deal with governments. We have alcohol program leaders who help the people with their addiction problems. We also have church leaders who help people when there is no priest around. We have group home leaders who help children who are having problems at home. Social Services workers also help people with problems at home.

♣ ♣ ♣

I like some of the White people's way of life, but not all of it. I also like the Innu way of life very much. I can make the things that Innu women used to make in *nutshimit*. I know very little about White people's culture because they use too much education and I don't have enough of that. Innu people don't use anything to learn, just their memories and their hands to make what they need.

I like to follow some of the ways of the White people, because sometimes we need them. For example, I am happy to learn their language. It is hard to find translators when we want to talk to White people, especially when we see a doctor and important people like the band manager. I get jobs from White people, because my family needs money to buy things. That is why I like to follow the ways of White people. I don't hate them.

Another thing that I follow of the White people is their religion. I don't remember much about Innu religion. I don't want to talk about it, because I don't remember it. The only religion I know is the one we use now. Some people say this religion is not ours. It comes from the White people, but I know I was baptized into it. I don't think I could ever change, because we changed to this one even before I could remember anything about our Innu spirituality. The old people love this religion now. They trust it very much. They always like to pray and, everywhere they go, they take their bibles and rosaries with them. I don't think they're looking for fun, like they used to. We young people are still looking for fun, like drinking, dances and all kinds of parties. We don't care about our elders and we don't listen to them any more. As young people, the only thing we care about is happiness.

I love my parents and I never thought of moving away from them until I was married. I stayed with them wherever they went. I missed them when I didn't see them. Today youngsters who have just turned 16 or 17 are already leaving home. They already have their own families. I have four children. Three of them are married and one is not. She is still with me, but she has three children of her own. I have 16 grandchildren. I might have more since I am only 52 years old.

Now I'm kind of worried about my children. Why can't I teach them the way my parents taught me? My children are poor at doing *nutshimit* work, because they have never been in *nutshimit* to learn, especially the boys. They don't know how to kill animals. I feel sorry for my children because I never go to *nutshimit* with them. It doesn't mean that I don't like to go to *nutshimit*. I will always like it. I was raised out there. I always think about how and when I will go with my children to teach them like my parents taught me. But maybe it is going to be too late now for younger people. They don't know how to make the things they need out there. They have to remember to take all these things with them, because without them they will never make it in *nutshimit*, especially in the winter. They buy all the things they need to go to *nutshimit*, but they have problems with this because of money. My children haven't learned or tried to learn the Innu culture, because they are too busy following the White people's culture.

♣ ♣ ♣

There are many articles written for teachers about how to teach their students an early Innu education in our school, but we need elders to be the instructors. Elders have already completed their Innu education. Some people think it is too late to learn now.

We still have time to learn from our elders, but soon it will be too late, because our elders will be gone.

It is hard to make things, but I am sure we can learn if we try hard. It is also hard to find someone to make them for us. In the old days people used to share the things that others might not have and didn't know how to make for themselves. The elders would share and make things for others. Today nobody does that. When a person needs something, he or she has to buy it from someone else. Nobody shares now like the elders used to.

I worry about younger people going to *nutshimit* without elders, or without a plane in the summer or a ski-doo in the winter. Most young people never learned how to paddle canoes or how to walk in the deep forest. Most of us don't know this anymore. We don't know how hard it is to walk all day long.

I remember a few years ago, some people went to *nutshimit* by plane. The younger boys went out hunting in the forest and their parents waited for them to come home that same day. The boys never returned. They went to look for them the next day. They had been lost in the forest the whole night, because they didn't know how to walk in the forest. They had never been and they had never seen elders walk in the forest before. We need to learn from our elders, before we start to walk by ourselves.

I also want to talk about when people go to *nutshimit* with a box full of medications from the clinic. This is good, but what if the box runs out of medicines, someone is sick and the plane can't go anywhere because of bad weather? This is another problem. We must learn about Innu medicines from our elders — what kinds of trees and plants, or animals, to use for which sickness. We need to know what parts to use and what we do with them before we use them. We can use these medicines in *nutshimit* or even in our community.

The elders still use these Innu medicines today. They say they are better than White people's medicines. They think White people's medicines only make them feel worse. My father used to say that, since we have been settled in the community, there are a lot of health problems such as heart disease, cancer, gall-bladder problems, high blood pressure, arthritis and diabetes. We never saw these diseases when we lived in *nutshimit*. Everything about the hospital is killing all the Innu medicines. There are all kinds of Innu medicines in *nutshimit*, but knowledge of Innu medicine is no longer around. Why has it been killed off?

♟ ♟ ♟

It is important to get our children to learn not only in school. If they want to follow an Innu way of life, they need elders to teach them. This kind of learning doesn't happen when you ask students to draw something on paper or on a chalkboard. It is very different. You have to experience the Innu way of life to learn to do the kind of work.

It is very important to keep our culture alive. A lot of Innu and other Natives have lost their way of life because of modern technology. A lot of teenagers don't care about Innu culture because they think life is easy today and it was hard yesterday. It is very bad to lose our traditional ways. This loss will take everything that matters away from our lives. If we lose our culture and language, it's like a person who dies and doesn't come back again. When our culture and language are gone, our life will be like a dried-up lake. We must work hard together, like the old people used to do, and keep our culture growing.

Retracing Our Footprints

Mary Adele Andrew

Mary Adele Andrew, or Mani-Aten in Innu-aimun, was 64 years old when she died in the spring of 1996. When she was 17, she married Matthew Ben Andrew (Matshieu). They had 15 children, 5 of whom were born in nutshimit (the country). In the early 1960s, her life changed dramatically when her family, along with many others, was settled to village life in Sheshatshu.

This story was told to Nympha by Mary Adele a couple of weeks before she died. Before Mary Adele settled permanently in Sheshatshu with her young family, she had spent her whole life moving from one place to another through the vast territory of Nitassinan, from Uashat (Sept Iles) to Meshikamau and Sheshatshu. People would follow the animals throughout their hunting grounds. They knew where and when to hunt and fish. The seasons would change, the wildlife would become scarce and they would move again. Distances were meaningless; survival was what mattered. People would spend the fall, winter and spring in nutshimit and return to a trading post for the summer — to places like Uashat, Sheshatshu or Kauishatukuants (Old Davis Inlet). Some would come to see the priest. Sometimes

*they were hungry and sought relief from the store agent
or the priest. On occasion they also returned at Christmas time to see the priest for baptisms and weddings.*

*In 1989 Nigel Markham and Marie Wadden were
making a National Film Board of Canada and Nexus
Films production,* Hunters and Bombers, *about the
Innu campaign against NATO's military flight training
on their homeland. They wanted to film Mary Adele's
reaction when she returned to her family's traditional
hunting territory, the site of the largest industrial development on Innu land, the Churchill Falls hydro-electric
project. She had never been back to the area since it had
been flooded, and her family had lost many of their
earthly belongings as well as a whole hunting territory,
travel routes and portages.*

I will tell you my story about the times I spent in *nutshimit.* In the
old days it would be some time in August when we left to go to
nutshimit. We travelled along where the train runs today. We
canoed and it took us a long time, two months usually, to get to
where we wanted to camp. We had to carry all our gear. It was
very nice when we lived in *nutshimit.* Even when the mosquitoes
were very thick and it was hard to be outdoors, we were still very
happy. The children had a hard time with the mosquitoes
because they couldn't play outside. An *espeshetshimeuean* (canopy), like a small tent made of cloth inside the tent, would be
put up for them to keep the mosquitoes away.

It would take us a long time to portage around the lakes. Our
family was big and we all had to fit in one canoe. My father,
Stakeaskushimun (Simon Gregoire), usually took us first, then
he went back to pick up the supplies. One time, without anybody
knowing, my sister and I took the canoe and went to pick up the
things. It was raining hard and we got lost. My father was very
upset with us because we got all the stuff wet. He told us never
to do that again. We didn't say a word.

We would arrive in *nutshimit* in the fall to where we wanted to camp, stay until winter and then move on. We would set our nets when the lake froze up. It was a lot of work making all the things we needed and trying to find the right materials to use. The food was scarce. It was a very big lake and it took us a long time to cross it. We usually headed back to a community in June. The community could be Uashat or Sheshatshu or, very occasionally, Kauishatukuants. Sometimes there was still ice around when we travelled back. The women and children would follow far behind while the men went ahead to push the canoe across the ice. When they got to open water, we would all climb into the canoe and the men started to paddle again.

I remember one year we stayed in the country the whole of the summer. The flies were very thick and the only time the children could play outside was when the smoke built up by the campfire. Our tents were very poor and full of holes, so the flies got in. They were very hard on us. And we didn't have much food, only fish.

�“ ☛ ☚

My father's land was around Mishikamau Lake, which is now part of the Smallwood Reservoir. In 1963 my husband, Matshieu (Matthew Ben Andrew), and I lost most of our hunting territory, along with our canoe, traps and caches, when the reservoir flooded this area. We were not forewarned.

The last time we travelled from Uashat to *nutshimit*, the land was being cleared for the railway. Bridges were already built across the rivers and the land was torn up. The land was also badly damaged in Wabush. My mother's brother Napetshish (Côme Pinette) lived there. He called it home. There is a river that goes around that area and that's where he used to hunt. My uncle never realized that the land where he lived was going to be damaged.

The non-Natives built their houses and their motel. My uncle was hired to help build these houses. He told me the people who did the hiring were very nice to him. I guess he didn't know what was happening. He mentioned that he didn't have to pay for anything. Everything was free, like sleeping in the motel, and booze was given to him for free as well. The place he called home got bigger. Houses were built everywhere and the place turned into a community. I guess the people didn't really need him and later abandoned him. They gave him a house and that was probably just to get rid of him, just to shut him up. He must have thought they were being friendly. He didn't know there was big money involved in this land where he was living. There were more and more people coming off the train each time it came in.

In 1989, I travelled to Mista-paustuk (Churchill Falls) with the people who were making a film. They took us to where the dam was built. We left by plane from Goose Bay. There was me, my sisters Elizabeth and Rose and my daughter Clem. When we arrived at the dam, I was very tired. I had a hard time breathing, but I was told to keep talking for the camera as I was walking. I was telling Elizabeth a story about how hard it was for a woman when she had to carry her baby on her back in the old days. The woman's family had to portage many lakes while they travelled in *nutshimit* and the woman had to rest to breast-feed her baby. She would nurse her baby and then start walking again to catch up.

After the dam was built, it was dangerous to go in that area. The same thing happened in Schefferville. At first there weren't many houses built. A few Innu people were working there and they would use the train to go back to the country. They were dropped off by the train at the places where they wanted to camp. But Schefferville got bigger and the people kept coming and the land got destroyed once again. I guess the people thought that things were easier for them, like it was easier to travel back to the country on the train. They only had to go on the road and get on the train.

But the things they were missing were the land and the lakes where we portaged to get to our hunting territories, which were very beautiful. And the wild meat tasted so good. The Innu always had fresh meat when they were paddling the rivers and lakes. We hunted mostly beavers, porcupines and ducks on the way. We ate healthy food and we were happy to be living in *nutshimit*. It was a healthy way of living.

Today we don't see Innu travelling to *nutshimit* on foot. In the past we walked everywhere. We walked from as far away as Uaskaikan (Fort Chimo, or Kuujjuaq) to Kauishatukuants and Nent (Nain). We also walked to where the land is recently being destroyed — the place called Emish (Voisey's Bay). The people used to go there all the time when they came from *nutshimit*. Many used to camp there until the ice broke up and then we would canoe to Kauishatukuants. Today the Innu are lazy. They can't even walk to *nutshimit*.

In them days the man and his wife were always travelling together to hunt. We didn't get money from Social Services for food, although we did get relief from the store clerk in North West River. That's how the Innu bought their food and boats. We always had enough food from this relief to go back into *nutshimit*. We mostly gave furs to the clerk to pay our bills. When we returned to the community, we had already cleaned the furs for the clerk. After we began leaving our children in the community to go to school, we always returned home with lots of food from *nutshimit*. We also had lots of furs to trade.

I'm sure the Innu didn't realize once again what the non-Natives were doing to them. I guess the Innu made the clerk very happy when they arrived from the country. He must have waited patiently for them. He was probably a wealthy man. The Innu must have made him rich, because he didn't give the people cash for their furs. He only traded food and he gave out liquor too. Sometimes he would just give an Innu a small glass of liquor for his furs. The furs must have been worth more than a small glass of liquor, but the people were happy with him. I guess they didn't really know what he was up to. They probably thought that he was doing them a big favour whenever he handed them a drink.

I think this problem is still happening with the Innu today. When an Innu person gives booze to his own people, it is a crime.

They are not doing them a favour. If people knew when to stop drinking and not get drunk, it would be better. Some people are having a hard time with booze. They damage their bodies and end up in poor health. In the winter when Innu get drunk, they can end up frozen to death. They don't know where to go when they are drunk and they don't know how to get home. As well, when couples are drinking, they leave each other and one of them might end up in a relationship with someone else. Sometimes they actually give up on their lives. They end up taking their own lives.

Young people are changing so much today. We were different when we lived in *nutshimit*. In the past when a boyfriend or girlfriend left, they didn't behave like that. They just wouldn't bother one another and they didn't try to harm themselves. They always found someone else to go out with. Today even older people are physically fighting with one another when they are angry. In the past we didn't do that to each other. Today everything happens because of alcohol. When the people are in *nutshimit*, they get mad and argue sometimes, but they don't fight. They don't dislike each other or stop speaking to one another for a long time. They become friends again.

Today husbands and wives don't speak to each other for so long when they are mad. A woman thinks that her husband doesn't love her anymore, but she won't talk to him about her problems and how she is really feeling. People are making each other suffer too much. Their children start drinking too. The parents then worry about their children. They wonder where their children are going to end up sleeping and what kind of stories they'll hear the next day. This is how I feel when my children don't come home. I can't sleep at night when they are drinking. I worry as I wait for them to come home. I feel sick sometimes from worrying too much. I used to go over and check on them when they were drinking next door. That was before I had a hard time walking. I worry that they will get beat up by other people and I am afraid that they will get themselves into serious trouble. This is where things go wrong today.

If I was a drinker I would end up in the clubs with my children. I mentioned this to them before. I told them I could go everywhere they go, hang around with them and shame them. They all laughed.

♠   ♠   ♠

Before my sister the late Mary Ann died, we were always asked to help out. One spring the men were out hunting. My sister and I were told to go to their camp, so we started to pack our stuff and loaded up the *utatshinakeaskut* (komatik). We were sent to look for sugar, flour, butter and tea. We were afraid to go by ourselves, but we had no choice. We had to do what we were told. We put up our tent before the sun went down, but we were too afraid to sleep. The next morning we headed out again. We arrived at the camp where our three uncles were.

We were too shy to approach their tent. We hung around in the woods and peeked through the branches. They caught us and told us to come over. They invited us in and gave us a meal. After I ate my dinner, I complained that my eyes were sore from snow blindness. My uncle cured me. He heated up some loose tea, wrapped it up in a cloth, then put it over my eyes. It helped me. My snow blindness was gone and it worked really fast.

The next morning we went home. We stopped one night on our way back. One of my uncles came with us and helped us pull the gear to our camp. When he left, the people at our camp gave him caribou meat and dried meat. I don't think he slept on his way back home. He probably just walked through the night.

After we picked up the food, we moved our camp further into the country, where we hunted caribou. My little brother Shuash (George) was just a baby. I used to mix the milk for his bottle — flour with water, that's what he had for milk. He got bigger while we lived in the country and then started to eat solid foods. Later than fall, we moved again. We left some food behind where we were camping, so we could pick it up later when we are out of things.

I remember that fall one of the children became very sick from hunger. Her mother tried to breast-feed her, but she wouldn't take the milk. We were all starving at that camp. My friend Matinin Selma (now Madeline Michelin) and I were asked to go back and pick up the rest of the things that we had left behind at our last camp. We packed up our tent and gear on the komatik. The nights were very dark and cold, with blowing snow. We couldn't walk on the ice, so we had to walk through the woods where we were more sheltered from the wind. We finally made it to our cache, which was marked with a stick.

Someone had been there before us and taken a few things. We followed his tracks to an island, where some stuff had been left. I asked Matinin whether we should put up the tent before it got too dark. It was a very beautiful night. I told her that we could make jam for our supper. She didn't want to put up the tent, because she wanted to find the people.

"Their tents can't be very far away," she said. "These tracks are fresh."

So we left to find the people and arrived at their camp. They invited us inside and gave us supper. One man at the camp was very sick. He couldn't even walk. The people pulled him on the komatik back to the community. We followed them when they left. We never thought about the food that we were supposed to bring back to the camp. We ended up in Schefferville, where we stayed for a while with the people. Finally we decided to go back, so we started walking to the place where we had left our things. We set up our tent halfway there and spent the night. After we were settled in, Matinin decided to do some ice fishing for kukumesh (lake trout). She made a hole in the ice and caught one, so we cooked it up for supper.

The next morning was very sunny and the sky was blue. We heard a plane coming. Matinin ran to the ice and started waving. They saw her and the plane landed. My mother's brother Shinipestiss (Sylvester Pinette) was on it. He called out to me and asked for my mother. I told him that my mother was camped near the area of the dam. He told us we could get on the plane with him. We rushed to the plane and left our tent standing there.

We were very excited to see the people for whom we were supposed to pick up the food. I could see my father's tracks. He was hunting partridge. We saw him running to meet the plane with partridge in hand. As we were landing, we were afraid our parents might get very upset with us, but nothing was said. They were all happy to see the food being unloaded from the plane. There was a lot of food. The people at the other camps were also out of food. We carried the food to our tents. The pilot was given furs in return for the food. They gave him every single fur they had at the camp and each one was in good shape. The pilot left and we were very happy to have so much food.

We moved our camp again, this time to Mishikamau. Matinin and I went back to fetch our tent. We were told that we shouldn't have left it behind. Our parents were upset. They told us we should have put it on the plane. We never thought of our tent when we saw the plane because we were too excited. We just hopped on. We didn't think we would have to go back for the tent. I often mention this to Matinin when I see her now. She keeps reminding me too. We were very happy in those days when we used to walk in *nutshimit*. Matinin was never afraid, but I always was. The country was very beautiful.

To the People I Lost

Marie Pokue

It's only a dream. I wish I could wake up
and see your faces again.
When I lost you, I thought I was dreaming.
But it's not a dream
it's real.

You were all gone, and I'll never see you again.
I'll see you someday when I leave this world
but I'm not ready yet.
There is a lot to do here in this world
without drinking alcohol.
You wasted your lives because of alcohol.
I'm trying very hard not to live the way you did.

Oh, I miss you all.
I'd better learn more
to not waste my life
like you did.

I see your faces in my dreams.
I talk to you in my dreams.
You talk to me in my dreams.

If only I could talk to you,
and tell you again not to drink,
you could listen.

I know you don't want to throw your life away
but something is controlling your life.
You're not strong enough,
you need someone beside you.
I know you can't do this alone.

You didn't make it.
It's too late now.
But I'm here.
I'm going to be strong.
I'll do it for you.

*Marie Pokue lost her parents, four brothers and two sisters
in an alcohol-related boating accident in 1979 when she
was still a child.*

This Land Is Still Our Home

Charlotte Rich

Charlotte talks about the days before trade, when the land provided the Innu with all their needs. The people made everything with materials that came only from the land and the animals. Charlotte also shares childhood memories of Emish (Voisey's Bay), a place she still thinks of as home. The giant multinational Inco plans to develop a large open-pit nickel mine at Emish. Emish has always been an area rich with wildlife. The Innu have already lost this important hunting and meeting place. All the activity of choppers, people and bulldozers has already disrupted the habitat. Where will the animals go when they, too, lose their homes? Fish are already scarce and the waters will become further polluted from acid mine drainage. The airstrip is planned near a key waterfowl nesting spot. This is not the first time the Innu have seen a mine ravage their land. They have seen the devastation of the mines at Wabush and Schefferville. Charlotte shares her feelings about the White man's plans for her birthright.

I am 52 years old or maybe I am 41. I am not really sure how old I am. The records must be at the mission. My mother's name was Etamanisheshish and my father was Shenapeu. Their Christian names were Ann and Ponas. After I got married, I had only three children, two daughters and one son. My son died. My two daughters, Justine and Mary Ann, are still alive.

There is a story of a long time ago about how our ancestors kept the fire going by using dead wood. One person would keep it going while they travelled in the wintertime. When they stopped to set up camp, they would pass the fire around to everyone in the camp. This is a very old story. They would set up their camps where there was a lot of wood, so they could be sure their fire would always continue. These people were fascinating. Where did they get this fire? I heard that they used gunpowder, and before that they used flint that was shaped like a pipe. I heard this works to start fires.

When somebody was sick with chest pains, people would use boughs for medicine. They would boil the boughs and drink the broth. The people also used caribou moss when they were travelling. They would carry heavy loads on their back, supporting the weight with the strap of their bags running across their foreheads. The moss protected their foreheads by stopping the strap from rubbing into their skin.

When people killed a caribou, they would have to carry the meat on their backs. Sometimes they would use boughs on their chests to protect themselves from the ropes. They used the boughs on their chests the same way they used the moss on their foreheads. These were the things Innu would do when they were in *nutshimit* (the country).

The caribou hides were also used for teepees. Six hides were used for one good-sized teepee. We would have to make sure the hide didn't burn. We would be careful that sparks from the fire in the middle of the teepee did not burn the hides. The sparks made me very nervous. People were very careful.

The Innu also used caribou hide for their pants. The hair was left on, but the inside of the hide was cleaned and softened. All the men used caribou-hide pants. In the winter they would dress all in caribou because it was very cold. They dressed like *kautashapits* — bow-and-arrow Indians! They also used caribou hides for blankets to cover themselves in the winter and they made shawls from caribou hides. They used these shawls, called *espikun*, when they went ice fishing.

In those days, the Innu made many tools. They used the birch tree to make *mekanepakan* (shovels) and *eshun* (ice picks) for ice fishing. For tobacco, they used a certain tree that looks almost like a birch. They would scrape the inside and rub it thoroughly until it resembled tobacco. Then they smoked it. There are also some bushes that can be used to make tobacco. Maybe it tastes almost like tobacco. There is a bush they use for tea. These bushes are called *mikuta* (Labrador tea). People used to collect these bushes and hang the leaves to dry. It looks like tea, but it has a strong, bitter taste. The Innu used so many things from the land.

When the Innu were out of string or rope, they used to cut caribou hide into strips, which they then braided. They also cut very fine strips of caribou hide to use for fishing line when they were out of string to go fishing. Even the big fish could not break this line. We had everything we needed when we were in *nutshimit*, even if we were poor and we didn't have very much. It was hard living.

🌲 🌲 🌲

I grew up at Emish with my parents and my sister, Muskamin (Alice Benuen), who passed away a few years ago. I remember I used to fish in the brooks for trout with an *espikun* to keep me warm. It was so cold, that when we caught fish, they would freeze solid. After fishing, I would play. My sister was bigger than me and she didn't want to play with me. She had cleaning-up work to do inside the tent.

I don't know what time we would go to sleep in the evenings. Usually it was when it got dark. We never used a watch. We used the sun to tell the time and, when the sun shone, we knew it was time to get up. I would play in the sand on the beach in the summer, making houses. They were like underground shelters. I would dig a hole under the sand with two openings on either side and I would stuff things inside it. In winter, my father would make me a swing to play on outdoors. There were no other kids around to play with. We didn't see other people very often. This made me very lonely, but when I was busy I wasn't so lonely. Sometimes I would help my sister in the tent or when she went out looking for wood or boughs for the tent floor.

My family liked to stay at Emish because there were a lot of fish there. My father would catch fish all year round. In the summer or the winter he would catch trout and char and another small whitefish we called *kauapishissits* (smelts). There was also every kind of animal at Emish: ducks, geese, bear, partridge, porcupine, caribou. I miss this food a lot. There was everything. I couldn't wait to eat the porcupine, because it was my favourite. Sometimes we used a net and other times we used spears to catch the fish. We would make the spears ourselves, using a knife to carve the end of a stick. In the winter, my father would put some trees around the ice hole to keep warm. We would stay a long time fishing. We would only go back to the camp after we had caught fish. That was often our only food. When the ice was gone, we would go out in our canoe up the river, which was not very deep. We went through all this and I remember these things as a child and as I got older.

Once when we were in *nutshimit*, we ran out of food. We had nothing to eat and couldn't catch any fish in our nets. My father had a difficult time catching animals. My mother boiled a bear skull in water, but it took a long time for the meat to become tender. I couldn't eat any, but my father did. We drank the broth. We ate only a little of the meat on the skull. This is what we went through while living in *nutshimit*. We hardly saw any other Innu, only off and on. My sister and I really missed people when they left after a visit.

Sometimes we travelled to Kauishatukuants (Old David Inlet), but we never stayed there. When my mother was lonely for her people, we would go back there. At Emish, we wouldn't see people for a long time during many winters. I remember we would also go back and forth from Emish to the interior — inland to *nutshimit* to hunt. We never used ski-doos or dog teams. We would travel on foot in the summer with our belongings on our backs, and on snowshoes in the winter with homemade sleds that we dragged behind with string.

In the old days, we would get supplies from Nent (Nain). The people there would give us used clothing. In the wintertime we used caribou-skin clothes that we made ourselves. I remember that we also got tent canvas from Nent.

Amos was the name of the person who lived at Emish. His wife was also there, but I don't remember her name. I never went to their house, because they had so many dogs and I was scared of them. The dogs were dangerous. Every time we got close to them, they would try to bite us.

I remember one time, when we were still at Emish, we canoed to Kauishatukuants. We paddled our way there because there were no motors or machines back then. I would get the wood for my grandparents when we stopped along the way, to cook up something to eat. We went to Kauishatukuants to visit people who have since died. The only people still living that were there at the time are Ueniam (William Katshinak) and Miste Etuet (Edward Mistenapeo).

Kauishatukuants is where I met my husband. We didn't get together when we first met. It was only the second time we met that we went together. We knew each other a long time before we were married. My father arranged the marriage. He thought Masku-tiskum (David Rich) would make a good husband. My mother died in Kauishatukuants before this time. I was happy to be married because I was with my father a long time after my mother died. It was the same for Muskamin. She also found a husband. In fact she was the first one to find love. After we were married, we returned to Emish and my father stayed behind. There were a lot of other Innu at Emish then and we felt this land was our home.

⚓ ⚓ ⚓

This land is still our home. The White man does things to this land behind our back, without notifying us. What came through my mind when I heard the land is destroyed? "The White man has taken my land," I thought. I didn't hear at first what was happening. I only heard about it after they had started. I was very upset and hurt. I couldn't say anything then, because they had already broken a piece of the land. I think those people are outrageous for damaging our land. The Innu do not go to the White man's land and destroy it. I will say this to them if I see them.

Shunin (Julianna Saunders) and I were born at Emish. I remember that elders are buried at Emish. My only son is also buried there. He died when I was giving birth. There was no medical help for me to save my baby at that time. My grandfather and the late Shanish are also buried there. My husband's mother is buried there in a place called Kakesekauts, where the river runs fast and we used to have to portage around. Tshenish (Charles James Pasteen) knew many people who are buried there right by Amos's house on the side of the hill. There may be a lot of big trees and bushes grown over around there now. Maybe I would remember where the house and the graves are. It is not very far and there are crosses that mark the graves. I know where they are.

I went back to Emish before all this mining business started. It is the most beautiful place where they are doing the mining. But I know that if I go back two or three years from now to see what the mining people have done, I will be very upset and angry. I know those guys will destroy everything. The elders used to be strong in the old days. Right now, akaneshau (White people), like the mining people, don't listen to elders. They just go ahead and destroy everything that the Innu own.

Artists Know the Spirits

Angela Andrew

*Angela is an avid craftsperson. She draws inspiration
for her work from the past, from the lessons of her
mother and father. Many tools and clothing of the past
were decorated with artwork — beadwork, painting
and embroidery done mostly by women. This art and
its symbols was a way of communicating with the spirit
world, a way of keeping harmony with each other, the
land, the animals, the plants and the spirits. Angela
believes her craftwork continues this tradition. It is how
Innu artists and craftspeople help to keep the culture
alive. She is best known for her tea dolls, a practice she
revived in the early 1980s. When the Innu lived as
nomads, the women would make dolls for the children.
These dolls would be stuffed with tea. This was to
encourage young children to help carry the load as they
travelled long distances. When the group ran out of tea,
elders would begin to use the stuffing of the dolls. Some
say the children would not mind, because a new doll
would get made when the group got new supplies.*

A long time ago, the use of crafts was strong. The Innu made their
own moccasins, canoes, drums and shelters. But these crafts are
beginning to die out because people now live in the community.
We are losing our culture, like the drum dance and respect for

the animal spirits. The people were strong because we didn't need European things. Now it seems the people are weak. We don't have to build our shelters or make moccasins to survive. We can buy these things.

I'm interested in making tea dolls because I remember how the people used to dress — the special hats they wore for the drum dance and the traditional clothing like the moccasins. It's important to me to make these dolls because people today don't dress like that anymore. I feel there is a frustration and depression in the community. People before felt peace inside themselves. I love to make tea dolls because I think my people were happy in the old days. They wanted to give thanks to the animal spirits who gave them food, so they danced to the drum. I make tea dolls to recapture some of this past.

I used to love to watch people dance, to watch them proud in a circle. We would hear the men shouting to the rhythm of the drum. We could hear how they felt good about themselves.

Tapatapinukueu (Maggie Antuan), an elder here in Sheshatshu, made the first tea doll I ever saw. There are different stories told about these dolls. Some people say kids used to carry tea dolls in the old days when the Innu travelled long distances in the country. Some say the elders carried the dolls. When the group ran out of tea, only the elders drank tea. I wanted to make this tea doll of the past, but I created my own kind of tea doll in the way I dress them up.

I started to make crafts when I was a little girl. I was 10 or 11 years old when I first tried to make moccasins. My interest came from my mother, Miste Atenin (Adeline Rich). She could make everything. She would do some sewing and I could see how relaxed she was. She looked very peaceful. She would cut out the moccasins, tiny ones so as not to waste the caribou skin, and she would try to teach me how to stitch them. I don't know how many years I tried to make them. She told me I was too hard-headed to learn. I asked my father, Tshetshepateu, or Early Bird (Edward Rich), and he sat beside me to teach me to stitch. Finally as a teenager, I could help my mother make moccasins.

I also watched my mother tan and stretch the caribou skin. When we were finished, we were pleased and so anxious to make moccasins to sell. I used to embroider flowers on my moccasins instead of beading like my mother. Sometimes we made beaver hats, beautiful, like factory-made ones. We also used to make rabbit yarn.

Maybe when Innu artists paint, they feel like I used to feel when I sat with my father. When I made my tea dolls, I was curious. I would ask questions. "Why do men wear long socks when the socks break so easy in the country?" My father then told me that the men don't wear their socks in the same way in the country. They wear them on the inside of their pants in the country and on the outside in the community.

When I look at the paintings created by Innu around the community, I see the animal spirits that we cannot see. We just hear them. We hear people say that the animals' spirits are very strong. Young people don't understand those things. The artists see and know the spirits. They know about the spiritual part of our culture. They help us to understand who these spirits are. When we talk about animal spirits, it's very dangerous. Let's say we take any animal — a dog, for example. It's very dangerous to abuse a dog. The spirit will always be after you. These spirits are powerful.

"Who is the dog's god?" I asked my mother one time.

"Do you see in the wintertime when there is a storm? Watch the dogs very closely," she said. "The dogs feel good about themselves in the storm. They play around. The storm is their god."

Innu artists usually draw animals of the land, leaves and plants. They are saying, "I am Innu." Their drawings tell the viewer about the Innu culture.

Arts and crafts are important to our culture because they remind us of the way things were before. In the old days, there was no teacher to teach us. We had to teach ourselves, the way our parents did. Now we don't have to learn all these skills, so craftspeople and artists make these things to keep our culture alive.

Will the young people learn how to make these crafts? I find young people are easily frustrated. The interest has to come from the parents. My kids know how to make tea dolls. The only problem is they can't design the faces I make. When I make the babies for my tea dolls, I have deep thoughts. I think about the children I see on the road. I find it very strange, this feeling. I stitch the faces from deep thoughts of those children. And I feel good about it. Once I stitched Phyllis's face, my daughter-in-law, and I showed her. It is strange how these faces come up — men's faces, my grandfather's face, my brothers', my father's. They come up from looking at them very hard.

It helps non-Innu people to understand us better when they get to see our crafts. For example, they learn more about our culture and spiritual world. I don't think people have a clue who we are. They think we are nothing. This might give them a clue, make them learn more about us, understand us, the way we were a long time ago before Europeans came, how we survived from the animals, the shelters we built. We are the most important people here because there was no one else here before on this land, just us, no Europeans.

We can't change now. One elder was talking about the thousands of caribou that drowned in Quebec. He said he almost cried when he heard this, just as if a person or family had died. But now young people don't have respect even when they hear about the animal spirits. The elders are really afraid. They cry when they realize that young people don't try. Children don't listen. Since alcoholism came into our lives, people don't care.

I Can't Forget You

Christine Poker

You have ripped my life apart
since the day you looked at me
and smiled. You asked me to
come in. I smiled back never
knowing this could be the day
that I would never forget you.
I have never forgotten your face,
your voice, your smell.
Whenever I look at the scars
on my hands I remember you.
I look at my daughter's hands
I remember you.
I sleep with my husband
I remember you.
You are always there instead of him.
I wake up in tears remembering you.
I have tried many times to get you out of
my mind, my life
But it still hurts even to mention
your name.

Like the Gates of Heaven

Elizabeth Penashue

Elizabeth outlines the systematic seizure over the last 40 years of Innu land by governments and industry for hydro, mining and forestry developments, as well as for NATO military flight training. She talks about how the Innu were manipulated to settle in communities in order to remove them from these coveted lands. She describes in heartbreaking detail what happened when the Innu culture became essentially illegal and social chaos replaced it. But in the late 1980s, Elizabeth and other women decided to reclaim their land and culture with protests that brought renewed pride and rallied the strength of all her people.

The Innu detest what the governments have done to our land. There has been heavy destruction of our homeland. We have been gentle and loving to our land, and we use it wisely. With the Churchill Falls development, all the animals were wasted away in the flooding. They dammed Mista-paustuk (the Great Rapids). Before this, we could see the mist of Mista-paustuk from very far away when we walked through *nutshimit* (the country). The governments didn't look at the Innu way of life. They never even consulted us. All that mattered to them were dollar signs, the profits, the jobs and the power that would be generated. The power lines go for thousands of miles, to places like New York and Montreal. Millions of dollars are made from our land every day. It doesn't matter to government and industry how much they destroy Innu land.

My late father, Stakeaskushimun (Simon Gregoire), was always very emotional when he talked about how his belongings, including his canoes and traps, were flooded over when the Mista-shipu (Churchill River) was dammed. He was not the only one to lose all his belongings. Many others also lost all the basic things they used to survive in *nutshimit*. My father lost everything, even his hunting land. He mentioned this many times, over and over again. He was so troubled about what had happened. Mista-paustuk no longer exhaled the mist, which was a landmark that helped us find our way from afar.

In 1984, there were 10,000 caribou drowned in Kaniapishkau (the Caniapiscau River). My father could not speak or understand English, but my sister Rose told him the story. He was almost in tears. That was how much he respected the caribou. He was so upset. Today, if my parents were alive, they would be so shocked to see what is happening to our communities, to our people, and especially the destruction of our land.

I remember seeing my husband's father play the drum in *nutshimit*. I sometimes find it hard to believe the power of the drum, but I do believe. One time at our camp, I saw a person taking a drum in the night to this old man's tent. The old man sang while he played the drum. Then another old man sang after he had finished. Then they announced the name of a place where they said we would find caribou. The next day, young hunters went out to get caribou and, sure enough, they were successful in exactly the place where they had been told to go by the old men.

I was born out in *nutshimit* on this land. Only my family was present and I am proud that it was my father who delivered me into my mother's arms. As I grew up, I never thought I should be in school. I felt like I was already in school, learning the Innu way of life in *nutshimit*.

⚜ ⚜ ⚜

The White authorities have always intimidated us. I guess they want us to give up our life on the land. Our grandfathers were free. They killed only enough for food and trapped all they liked. I never saw any wildlife officers when I was young. We were never restricted by foreigners. Then Innu hunting became regulated and we were required to buy government licences. Even the smallest of all animals, rabbits and partridge, were regulated, and of course the caribou. For many years, we were not allowed to kill animals for food.

Sometimes I would hide the meat deep in the snow. We used to control our own hunting by making sure to never overkill the animals. The Innu hunter was happy because of the sense of accomplishment he had from providing for his family. His children were very happy because they ate good food. But for years the Innu hunter felt uneasy, nervous that the wildlife authorities would know and come to raid his camp. He hid his kill. He knew he would be charged and brought to court to face a judge and a jail term or a heavy fine. His possessions and guns would be confiscated. How did the government think the Innu would survive in the country if he couldn't kill animals for his livelihood? To me, this is the crime, what was done to the Innu.

But we struggled against the government's wildlife laws when we protested in Akamiuapishk^u (the Mealy Mountains) in 1987 and hunted the caribou. Our men were thrown in jail for no good reason. We only wanted to protect our culture. Our people had always hunted there. The elders told us how many caribou we could safely kill so the herd would remain healthy. The government told us we were endangering the herd, but in 1988, the very next year, they opened the herd to a public hunt.

At the protest, the wildlife officers came with their helicopters, but the elders, women and children sat down on the caribou that our hunters had brought back to the camp. One wildlife officer tried to get just one caribou, probably to bring to the court for evidence. But the people screamed and we stayed close together and we stopped him. We were so happy and proud when the officers left empty-handed. We felt so strong.

After this, the wildlife officers seemed to lay off for a while. They didn't harass us any more.

But in 1989, when we were out at Minai-nipi near the NATO bombing range, Innu rifles were taken by game wardens and police. One of them was my son's rifle. The hunters still have not got their rifles back today. The game wardens took geese as well, and then they were no good to us because they had spoiled.

The wildlife officers leave us pretty much alone now. But the animals are scarcer, especially along the brooks or along the roads, where there are cabins owned by White people everywhere. The White people always want to be the first to hunt in areas where the Innu have always hunted.

♣ ♣ ♣

We always regarded the priest as a very sacred person. We didn't understand what was planned for us. We treated the priest with great respect. There was no school when I was young. Father Pierson taught us and he always told the parents, especially the mothers, not to go to *nutshimit*. Many Innu thought it was wrong not to obey the priest. I guess we never foresaw what the future would be like once we lived permanently in the community. My mother and father did not understand back then about the abuse and wrongdoings of the church.

The priest would go to my mother, Miste Mani (Marie Gregoire), and sit close by her, talking to her for a long time. He lectured her on how to bring up her children. He would say he was the only one with all the answers.

"If you take your children into the country, the government will take away your family allowance," the priest would say to my mother. "If you take your children into the country, they will be hungry and cold.

It's better to stay in the community year-round. Your children will be schooled."

He encouraged my father to go to the country alone. I remember my parents had this surprised look on their faces. They were very concerned and unhappy about the priest's advice. "Why don't you go out in the country by yourself?" the priest said to my father. "Leave your wife and children in Sheshatshu. This way you won't lose your family allowance."

"No! We will all go out to the country," my father said, after the priest had left. This caused an argument between my parents. I wondered if the priest was making my parents fight. My mother thought we should listen to the priest. She did not know what to do. I now realize how my parents were manipulated by the priest.

Many other parents also felt intimidated. They were scared, so they reluctantly sent their children to the White school. The Innu people listened to the priest as if he were Jesus.

The Roman Catholic Church had a very negative impact on the Innu. Now we understand the destruction the church wreaked on our lives. The abuse of the priests — sexual, physical and even spiritual abuse — has been exposed to the light of day.

I speak personally when I tell this story. I cannot use the words to describe what the priest did to my sons. As a mother of nine children, I carry a lot of shame and guilt over what the priest did to my sons when he sexually abused them. My sons, too, must carry this pain and suffering throughout their lives. My children were innocent and pure. The priest stole their innocence and broke our hearts and souls. My husband, Kantuakueshish, or Porcupine Hunter (Frances Penashue), and I get very upset and angry when we remember what the priest did to our children. At times we wonder if we could have changed the past, if only we had known. I wonder now what kind of holy man this priest was. I say to myself he was not a holy man. He was a man who came to destroy my family and our lives. I thought I was the only parent who had endured this, but I found out there are other parents like me, who have the same stories.

♣ ♣ ♣

The priest's mission was to teach Innu children about the White education and religion. First we attended school in his house, and then he built a small school. Every few years a larger building was erected. I believe the buildings changed five times, until we had the big school up on the hill. With each new building in place, our connection to our culture was lost even more.

In the school, there is no teaching of the Innu way of life. Innu children learn from White books and then they go home to watch television. They learn and copy from what they watch on television. The school only makes Innu children lazy. Sometimes the children feel good about learning in a White school because they are told they will find proper jobs when they finish school. The children are very young and can easily be convinced. It becomes harder to break away as years of teaching about another society continues. The children become really convinced about the promises that have been made to them.

But these are broken promises. Innu children find nothing once they finish school, only an unpleasant life full of wrongs. They find themselves in court. Today, there are courts for very young Innu children and they are being sent to jail. Our children seem to be appearing in court at a younger and younger age all the time. This kind of behaviour comes from learning the White society. As a parent, I know from experience that prison does not help our people. It seems they just get more angry and abusive to one another. Our children would benefit more if they were sent out for treatment in the country so they could learn more about their culture.

When Innu children were in *nutshimit* all the time with their parents, they were happier. The children learn about their culture in *nutshimit*. Young girls learn from their mothers, while the boys hunt with their fathers. Today the children are led into a life that is strange to their parents. The children get frustrated because their parents can't give them any direction in a society that is foreign to them. The children get upset and vandalize the school. One time a teacher made my son Max leave the school. He was angry and frustrated, and broke a window. He never went back.

♗   ♗   ♗

I see so many changes in our lives. For example, the elders dress differently today. When I was a young girl, we would dress in traditional clothes, with an Innu dress and hat, according to Innu custom. Now you don't see one Innu person dressed this way. Children are so fashionably dressed. They have become so modernized by the White culture. They are now so critical of themselves because they don't have toys or clothes the same as or better than those of their friends. They compete so much with one another, like the White man. Innu children don't act like Innu. They are so unpredictable. They seem so angry and rebellious toward one another and toward themselves.

The Innu people are being bombarded with all these pressures. The Innu don't know what to think any more. We are all exhausted with emotion. The government should never have come here and forced its laws and ways upon the Innu. We wouldn't have any of these problems today. This leads the Innu to turn to heavy drinking. Alcohol never existed in our lives like this a short time ago. Our children are confronted with other unhealthy products as well, such as newer drugs and gas, which they sniff. People may have new vehicles and a higher standard of living, but there is so much depression and frustration. The Innu don't know where to turn. We are confused. Sometimes we feel hopeless, because it seems the White man is going to control us forever. The governments must be happy to think the more we drink, the less we'll care about our land.

♗   ♗   ♗

After I got married, my husband and I had all sorts of problems living in the community. I always liked to listen to my parents when they talked about their lives together. Their marriage went very well. My mother was happy because she was out in *nutshimit* all the time with her children. I often think my marriage would have been like that if the governments hadn't forced us to live in the community permanently. My marriage was full of unhappiness. My husband was always drinking. I find it hard to talk about this. It hurts me deeply. My children didn't have happy years growing up. The unhappiness caused everyone to drink.

The other thing that really saddens me is when I think of how I was injured because of the drinking. I almost died. My husband broke all the bones in my face. There are metal wires attaching my bones. My jaw was all broken on one side of my face. I was out in St. John's for one week. Then I was brought home to Sheshatshu with all my stitches. My daughter Kanani was just big enough to sit up. When I walked into our house she was scared of me, scared of my face. I felt so depressed that my own child was afraid of me. I was so happy to go home because I longed to see my children. I thought I would be so happy to take my child into my arms, but she was scared of me.

I was always hurt emotionally because I knew my children were also hurting. I would look at them when they were sleeping and know life was hard for them too. I would wake them up to try and hide somewhere else, somewhere away from our house and their drunk father. Before I woke them, I would look at them for a long time. Some had grown up a bit and some were still small.

"Am I really going to wake them up?" I would think to myself.

I would put on their clothes while they were still lying there asleep. I would wake up the older ones and we would all go out to hide in someone else's home. We went out into the cold many times. I would have to search for a house to stay in.

"Who will have the heart to put us up for the night?" I always thought. "Who will take me and all my children?"

Sometimes, I would go to my older sister Mani-Aten's house, sometimes to my mother's. Sometimes they would not open the door for me because they were afraid of my husband. Many times we were put up in a house where I wasn't related to the people at all. I was very depressed and saddened to see my children in that state, having to watch me being beaten up. My young boys were too small to fight back for me. But when they got bigger, they could stop their father from fighting with me.

Alcohol is the number-one problem we face in the community. My husband's will to stop drinking was weak for a long time. I drank too. My husband and I hurt each other too many times, and we started to hurt our children. We didn't care for them. There wouldn't be any food for them and we didn't give them the love they needed. Then all my sons began drinking a lot as well. I don't know about my two girls. For a while one of them did, but then she stopped.

When I went for help to stop drinking, I did not realize how much it would hurt me to realize that I had not cared for my children. It hurts me today when I think about it. My husband and I went to a treatment centre for help. My five sons also went to get help for their drinking. Two of them went back to drinking and one is drinking a lot again. I still sit with these two sons and try to talk to them about my experiences abusing alcohol. I tell them it is a hard way to live if they continue to drink.

You get worried sick about your children's safety. Nowadays, when the children get mad, they try to commit suicide by taking an overdose of drugs. The parents find it hard to sleep when they know one of their children is drinking. They always wonder how they are. Are they in fights or vandalizing the belongings of other people? Alcohol causes great pain to families and their children.

We brought our children to *nutshimit* to help them to heal. For example, before my son Jack went out to a treatment centre, my husband and I took him out to *nutshimit*, and I felt so proud and happy for him. I don't quite know how to describe these feelings. I would see him working very hard. He would hunt and set traps during the day. Sometimes he went with his father on hunting trips. But when he was here in the community, he was always in trouble drinking, and once he took an overdose of pills. He almost died and was taken to the hospital. When he was in nutshimit, he lived very well. He was happy and he didn't drink alcohol.

Nutshimit is like that. People go to *nutshimit* to stay healthy, but once they return to the community, all their problems come flooding back. They come back to a life of confusion and chaos. That's when the Innu turn to alcohol sold by the government.

We talk about how things were so good in the past. There was no alcohol and people would visit each other often. They shared everything they had. I remember what they would talk about.

"How many animals did you kill? Where will you go hunting tomorrow?"

"How far did you walk today? Was it dark when you got back to the camp? Did you have a hard time finding your way?"

There were so many things they talked about. I used to listen to them and it was so nice. Now the people's talk is dark.

"Where will we go drinking this weekend? Will we go dancing again?"

"Are you going to play bingo tonight?"

All the talk is about money. People want what others have — a job or a new car. The child might be happy that his father finally got a new job. He thinks maybe now they will have food. Maybe he will get a new bicycle. But his father wastes the money on alcohol. The child only ends up more hurt.

So we talk about the past, about all the things we should do to bring the things we value from the past back into our lives. But we don't do anything about it. I want to believe it when we talk about Innu traditions and values, but then we don't do anything. People tell me to wait, "Wait for the band council," "Wait for the Innu Nation ..." A few years ago, when the people wanted to do something because it needed to be done, we would just go ahead and do it. Now we spend all our time waiting and nothing happens.

🦫 🦫 🦫

We protested the NATO presence on our land because we want to maintain control of our land so that Innu children in the future, our grandchildren and their children, will have land that is rightfully theirs. We struggle because we know what the future has in store for us if we don't do something. The struggle is for every Innu — the old people, the adults and the children.

Ever since the military presence and jet manoeuvres appeared on our land, hardships have increased for us. Today we are often frightened in *nutshimit*. We never used to have to endure this kind of pain. We used to be free in *nutshimit*. Today we live in fear because the jets fly directly over our camps. They come so unexpectedly. It is difficult to imagine how frightened the children are. It's harder for women who are pregnant or for people with heart conditions. They could die right there because they can't hear the jets coming until they are directly over them with the loudest noise ever heard. The military wanted to build a big NATO base that would bring in live weapons, and they wanted to designate nine new bombing ranges, apart from the one at Minai-nipi. Maybe our protests helped to cancel their plans for this base. Still we feel uneasy about what is happening to our land.

The military say they have an avoidance strategy, but they still fly right over our camps. It's a little bit better, but we still have problems with the low-level flying. The animals are every-where. They are also terrorized. I don't only think about the jets flying over the small spot where my tent is in *nutshimit*. I worry about all the places where the animals live as well.

In 1988, once we set our minds to protest against the military, we weren't afraid. We had to do everything in our power to stop them. We had to take our protest right down to the runway. We all just rushed through the gates. The feeling was so good. Many Innu children ran through, big and small ones alike. Their hearts were strong and they had no fear at all, because they knew their future was at stake.

Like my son Peneshish, who was six years old at the time. One morning, I asked him why the police put me in jail and he said it was because of our land, Nitassinan. I knew immediately that even at his young age, he knew why we struggled.

We chose to go on the runway because we wanted to expose what is really happening here and to let others know that this military base is located on our land. Neither the government nor the military owns the land. We are the owners. Our ancestors have lived on this land for thousands of years. We truly love our children and we know they will have nothing if we never gain control of our land. That will be the end of the Innu race on this earth. We will have nothing, only pity. We will die off. Many military men will be around. There will be all kinds of strange diseases like AIDS brought into our communities. All kinds of negative things will happen to the Innu, like the military's PCBs, which we had to live with for many years.

Many times we protested and crossed the gates to go inside the fenced perimeter of the airbase. When we marched inside, along with our children and elders, we felt so good. Those actions were done in unity. We were very emotional. We felt proud of one another. We felt like the gates of heaven had opened up to welcome us.

Once we thought we were a powerless people. That feeling was suddenly gone. We felt strong and the future of our people was now in our hands. The children were proud of their parents and grandparents. They could not believe we had done this with so many soldiers surrounding us. Many children doubted they could go through the gates, but they did.

The military and the police told us many times that we were endangering our lives and the lives of others. But don't they realize that low-level flying and other military activities are endangering our lives in *nutshimit*? Still they continued to make their plans to expand. If only people could see what the jets are doing to Innu families in *nutshimit*. Ever since the jets and the military have multiplied in numbers, there has been risk of Innu lives being lost.

The first time we camped at the end of the runway, we weren't stopped from putting up tents. We entered the runway about seven times from that base camp. We had about 25 tents at that spot. We used to watch the struggle in South Africa on television before the fall of apartheid. We saw how the White people used to kill the Black people and their children. We were frightened about our children's and Nitassinan's future. We felt one day that we would be treated like the people from South Africa if we did not do something. That is how roughly the government and the military would treat us.

With our protests, we began to cry out and say we'd had enough. First the women started to organize and the movement built up from there. Innu women used to think it was the men's business to be involved in politics. We always thought it was the job of the chief, the councillors and the Innu Nation to look after politics, but the more the women talked, the more we realized what the future held for the Innu if we didn't do something. We asked ourselves where we would be once the military had a firm hold on our land. After the women became involved in the struggle, we realized how much power we had.

We also took action on the military's bombing range at Minai-nipi. I have been there twice. There were five of us who went to the bombing range the first time. We saw the damage done to the land. We saw the craters made by those mock bombs. Trees were destroyed and bombs were also dropped in the lake. Some of the bombs were huge. We have always gone to hunt and fish near that bombing range, but now the military won't let us go any more. The military has only a 40-year history on our land. How can they tell us they own the land? We have thousands of years of history on this land.

As the struggle went on, we found ourselves more and more united, and stronger. We understood more about ourselves and about the things we should strive for. Now the military has installed all kinds of barbed wire in their efforts to permit the military activities. But we never armed ourselves. We had only our legs to march around on inside those gates. We didn't get violent. We didn't damage the jets and we never picked fights with the military people. We protested then and we still protest now in a non-violent manner.

The Innu have grown to understand each other as we strive

to get control of our land. Sometimes we feel close to achieving this. We feel strong. When we have women's meetings, we talk about how we feel. We console each other and gain strength from each other. We feel we can't give up now. It feels good when other Innu encourage us to go on. They tell us that what we are doing is right and powerful. "We will stand behind you," other Innu people say to us.

⚜   ⚜   ⚜

Being in prison was the hardest part of the struggle. All the women who were jailed had many children. We left our husbands, our friends and all our relatives behind when they put us in jail in Goose Bay. We sat inside those cells, emotionally torn, thinking about our children, who we knew longed for their mothers. We were never at ease. When we talked about our children in the prison, we cried. We felt for one another because we knew the pain we were all going through. We were treated like criminals. We couldn't sleep properly, because there were no mattresses or beds. We were reluctantly given one blanket each, no pillow. The cells were filthy dirty. We cleaned them up ourselves. The toilet tissue had been thrown all over the ceilings. We were in cells in which they usually put drunks. The toilets were filthy. How could they expect us to eat by an open toilet? It was a very hot summer and there were so many of us in one cell. When we asked for water, they wouldn't give us any. When they did, it was warm. Who could drink warm water in hot conditions like that?

Trying to sleep was very, very hard. I would wake up every now and then. Sometimes I dreamt about my children, because I was thinking about them most of the time. Twice one night, I had trouble breathing in my nightmare. I woke up and looked at a book, hoping it would help me sleep. I fell asleep again and had this nightmare. I dreamt that my house was on fire and all my children were inside screaming. I tried to run in but I couldn't. I woke up and tried to wake up one of my friends in the cell. I told her I couldn't sleep. She stayed awake with me for a while.

At our court appearance for the protests on the airport runway, I personally understood only a bit of the English spoken in the courtroom, but some of the others understood. I thought I would be wrongfully put in jail, without having committed any crime. I had just wanted to save our land so that my children would also have a future. I thought I would not be able to see my children for a long time. After Judge Igloliorte's decision, I was so overjoyed that I wouldn't be jailed. I ran over to my children and my husband, put my arms around them and kissed them. I was set free. I was so happy when the court decision was explained to me.

I would get out of jail, go to court, go back home, call another meeting, we would plan another action, bring more women, and I would land in jail again. I did this three times. Some women ended up in the women's prison in Stephenville on the island of Newfoundland, far from home.

They can throw us in jail, but now we won't forget the struggle. We can't give up. We won't be silent any more. Once my generation gives up, the next generation will pick up the fight, and then their children will. If further militarization continues on our land, there will be no future for the Innu. This land was meant to be used for hunting. This is not a land of war.

⚱   ⚱   ⚱

When the women became involved in our struggle to gain our land back from foreign domination, we began to make trips to the outside to explain our struggle to ordinary people. Innu women never used to go out to meetings, but now we are constantly going to many cities and towns. We even went to Europe. I remember one big women's meeting in Ottawa. It was a meeting of the National Action Committee on the Status of Women. Obviously the government feels ashamed of what they have done to us and the damage they have done to our land. The government people weren't present, but their officials were. There were many supporters there. They had heard a lot about our fight and struggle, but were not well informed about what was going on. They told us they understood much more after they heard our presentation.

The support continued to build from all these meetings. The Innu made many friends. The outside support from non-Innu people is very important to us. We feel that maybe we will regain control of our land, because many other people are helping us in our struggle. People sympathize with our cause and, with them, we gather strength.

♟ ♟ ♟

I thought low-level flying was a very big development. I could not imagine that the government would still want to put more and more developments on our land. First there was Mista-paus-tuk (Churchill Falls), the iron ore mines in Labrador City and then forestry projects, which continue today. They take our trees and send them away. Every time I drive to Goose Bay, I see huge trucks full of wood. By the side of the road, I also see piles and piles of wood waiting to be picked up by those trucks. It hurts me so much. Innu people never killed so many trees. We only chop down trees to use to set up our tents and for our small wood stoves to cook food and to keep us warm in our tents. There are more and more companies who want to come to Nitassinan to destroy our land. These days we have to fight against the Trans-Labrador Highway; the Lower Churchill hydro development, including Gull Island; and a big mine at Emish (Voisey's Bay). How will the Innu and the animals survive all these assaults?

Emish is a very beautiful place with marshes, nice rivers and lakes, trees and mountains. I have seen Emish and many other beautiful places like it all over Nitassinan. My mother and father showed me all those places, special places where the caribou, porcupine, beaver and geese like to live.

What will happen if the mine grows non-stop? Emish will die. The animals cannot talk to people and say what they think about what is happening. But the Innu people know how the animals feel because we live so closely together. The animals eat in the marshes, from the plants on the ground and from the trees. The fish live and feed in the pure waters. People will eat the animals and get sick when the land has been damaged and polluted. Their food will be spoiled.

When I was at a protest in Emish, I saw gas all over the ground. This is something else that the animals don't like. They never smelled that before. They can't stand it and they stay away. There is also a lot of noise at Emish from the drilling and from all the helicopters and planes. The animals like to find a peaceful place to stay for a while. Now they can't stay in one place. They are always moving. Animals can't stay at Emish anymore.

The mining people don't know me, or how much I know about life in the country. But I know what a mess they will make at Emish, how much dirty stuff and pollution they will leave behind after they are finished with their mine. I have seen Schefferville, where they left their big hole. I worry that the pollution will make the people sick. The children will get diseases like asthma. The Innu at Schefferville thought that the company would clean up its mess after it shut down, but it just left a mess.

I have seen how the military don't clean up their mess. I have seen all their fuel drums and all the bombs that they drop on our land. The military and mining people think that the Innu are nothing. They have no respect for us.

People in Utshimassits (Davis Inlet) and Sheshatshu are very worried about this, confused about what the government is doing to our land. It is true that some Innu and Inuit people are working at the mine at Emish. Younger people don't understand what is going on, what will happen 5, 10 or 20 years from now. You don't see elders working there. Young people just worry about the money. They see their friends working there. They have cars and lots of beer and lots of friends. That is what is attracting young people to work there.

But Innu people don't put money in the bank. They just spend it and waste it. It is not in our culture to want to be rich, to save money for the future. This money will kill our young people. We see this happening already. I've seen the young men coming home from working at Emish. They are drinking a lot and there is violence happening. I don't want to say bad things about people. I just really worry about what will happen to them. I worry that my sons might work there and get into fights. One of them might assault somebody, drive a car when he has been drinking and get into an accident. Innu don't want to work there long. They end up getting fired. They lose their jobs or end up injured in the hospital.

The *akaneshau* (White people) who work at Emish, they put their money in the bank. When they are old and can't work, they will go back to where they belong and they will get their pension cheques. This is all they will worry about — their cheques coming in every couple of weeks. But what about what they did to the people's land? They will have left a mess for the Innu and Inuit children of today to live with. They will be very sad and angry. They will ask: "Who did this to our homeland?"

Now our elected leaders are sitting with the governments of Newfoundland and Canada to negotiate land claims. I remember in 1988 we had a community meeting about land claims. The people were not happy about this government process. Some people said they wanted to try and begin negotiations, but more people said no. We were strong and I was happy that we stopped negotiations. A few weeks later we walked onto the Goose Bay runway and stopped those military planes.

I've been to many places across Canada, like Toronto and Halifax. I have met many Native people who have been through negotiations and have signed agreements or treaties. They live like *akaneshau*. They have nice offices like the *akaneshau*. But they have only a small piece of land that they can call their own. The *akaneshau* are all around them, crowding them and pushing them off even this small piece of land. What about their children and grandchildren? There will be no place for them to live. Will this also happen to the Innu?

Many Native people I meet tell me they are very jealous that we have never signed an agreement to give away our land to governments. They say it is too late for them. I worry so much about these land-claims negotiations. In the old days we never had band councils or the Innu Nation. Our *utshimaut* (leaders) were not like our elected leaders today. Now when I listen to the *utshimaut* talk about the negotiations, I really try to understand, but they make me so confused. Sometimes I feel like I should just shut my mouth. But what will happen with negotiations? I am afraid for the land and I worry that I will get lots of money. This money will bring more alcohol and drugs.

A lot of other people are also confused. We don't know what these negotiations are all about. We need to understand what it all means, like me, Mary Ann Michel (Miste Mani-An) and other women. We need to get on top of this.

I am more interested in actions. Next March I want people to join me on a journey by sled and snowshoes to Minai-nipi once again. I want the military to know we will not go away. As well, in August I invite people to canoe with my husband and me down Mista-shipu (Churchill River) to let the world know that the Innu will continue to care for these waters and all Nitassinan.

Life on the Edge
of a Bombing Range

Mary Martha Hurley

In 1988 Mary Martha joined a number of women from
Sheshatshu to organize several actions on the military
airport runways in Goose Bay to protest NATO military flight training over their lands. The following year,
Mary Martha and her family set out for nutshimit (the
country) in the spring. Joined by four other Innu families, this exodus to nutshimit was more than their usual
seasonal migration to fish, hunt and tell stories under
the stars. This journey included plans for a guerrilla
action to protest the low-level flying. They set up camp
and occupied the Minai-nipi bombing range, designated
by the military for laser-guided smoke-bomb target
practice. They were periodically joined by a handful of
supporters, including members of Survival International, a British-based solidarity organization that sup-
ports indigenous peoples all over the world in their
human-rights struggles. Nigel Markham also visited the
camp with anthropologist and author Hugh Brody to
shoot some footage for their National Film Board of
Canada and Nexus Films production Hunters and
Bombers about the Innu campaign against NATO's
military flight training. The rhythm of life in nutshimit

allows for moments of reflection, and the following are
excerpts of Mary Martha's musings, which she wrote
in her journal that spring.

May 24/89   Shores of Minai-nipi (Burbot Lake)

In the country we are here as family and friends. We feel so safe
in Nitassinan when we don't hear the jets flying over us. It is so
peaceful out here. It is very good for every one of us in my family
to feel the closeness of each other. We care about and love each
other. Being united with the people makes us feel strong. In the
community the people are divided. We see different kinds of
problems that arise. Everyone must know that alcohol is to be
blamed for all of this. It makes us weak and have no power.

When I look at my brothers today I feel so proud and happy
for them. I know deep inside they are hurting because they, too,
wish our father was alive, but I suppose that's the way it is. I watch
my mother struggle so hard to do everything she can for my
brothers. We should be so thankful to her that the Innu have
never given up our land to Canada or to any foreigners. We have
never given them the right to use or claim Nitassinan.

The other day I was listening to a tape of an Innu elder singing
and beating the drum. Before he started to sing, he first talked
about how the Innu people respect their belongings and how these
are so sacred to them. For example, he said if you ever see an old
snowshoe that is worn out and lying on the ground, you have to
pick it up and hang it on a tree. I started to think about my people
and how they sure were strong fighters to prove who we are now.

If a NATO base is established in Goose Bay, it will destroy the
Innu culture, and everything that we once loved will be a huge
mess, with war toys all over the land. Whenever the Innu go out
in the country, non-Natives always bring up the point about how
the Innu leave garbage behind in their camps. But just think about
it a minute. Do they ever complain about what the military are
leaving around this area? They drop dummy bombs around our
hunting grounds and leave a mess of them in the rivers. This kind
of thing is more dangerous to the environment — to the lakes

and rivers and fish that live in the water. More and more of these bombs will be seen if there are to be more bombing ranges in hunting areas. But when I begin to think about how the land will be destroyed, I am encouraged even more to keep on struggling for Nitassinan.

This morning we saw loons on the water and Guy shot one. My nephew ran over when his canoe was coming ashore. I observed from a distance and saw how proud he was when my brother passed the loon over to him to take to his grandmother. I truly believe that if anyone decides to go in the country, it is a very best place to let out feelings. Here you have people who really care and understand what you are saying. When I talk to my mother in the tent, I can really see that she has time to listen and give me advice. When we are in the community, I feel that no one has the time to listen. In the country, elders are always telling you how long ago people used to suffer in order to survive. You listen to their stories and wonder at how the Innu were so courageous and brave.

I used to always think that I was a useless Innu. I felt that non-Natives would always beat the Innu. But now everything has changed since our protest began. We are much stronger now that our feelings of frustration are being let out. Now Canadians and other aboriginal people are familiar with what is happening here in Nitassinan.

From what I see around the campsite, people are enjoying being here at Minai-nipi. I often ask myself, "Is it wrong for us, the Innu people, to walk in the footsteps of our grandfathers and grandmothers? Is it wrong for us to continue practising the Innu traditional way of life?"

Mitshen (Bart Penashue) and Jim Roche and our youngest adopted son, Trevor, went to check the fishing net. They caught 13 trout — all a nice size and they tasted real good. This evening my mother, Mary Adele Andrew, her grandson Matthew, Michel Andrew, Jim, Martha Rich and Mitshen went to put out my brother Ben's net across on the other side of the lake. I wonder what their catch will be?

When we checked my mom's net yesterday, there were 11 more trout. Mitshen had caught four trout and the last one was a big one. We had a lovely time in the boat. If the weather had cooperated, it would have been even more enjoyable. Eric shot two ducks on the way to check the net. We also saw a beaver dam, and the children were really interested in the dam. I started to think about how young children should be taught what the Innu do in the country to live. It is their culture, so it is very important that we do not lose it.

May 26/89

Yesterday wasn't a very nice day, but a few men still went out hunting. Others stayed at the camp to get wood and smoked fish so they wouldn't spoil. I cleaned my goose and two ducks, while my neighbour was washing clothes. It was a busy day. One family moved across the lake to another new spot. The people are catching a lot of trout in the nets, especially in my mother's net.

My mother shared some memories that came to her when we were checking the nets. She said she wished she could participate when people from our camp return home by canoe at the end of the season. She said the only difficult time she would have is when she would have to portage and do quite a bit of walking. She used to be quite healthy in those years when they travelled by canoe and portaged. She isn't quite as healthy now and she couldn't do it because of her illness. I just wish she could go with us. When it will be time to leave the campsite, there will surely be tears in her eyes, she said.

May 28/89

I will never forget today. It was a very frustrating day and I could tell just by looking at the men's faces that it wasn't a very happy day for them. When we heard the helicopter flying around the campsite earlier, we knew it must be the wildlife officers and some RCMP. Ben left the camp with John M. and another fellow who works for Survival International. They took quite a few photographs of the police taking the gun from Ben. I walked down along the shore, where it was still safe to walk on the ice, to see what was happening. I asked myself, "Where is his gun?" And as he came closer to the tent, I knew from the look on his face that he was very angry. He dropped his game bag and went on to inform the others about what had happened. Chief Daniel Ashini was sent a message on the camp radio to look into the matter.

A few minutes later, two of my other brothers and my nephew came back. They also had been harassed by the helicopter. The wildlife officers had also seized their shotguns. By just looking at their faces, I knew they were hurt and angered. They described everything that happened. They were in a canoe, hunting geese, when suddenly a helicopter flew over them. They thought it must want them to go ashore to seize their guns, so they figured they would stop hunting. The boy, who is eight years old, was very frightened of the helicopter. He jumped out of the canoe onto the ice. The older men never had the chance to test the ice to see if it was safe enough to walk on. This type of harassment could have caused the young boy to drown or the canoe to tip over. The wildlife officer yelled at my youngest brother and said, "Give me your bullets!" My brother was very nervous and he did everything as fast as he could to give them everything they asked for.

Then the third hunting party arrived back to the camp. It was Eric and Mitshen. They had gone goose hunting and it was a successful and frustrating hunt. They killed two geese, but these were confiscated and their guns were taken away as well. The two young men said they were just having a boil-up when the helicopter landed. They were warming up leftover goose. They felt really angry when their geese were taken away. When the men saw the wildlife officers and RCMP walking toward them, they thought they were there to bring them a summons to attend court because of the protests. But instead they wanted their geese and guns.

They never even tried to land at our camp. You should have seen the people gathered around outside the tent, telling each other what had happened. One of the men said, "It hurts deep inside of me. Right now it feels like my heart is burning. What do they expect us to do? We use the shotguns to kill the geese and to bring home food to feed our family."

The reason they come and confiscate our guns and wildlife is that they are trying to make it harder for us. They really would like to see us leave Minai-nipi, because we are close to the bombing range. But after what they have done, we are more determined. They have given us courage to stay as long as we can. What is it they want us to be? They don't want us to camp near the Canadian Forces base, they don't want us to protest, they even come to take away our hunting guns from us in the country.

We have said it over and over so many times. What we are doing is not illegal to us. If the non-Natives were here before the Innu, then we would feel that whatever we were doing was illegal. But our ancestors were here first. Our people never had to go through what we face today. We want to control Nitassinan. I always feel that what the non-Natives or the Canadian and Newfoundland governments don't realize is that the Innu would be more capable than they are of handling our own problems. This would be better than the White society telling us that we should be happier to live the way the non-Natives live. I am not saying that their way of life is not normal. I am just trying to tell the world that we Innu cannot be changed from the way we are. We can't live like non-Natives, no matter how hard we try. We have our own culture. We would never ask the non-Natives to live like the Innu. You can imagine the type of reaction we would get if non-Natives were told to live like the Innu and to practise our traditional way of life.

May 29/89
The weather today is still raining and foggy. But everyone had a nice sleep listening to the raindrops falling on top of the tent. There are two families over across the lake now. We are preparing to move across tomorrow.

Now I will write about how I felt when the four people were acquitted by the judge. They were charged with mischief for protesting on the runway. That was the first time in my life that I ever felt so happy. I thanked the Lord on that day when I heard they were going to be acquitted. It showed us that we are struggling very hard and finally a judge recognized what we are saying out to the public.

May 30/89

The weather is clearing up and the sun is beginning to shine. There was snow on the ground when we got up this morning. It started off wet, but at last we are beginning to have a good day. My mother has moved across the lake and her bed has already been set up. Me and Melvin, and Ben and Lyla will move tomorrow. Big decision, but after Mom's stuff was moved, all of us decided it was time for us to go as well.

June 1/89   12:00

A number of people left to go to the bombing range. We aren't quite sure when they will return home, but they were anxious to put up the Innu flag on the range. We are anxiously waiting to hear back from them to see what the word will be for us women to walk in there. I asked Tshaukuish (Elizabeth Penashue) if we should walk in there after the men come back. Some people came back today around 3:30 p.m. Before they arrived, the military helicopter flew over us twice to the spot we had cleared for a helicopter to land. The people all scattered around everywhere so they wouldn't be able to land, but the children were getting frightened of the helicopter. Some were asking their mothers, "Is my father going to be arrested? Will they find them?"

June 3/89

The guys who went to the bombing range returned this evening. They all looked well and people were happy to see them back home. They said it was hard going in the woods. They had to portage through the woods. They were seen by the military helicopter, but they weren't bothered by it.

It's such a beautiful evening and for supper they had some beaver, which my mother cooked. It seemed so different when they were gone. My mother described it as a feeling of loneliness without them. Same with Mitshen, I felt like it wasn't the same without him with us in the tent. My husband brought back a small dummy bomb, which he picked up on the bombing range. When I saw it and the young children examined it closely, I felt a pain go through me. I said to myself, "As they grow older and we continue to teach them what is going on, gradually they will learn that our land is being demolished because the military is using it as a playground for wars." This is a big threat to our lifestyle. Once every area is bombed our culture will slowly die, but we will continue to hang on to it and never let it be destroyed more and more.

June 4/89

Today it is raining off and on, which isn't that bad. We were all supposed to go on a picnic but, due to the rain, it looks like it will be cancelled.

I am all alone in the tent, preparing to make fish cakes. When I am by myself, that is the perfect time for me to think. I feel the strength from my people. Some aboriginal people have lost their language. Now they are using a second language, which isn't their mother tongue. It's so sad to see this happening. In our community, everyone is still communicating in our own Innu language. And the other thing is that no one on this earth can convince me that this land doesn't belong to the Innu people. We were here first before any non-Native person ever walked here. An Innu elder said to the minister of National Defence when he came to the community, "Long, long ago, whenever we used to meet any non-Native persons during our journey through the country, we were always willing to share anything that we could spare with them. But today I look around and see the treatment we are getting back from the government. It is like we are being driven and pushed off our own land."

I asked a question to my 10-year-old daughter about how she feels about the bombing range. It was around 10 o'clock last night when I asked her to write down how she feels and what she thinks will happen. At first she said she couldn't find any easy answers. Then I explained to her that there weren't any wrong answers to the question. I was surprised at the list of answers she came up with. I watched her when she was writing, and these are the things that went through her head about what she thinks of the bombing range:

1. It will destroy our land and culture.
2. It will contaminate the animals that are there.
3. I think it is stupid for jets to be there.
4. It will hurt people's ears from the noise.
5. The children get scared when they see the jets.
6. I think the use of our land by the government is no good because it's not their land.
7. The jets are only playing with our land.
8. I don't see why the Innu have to go to court over their own land.
9. I think the bombs should not be there.
10. And neither the bombing range.

1:30

Pat Rich, Guy, Eric, Jim Roche, Nigel Markham and Louis went to the bombing range. Ben and Francis will stay overnight and then come back tomorrow evening. At the camp, we were planning to play Innu baseball. There are mostly women left here.

5:00

A military helicopter flew over our camp. It got so close to our tents, we could see them taking pictures of the people, and we took pictures of them as well. Clem recognized one of the police as Constable Walton. I noticed that the constable was talking into some kind of a microphone. The only welcoming signs were fingers.

We finished playing ball and other games around 10:00. Everyone was very happy and even the little audiences were excited about the games. Afterwards we made a big fire and listened to the tape of the Innu man beating the drum. All of us danced around the big fire. Even my mother was dancing. We had an enjoyable evening. Later, Mitshen checked his net and he had caught seven lovely trout, which he will start smoking tomorrow. We remembered the men that went to the bombing range and the two who will bring them back.

We radioed Sebastian and Christine Nuna's camp to ask them to inform my brother Alex Andrew, the outpost coordinator, about the military helicopter always harassing us. The radio in Sheshatshu is broken and the people there can't hear the people who are in the country. We can't communicate back and forth to send our messages. We want Alex to ask the RCMP why the military helicopter is flying around our campsite so low and why the RCMP are taking photos of us in the tent. The children get very frightened by the helicopter. What is it they want from us?

June 6/89

Today is Pat Rich's birthday. Early this morning we could hear a helicopter a long distance away. It must have been a Universal or Sealand helicopter bringing fishermen to the fishing camp nearby. This afternoon we saw a military helicopter flying toward the bombing range. Tshaukuish and I were looking at it with the binoculars. Then it went behind the mountains. Later on, a jet flew over but it was flying high. It may have come from the bombing range. That was the only jet we saw.

Paul Rich shot an otter this evening with Dominic Gregoire. It must have been exciting for Dominic to observe what was going on when the otter was shot. Tshaukuish made yeast bread and placed it in the hot sand to bake. Melvin smoked fish and then went to put out my mother's and Ben's nets in the water.

Today the only way to send out messages was to pass them on to my brother Pat, who is in Utshimassits (Davis Inlet). He told us that the radio in Sheshatshu was broken down and they were trying so hard to repair it. This afternoon people could hear them so plain and clear, but no one could talk back to them. Maybe tomorrow the radio will be fixed. Tshaukuish wanted to talk to Alex to ask him if he could find two canoes for the canoe trip back home.

June 7/89

A jet flew way off in the distance earlier, heading up to the bombing range. Tshaukuish came to our tent to tell us that Janet Pone had heard on the radio that the military had taken down a tent and flag on the bombing range. These were put up by our men yesterday. The news on the radio was saying that the Innu have been trying to get onto the bombing range for three days now, but with no success. They said the bombing range was well secured and no one could go there. But now we can show them they were making up lies, because some Innu people have already been in there.

I don't suppose any human being or group of people wants to lose their culture. For example, the people in Newfoundland have their own lifestyle of fishing, which they have had for so many years. Today foreigners are coming in and over-fishing their waters. Well, the people in Newfoundland are angry and frustrated that the Canadian government would let this continue. I believe Newfoundlanders have every right to be angry when they don't agree with something they see happening in their land.

The fellows returned from the bombing range and they all looked tired. We were all surprised to see them return home safely from their journey.

I feel the only way people in other places will know something is terribly wrong here is when we start voicing our concerns. A group of people must strongly oppose something when it is a big threat to their lifestyle. How would other people feel if they were in the country and overflown by a low-level jet? The jet suddenly comes from nowhere. When we are in the country, we can't do a thing about it, but just look up. It angers us a lot, especially when small children are in the country camp. Just imagine for a moment, how the elderly people in camp feel. The noise startles them and they complain about their hearts beating rapidly. One of my children woke up the other night, screaming in terror, saying he was frightened of the jets.

It's frustrating when the commanding officer accuses us of exaggerating, but what do they know? They aren't in the camps. We know because we have experienced these terrifying flights. We have CB radios in our camps and the base commander says we should tell them where our camps are so the jets will fly around them. But we haven't been giving out that information. We know that the jets will still come around to our camps and disrupt the hunters and people. I say to that base commander that he can't be on every plane to order his pilots where to go and where not to go when they fly low. Once they board their jets, they don't care where they fly.

I always feel like my own people are underestimated when they want to speak out. What hurts deeply is when Innu people express themselves in public and are accused of lying. We get very upset when our elders are denied a voice and not taken seriously. The Innu admire the country the way it is now, so we try to protect it.

June 8/89

Today we were all at the tent with the radio to find out information from Alex. He and Rose Gregoire were giving us updates of what has been happening. They told us the Minister of Indian Affairs will be coming to Sheshatshu on June 21. We told them we were planning to canoe back home to Sheshatshu, so they were pretty worried that we wouldn't get back to the community in time. Hugh Brody was supposed to film our trip by canoe back to Sheshatshu, but his camera crew can't be here until the 17th of June. There are so many things happening these days. Some people need to stay behind to walk back to the bombing range, which was closed for a day and half yesterday.

June 9/89

No contacts can be made to anyone on the radio. We don't know if the plane will be here today. The camp radio is dead, no sound, we can't hear a thing. Some people heard on the news that the bombing range was re-opened again for the military to continue to bomb Nitassinan.

June 10/89

This morning, when we woke up, the film crew from the National Film Board came to our tent and wanted to film my family. One thing they could not film was me reading from this journal. After I had read about five pages of my diary, the filming came to an end. I just burst into tears. I was holding back my tears and I couldn't go on any longer.

When I describe everything about how I feel every day, I always think about my grandparents and my father. I think about when my brothers were growing up. My father used to say to them, "When I am gone and can no longer be with you, my sons, never ever let anyone convince you that this is not Innu home-land. You can pick up where I left off when I am gone." So whenever I see my brothers try so hard to be good hunters like my father, I remember him. It's even more difficult for our mom, who has been a widow for 12 years now. It has been a very painful time for her. She talks about all the years the boys lost of their father's guidance and of the skills he could have taught them.

We didn't do very much today, because we thought the plane was going to pick up passengers. Instead, only one helicopter came to pick up the NFB crew. We kind of waited around for the plane and helicopter to come. It was a hot day and there was not much we could do. This evening around 7:45 my mother, Tshaukuish and Francis went to take up his traps for now. They came back around 10:00.

June 11/89

This afternoon Pat and Ian Rich and Jim Roche left to go to the bombing range again. Mitshen went to drop them off at the trail.

My mother, Tshaukuish, Germaine, Clem, Eric, Guy, Ben and Lyla were all there to see them leave Minai-nipi. We will miss their company. We will be with them in our thoughts throughout their journey to the bombing range. Around two in the afternoon, a military helicopter flew around the campsite and took pictures. About 5:30 a Sealand helicopter flew over our campsite. The pilot couldn't see the camp, but he finally landed. Alex, Simon, Peter and Mitshen left to go back to Goose Bay.

The people at our camp this spring were my mother, Mrs. Mary Adele Andrew; my brothers Guy, Eric and Max Andrew; my nephew Matthew; Jim Roche; my brother Ben and his wife, Lyla, and their family: Elena, Jeremy and Penute; my husband, Melvin, and I, and our family: Pamela, Natasha and Trevor. My sister Clem arrived on June 2nd. There was also Angela Penashue and Paul Rich, Dominic Gregoire, Janet Gregoire, Francis and Elizabeth Penashue and their family: Mitshen (Bart), Caroline, Frederick, Robert and Kaputshet Penashue. In another tent were Pat and Germaine Rich, and their family: Roxanne, Desmond, Ian, Lisa, Antonia and Patrick Rich Jr.

The Trickster and the Ant

Nympha Byrne

Kuekuatsheu, the wolverine or trickster, was in love with a woman hunter. He didn't want his brothers to see this woman. He called all the different animals — beaver, lynx, ant, geese, muskrat and so on — his brothers. One day his brothers found out Kuekuatsheu had this woman. They followed his tracks. They left a goose and an ant to keep an eye on Kuekuatsheu while he slept. The others took one of his leggings, hid it inside a dried caribou stomach and hung it inside the tent. The brothers went on to find his girlfriend. When Kuekuatsheu awoke he would be slowed down because he would be looking for his legging. When he asked the goose and the ant where to find his legging, they refused to say. He finally found it, wrung it out, put it on and took off. The goose and the ant followed him.

While they walked, the goose told Kuekuatsheu his scarf was falling off. Kuekuatsheu helped him put it back on. The ant removed his belt and told him his belt had fallen off. Kuekuatsheu helped him out with his belt. They kept stalling him until Kuekuatsheu caught on and became suspicious. When the goose took off his scarf again, Kuekuatsheu became angry about being slowed down again. He was worried that someone else might have caught up with his girlfriend. He tied the scarf really tight and threw the goose into the marshes. He told the goose that the marshes would now be his home. That is where they would lay eggs and feed. That is why the geese now spend their time in marshes.

The ant removed his belt again and asked Kuekuatsheu to help. By this time, Kuekuatsheu was really upset. He stopped to help the ant. He twisted his belt very tightly around the ant in two places and he threw him into some dry dead wood. Kuekuatsheu told the ant that's where he would keep himself warm in the winter. That is why this kind of wood is the ant's home today.

Kuekuatsheu was like a god, the way he changed the animals. He took care of them.

Fifty-seven Days in Jail

Mary Martha Hurley

Mary Martha was one of a number of Innu women
arrested for their part in the occupation of military
runways to confront NATO's murderous fighter jets
as they prepared to take off in Goose Bay. Other
women arrested included Tshaukuish Penashue, Anne
Marie Andrew, Janet Pone, Helen Gabriel, Jackie
Ashini, Ann Hurley, Rose Gregoire, Francesca Snow,
Mary May Osmond and Germaine Rich. The local
lock-up in Happy Valley (next to Goose Bay) can
accommodate only small numbers and for a short
period of time, and the local penitentiary is a men's
facility. The women, who refused to sign undertakings,
which included a promise to not protest again on the
runways, were shipped to the provincial Women's
Correctional Centre in Stephenville, on the west coast
of Newfoundland, to await their trial. This happened
on two occasions. Mary Martha spent the most time
in jail of all Innu who were arrested for their direct
actions. She received a number of visitors in Stephenville, including Innu family and friends, women from
the National Action Committee on the Status of
Women, and a film crew shooting the Innu campaign
against NATO military flight training in Nitassinan.
The following are some of Mary Martha's thoughts

while she sat in her jail cell during one stint awaiting her trial.

Sept. 9/89   Happy Valley Lock-up   11:00

This is the first time I ever had to go to the Supreme Court. I was so nervous. There were two policemen sitting one on each side of me. That made it even worse. My honest feelings of the day are that I felt like I had committed a serious offence. But I was only protesting to protect our land and I did it mainly for my children. Finally when the court was over, I was so frightened. I didn't have a clue what was taking place. I started to cry when I saw some of my relatives cry. I was so worried. But when I got back to the cell at the RCMP detachment, Joe MacDonald told me that everything wasn't over yet. I didn't need to get real upset. My husband came in to see how I was doing. He was allowed to visit for a few minutes, so we talked. I felt a lot better when we had finished. He told me not to worry about anything.

As each day passes, I am still hanging on and stronger. I hope my children won't be at the airport when I leave to go back to the women's jail in Stephenville. It will just tear my heart in two. I am suffering enough in here. I will surely miss them, but they will always be in my heart.

Friday, Sept. 22/89   1:30

We rushed down to the Supreme Court office. Melvin and my kids were there, and Mom, Clem and her son Matthew, Tshaukuish and Francis Penashue, Lyla, Penute, Elena, Janet and her baby, Louisa and Joseph Penashue, Ben Michel and Janet, Marty Andrew, Frederick Penashue and Terry Andrew. We waited for the judge to let me know what was going to happen after the rebuttal from both sides. I didn't have a clue what the judge said in the last part of his speech. That was the frightening part. The court was adjourned for a few minutes and two policemen were in a small room with me. My husband, Melvin, came in. We couldn't do any talking, so I just wrote on a piece of paper if I wanted to tell him something.

When the judge said I would be remanded in custody, I cried. I didn't hear what he was saying. Was it months or years? I didn't have a clue what was going on in there.

I was very tired this morning and didn't know what to expect. My head is still aching from the crying I did after court. I didn't expect they would keep me in custody. I thought they would give me an option to choose. Instead I have to wait until a trial date in October sometime, before they will see what they can do for me.

My headache is finally gone and I can write about how my day went. It would be so lonely otherwise. My friends are still in Stephenville — the other women who protested with me. It has been very hard to be in here by myself. I really haven't got anyone to communicate with. But my prayers each day give me faith and strength. It is so quiet. I can't hear a sound. I can't wait until tomorrow when I am out where the other ladies are. I wish that I was there tonight instead of in this small cell. You can't roam around in this small place. I can only read and smoke. I just hope someone will drop by this evening so I won't find it too long a day.

I wish the non-Natives could understand why we are doing everything to stop low-level flying. Maybe one of these days, citizens here in Goose Bay will regret that they welcomed a NATO base. A jet might crash not only in the country, but it could happen in a residential area as well. Does it ever occur to any of them how the environment surrounding us will be damaged, including the animals, rivers, lakes, fish that live in the water, the wildlife that people depend on for food?

Whenever non-Natives speak or write about our people, they always say something bad. They say we always depend on social assistance and we are too lazy to work. They never look on the good side. It's very hurtful when someone writes these kind of false stories about my people. That is the reason we try so hard to keep up with the struggle, so non-Natives will know we can stand up on our own two feet. We just can't watch or listen to people saying or writing these things about our people. I hope someday non-Natives will understand the aboriginal people from here and across Canada.

3:30

My husband came to the RCMP detachment. I felt a lot better after that. Melvin said I didn't need to worry about anything, and the children were all right. And my mother was fine. I felt a lot better when he encouraged me to be strong.

The judge said a bunch of words. He said I signed an under-taking before. I broke my promise. He said something about how he was doing this for the safety of the civilians, the military, the RCMP, crew, people, the residential area. I don't know much of what he was saying.

Lyla and me hugged and cried on each other's shoulders for a few minutes. Someone knocked on the back window of the police car. I turned around and it was my nephew Marty. He waved at me with tears in his eyes. I will never forget that. I love and miss them all.

Joe MacDonald said I will be taken to the Women's Correctional Centre tomorrow morning. I can't wait to see my friends and hear their laughter again. I know they are waiting for me. They must be out of their rooms right now having a big chat and laughing. I am so lonely in here by myself. I am always asking the woman guard the time. I am getting sleepy, but I don't want to go to bed yet.

When I had supper this evening I didn't really feel like eating. I was wondering if my children had any supper. Whenever they bring my food, I always remember the kids at home, but I know they are eating and well looked after. Thank the Lord for the help I get with my children. But I wish they were here beside me now, just for a few minutes, just so I can see their smiles and hug them. I love them so much. I pray for them each night before I go to bed, that God will protect them while I am not there to watch over them. It's heartbreaking to leave them and go so many miles away. It will be nice to find out how they are when I get to use the telephone.

Sept. 23/89   4:00 a.m.

I woke up early and had a cigarette, then went back to sleep. I woke up again and it was eight, which was good to hear. This cell is so lonely and I can't take another day in here by myself. Later I had a shower and I felt a lot better.

Sept. 29/98   Women's Correctional Centre,
                            Stephenville, Newfoundland

I have been here one week. I couldn't write in my journal for the past few days because I had to be here one week before I could get my personal belongings. I have 25 more days to spend here. Our trial date is October 24. I can hardly wait for that day to come. I don't know what I'll get, but I am anxiously waiting to be released and have some time with my family.

How can the Canadian government be so cruel to the aboriginal people? We all know that all Native peoples have problems with the land. It is part of our culture to respect and protect the environment. If we just sit back and watch the land being polluted, maybe someday it will be just too late for anyone to voice their concerns to their government. We want to keep on struggling before we are all covered with pollution floating around us. By then no one will hear or even see us. We will not be able to breathe clean air again. We should not forget what this will bring for our children and everyone else's. We should appreciate the land the way God created it for everyone. The animals that we depend on are in the country and live off the land as well. Once the land is polluted by the fumes that low-level jets drop on the ground, the animals will be affected when they eat things that are harmful.

Non-Natives have misunderstood why we are protesting and why we decided not to enter land claims negotiations. They think we are trying to take over all the land and to kick out all the non-Natives living here. But we aren't being selfish in fighting for our homeland. The Canadian and Newfoundland governments have said in public that we have missed our chance by not entering land claims negotiations. Let's face it right now, land claims will not be solved right away. It might take 50 years or more to come to an agreement. Then if the Innu sign an agreement, it will be like we will be signing away our lives forever. We are not that dumb. We have learned from other aboriginal people who have signed land-claims agreements. They say to us, "Please don't do what we have done. It was all a big mistake." They regret it very much.

All along the Innu have been quiet, because our people didn't speak any English. We couldn't communicate with the government officials. In those days, like when our land was flooded, the Innu were quiet and we didn't know how to inform the people across Canada and internationally about how we were being treated. But the younger generation is willing to fight for our people, to speak out and write for them. We want others to know how we have been forced to live in communities. I believe the governments are trying in every way to divide my people. They want the Innu to feel weak and to fight among ourselves. But when the people are together, we can feel the strength that we have.

Sept. 30/89

We have been doing much the same thing over and over again. The chores are pretty much the same day after day. I enjoy the things we do, but when everything is completed, it is so boring. I feel so restless. I wish I was out in the country with all my family in the tent.

We received letters from home and they made us homesick. My husband wrote and I was glad to hear from him. My aunt Rose was upset this evening, worrying about her children. I sympathize with her. I wish there was something I could do to help. She is in a difficult situation. Three of her children returned home from being in Newfoundland. I pray to God that everything will go right for her. She will be speaking to her oldest daughter tomorrow to find out how they are getting on. It is some hard to live so far away from your family.

Oct. 3/89   6:30

We got up to have a shower and cleaned our rooms. Jackie Ashini counted the days left on the calendar and she said we have 19 more days left.

On the evening news I saw my children and the people who went to the Court of Appeal. My tears just came streaming down my cheeks.

Oct. 4/89

We were surprised to see the people from Sheshatshu standing outside the gate of the prison today. The first little one I saw was my son Trevor and the tears started to flow. I cried because I knew he didn't have a clue about prison and why I am in here. But my daughters Pam and Natasha understand quite a bit. Thank God, I could hug and kiss them in person at last.

Oct. 5/89   10:30

We had another visit, this time from Tshaukuish and Francis Penashue, and from Rose's children Janet and Theresa, and their father, Richard. We had a long chat and it was very good to see them all again. It was very emotional when everyone had to leave, especially listening to Rose's children crying.

                                                                 3:00

We anxiously waited for a visit from my husband, Melvin, my mother and Jackie's sister Janet. At last they were here and we were very happy to see them. It was hard to say goodbye to them, but it was helpful for us to have them visit.

Oct. 6/89

Rose received a call from the RCMP detachment. They wanted to know if she would sign an undertaking to be released, but she still refused to sign because of their conditions.

Oct. 8/89

I was told by a correctional officer that I was going to be taken to Goose Bay. I finished my dinner and they told me someone was here to pick me up. I was very happy to hear I was going back, but the constable told me I had to overnight at the Corner Brook lock-up. I was pretty nervous because this was my first time there. I did not know what to expect. I thought I would have to share the room with some other women. It was an empty cell, but I was still scared.

Oct. 9/89   Happy Valley Lock-up
I didn't sleep well last night. I will never forget that I had to spend a night in the Corner Brook lock-up for my sixth wedding anniversary and today is my little boy Trevor's birthday. This will be a month and a year that I will never forget as long as I live. Melvin told me my oldest daughter, Pamela, was making a birthday cake for Trevor today.

Oct. 10/89
My trial date is set for Nov. 6., but I put in an application for my release until then. My lawyer, Mr. Kearslie, and the Crown will argue this on Oct. 17 and then decide if I can be released. But I will be taken back to Stephenville tomorrow. I was happy to see all my family today, especially my mother. Rick, Louise and their daughter were there. And it was good to see Germaine, Paula, Elizabeth, Clem, Anastasia, Alex and Mary Martha, Matthew, Tshaukuish and Francis, Frederick, Nigel, Marie and Hugh Brody. The painful moment was when my girls called out, "Goodbye, Mommy." I started to cry. My mother told me that she and Hugh and the film crew were going to Churchill Falls to do a film about the flooding. I was given about a half-hour, but I thank the Lord they came to see me. It's so good to see that people care, even if they can't be with you all the time. I could see tears in my mother's eyes, but I didn't want to make it any worse for her. I tried so hard not to cry and I did it. I know it is very upsetting for her.

Lyla told me that a part of my journal was used by Peter Gzowski. Jeannie Andrew was doing the reading on the "Morningside" radio show.

Oct. 11/89   Women's Correctional Centre,
                          Stephenville, Newfoundland

I gave Tshaukuish the things Rose had for her, and on the same piece of paper I told them Jackie wanted a bag to put her clothes in. I waited for someone to drop off our stuff, but no one showed up. I told Tshaukuish to check on Rose's kids and see how they were doing for food.

I hope my lawyer, John Olthuis, phones me when I get to the centre. He will try to find out when my trial date is going to be — the one to apply for an earlier release before the real case is to be heard on Nov. 6. This travelling back and forth from Goose Bay to Stephenville is getting to be hectic for me. Yesterday I felt terrible and I didn't eat well. I kept thinking about my children crying when I was taken away. And to see my mom cry made it even worse. But afterwards Ben and Lyla phoned to find out if they could visit. I felt much better after that.

5:00

Well, it's almost suppertime and I will be glad when it is over. For the past couple of days I haven't got much appetite. Nov. 6 is weeks away, but still it isn't so bad. By then I will have served seven weeks in prison altogether. I will be very happy when I am released. I am always counting the days until Nov. 6. The hardest part when I am in prison is when I think about my children. I ache so much to be with my children.

I have decided to continue with my writing, since no one came around and it is around eight o'clock in the evening. I have so many things on my mind that I can release by writing in my diary. Maybe my husband will bring up the stuff tomorrow morning before I leave.

Oct. 15/89

I am 29 years old today. I have to be in prison for my birthday. I wish I was home to celebrate with my family.

Oct. 20/89   10:00
I have received word from home that the RCMP called to inform
the centre that Rose and Jackie have agreed to sign their undertakings. They will be leaving for the RCMP lock-up in Goose Bay
this afternoon. I know it is too hard to be in prison, especially
when we know our children are so far away. But I know I will be
able to last two more weeks in here by myself. Praying will give
me the strength to have faith in myself. He will take care of me
if I put everything in His hands.

                                                    2:15
Rose and Jackie left for the Goose Bay lock-up. Both of them
hugged me and said farewell. They told me to stay strong. After
they left, Lynn Kaye, president of the National Action Committee on the Status of Women (NAC), came to visit. Too bad Rose
and Jackie didn't get a chance to meet her. I tried my best to tell
Lynn whatever messages Rose had for her. She, too, felt bad that
the women had left before she could see them. She told me so
many people are supporting us, which is always good to hear.
This was my first time meeting her and she had a nice personality.
It was encouraging to hear from an understanding person that
the Innu weren't alone in their struggle.

   This evening I was asked by one of the guards if I needed to
take a shower. I was happy to hear her say that, because I really
felt good after my shower. Around nine o'clock, she offered me
a cup of coffee, which was very nice of her. I find this guard rather
friendly and I always feel comfortable when she comes to work.

Oct. 21/89   4:30
I got another visit I was looking forward to — Marion Mathieson
and Michelle Seguin from the NAC. Both of them hugged me.
I saw tears in their eyes, but I held back my tears. We talked and
I told them why I felt so strong about being in here. These ladies
listened very well and I wanted to thank them for their visit. I
felt like I have known them a long time, but this was my first time
meeting them. They were just like family to me.

We will soon be going down for our dinner — tossed salad and grilled sandwiches. Maybe after dinner we will be doing crafts, which will help pass the time. I have been thinking about Rose and Jackie ever since they were taken back to the RCMP lock-up. Rose told me to expect her back here. I am anxious to know what she will decide to do tomorrow. I believe Jackie was going to sign the conditions, because she could be a help to Rose's family while Rose is in prison.

Oct. 22/89

My husband called at 4:30 and I was happy to hear from him that the children were fine. It is so lonely here without Rose and Jackie. I only wish someone was here to speak in my own language. It is hard when I want to speak Innu-aimun. The day was long, but I managed all right.

Oct. 23/89

As of today I have been here for one month exactly. I slept real good last night. I didn't even wake up in the middle of the night. Every morning we get up 6:30, except weekends. We did our chores this morning and then knitting at 10:00. I believe whoever has to go to court shouldn't be remanded for more than 30 days, unless they are in for a serious offence. My only offence is to protect my culture and Nitassinan.

Oct. 26/89

It is Thursday and I am pretty excited about tomorrow's hearing. I only hope and pray that I will be released. I have served one month and eight days total as of Friday. It has been so hard, but if I am released, it was sure worth it. It will be the happiest moment in my life when I see my family again.

Nov 5/89   Happy Valley Lock-up

I was taken back to Goose Bay today. I first got aboard the RCMP aircraft in Deer Lake *en route* to St. John's, where we waited a couple of hours at that airport. I was inside the terminal building when this pilot began to catch the attention of the other few passengers. I was so angry. First of all, he said he had gone to a party the night before and the band sounded like the ones from Sheshatshu. "La Bamba!" he said. I knew right away he was poking fun. Then he was talking about me. "She likes our planes, but she doesn't like the military aircraft that fly at a low level," he said. "Our planes don't hurt the wildlife in the country."

I never answered or said anything, but a young woman at the desk defended me by telling the pilot what she thought. "I wouldn't want those jets flying low over me! I don't blame them for protesting against the jets," she told the pilot right to his face. "I see great big military aircraft landing here in St. John's," she told him, "and I can't even stand them." I appreciated very much that she was aggressive with that pilot. I remained silent, because I felt out-numbered. It was only me who was Innu, with all rest non-Natives. The only regret is I wish I had had a choice to travel on another plane instead of with this grouchy person.

It surprised me that I didn't have a matron or a woman police officer travelling with me. Then I noticed a couple whom I have seen working at the RCMP lock-up in Goose Bay. It was an old married couple, so she must have watched what I was doing. It was a very tiring day for me, but was I ever glad to be back home again!

Nov. 6/89   Sheshatshu

In the morning I was released because my husband posted a bond of $500 for me. The judge said he didn't need to deposit the money right away. Was I happy to be home with my children! I was interviewed after the trial and the reporter asked me if I would go back onto the runway. I said I wouldn't, because my husband had posted a bond for me. But I told her right there that I still felt the same way and I would continue to struggle for the land. My children were ever so proud to have me return home. It was a difficult way to spend 57 days. Thank the Lord so many people have heard of our struggle and why we choose to protest like this.

Dec. 4/89

Today as I begin to settle back in at home, I am going back to write in my journal. It has been a hectic year for me and my family. The time in prison was a time for me to think. After being released, I went straight into the country. I had to because I still felt like I wasn't free yet. In the country, I could roam around anywhere I felt like, not like in prison where I always had guards around me. It is good to be with all my family again, to stay home and to go back to my normal responsibilities as a mother. While my husband works and my two girls attend school, I have to make sure meals are ready for them when they get home. My youngest son is at home with me. I realize how important it is for me to be at home with them. My family is the most important thing in the world for me and that is why I did everything for them.

Life on a Roller Coaster

Cecilia Rich

For many years, Cecilia kept a deep dark secret. She worried that, if people knew, she would never be accepted for who she was. Finally, in 1991, Cecilia fell in love and came out as a lesbian to her family and her community. This caused a great deal of turmoil and conflict for Cecilia and her partner, Germaine, but they say that the razzing has now subsided. Cecilia was the first person to come out in Sheshatshu. The community was shocked and the women's relationship caused a lot of debate. Although there are others, no one else has had the courage to come out since, even though many people now say they accept this lifestyle. Younger people who have travelled have been quicker to accept homosexuality. But some people are still uncomfortable. Elders seem to have the most difficulty grasping this new phenomenon in their lives. Many cannot reconcile it with the teachings of the Catholic Church. They blame the introduction of homosexuality into the Innu community on the non-Native media. As the debate goes on, Cecilia says she has never regretted her decision.

My story begins with my childhood. My parents died when I was very young. I was placed in different foster homes around Sheshatshu. In one foster family, I was treated like a Cinderella.

I was the hard-working person cutting and splitting wood, getting water and doing the household chores. There were a lot of sons and daughters in the family, but I was the one who did a lot of the chores, both men's work and women's work.

Word got around the community that I was the only one working in that family. The priest approached my late sister Ueuistum (Theresa) to ask if she could take care of me, because she was looking after my sister Manishunin (Julianna) and my brother Antane (Andrew). He asked her if she could adopt me as her own kid. So I lived with her after that and she treated me as part of the family. She had five kids of her own. I was around 13 when she adopted me.

During those years, I managed to go to school and finish my education. I had gone to school when my parents were alive, because Father Pierson would force us all to go to school. If you missed a day, your punishment was to write the prayer "Our Father" on the blackboard a hundred times. If you missed any school, the priest would also make you kneel down facing the wall as a punishment. Even if you were just late, you would have to do this. The priest was a really hard man, really strict. But I managed to finish school when I was living with my sister.

I was the only person in that family who finished her education. There was no Grade Ten at Peenamin Mackenzie School, so the principal, Sister Coffey, made arrangements for us to finish high school in St. John's. I went to Beaconsfield High School along with two other Innu girls. Those two managed to do a little bit of going back and forth to school, but they couldn't cope with city life. They couldn't cope with the culture and they didn't make it. They were somewhat lost, I guess.

I went home after high school, and that's when I started drinking. That's when I knew I was interested in the same sex. I was probably 16 years old when I started feeling attracted to the same sex. I never mentioned it to anyone, and I took a lot of alcohol as a coping mechanism to hide it. I had also suffered sexual abuse from my own father when I was small and I had found out that I was an illegitimate child.

I had always thought I was different from my brothers and my sisters. The person I thought was my father was not my biological father. I started making the connections and understood why this person had abused me sexually, physically and emotionally. I don't know who my biological father is yet. I always felt different toward my sisters and brothers. "Hi, how are you?" they would say. But I always felt different when I was around them, like I didn't have a real sister/brother type of feeling. I got the news from Theresa, who is the oldest in my family.

"Listen, your father is crazy, your father is stupid," I simply say to my brothers and sisters, since I've known that their father is not my father.

I started being on my own, although I had always tried to be alone before too. I didn't need any support from my family or anyone. Both my parents were alcoholics, so I grew up in a dysfunctional family. I always wondered how I managed to survive though the years. I did a lot of writing. I had my notebook and I would just write down the things that bothered me about people, about what was wrong with me, what was going on. The writing helped me stay sane.

But I never shared any of my intimate inner soul with anyone, not with family or with anybody else that I met through the years. I always kept it inside. I turned to alcohol and let my anger out when I drank. And I got into a lot of trouble, like I always ended up in jail when I was drinking. That part of me, that anger, I still need to resolve. I need to deal with this anger and with the other side of it, which is the pain.

I started going to different treatment programs, like the one at Emmanuel House in St. John's. I was in a correctional centre for women for nine months when I was 19. That was in 1985. The offences I commit are all alcohol-related. I wouldn't be able to do those things when I'm sober. I started to realize I was always getting into a lot of trouble when I was drinking. I wanted to do something about me.

I always listen to other people who want help from me. They need me to interpret or translate for them, or to do other things like paperwork. They ask me to help them fill out application forms, income tax forms, or they may want to apply for their old-age pensions, for child tax benefits, for family allowances. Sometimes they need me to do a letter for them explaining why they need housing or funding. It's like a service I provide, I guess. That's what I've been doing all my life, but yet I get into a lot of shit when I'm drinking.

I still have a problem with alcohol, and I ask myself whether the reason could boil down to the kind of relationship I am having. Is the community putting a lot of pressure on me because of my sexuality? Since I came out in 1991, I've been getting a lot of intimidation, a lot of threats.

"If you go after my woman, I'll kill you," this guy said to me once. But it didn't really bother me.

"Listen, I'm not interested in anyone, only the person that I'm with," I just said to myself.

People automatically assume that, whenever I'm out drinking, I'm going to be after this or that woman. But I have no interest or desire to be with anyone but the person I'm with now. A lot of people think they made a mistake about who Cecilia Rich really is. Who is she behind the mask?

"All those years we saw her as a nice person," they think. "Suddenly she turned into a person we didn't know before."

At the same time, a lot of people knew all along who I really was. I was a tomboy when I was young and also when I was teenager. People would make a lot of assumptions about who I was.

"Hey, you act like a man," they would say to me. "You look like a man, you walk like a man, you even talk like a man."

People would say things that weren't true. I would talk to them and they would call me a boy. "Yes, boy," they would say. Even the term "boy" would kill me and get on my nerves. I was angry at first, because I was really afraid that they were going to notice me inside, like I was somehow transparent and they would know the real inside of me. I was really scared of people finding out who I was. I was scared they would know from my actions and behaviour. I was worried that people would see I was interested in women.

But now, I don't care what people think or say. The more they tease me, the more strength they give me. It's amazing. That started happening in 1991 when I was first involved with Shanime (Germaine). The whole community came to see us. They wanted to know if Cecilia Rich was really with Germaine Penashue? Even the nun came over to see us. She carried on a conversation as if she knew us. She never actually asked us about it. I guess she just wanted to find out if the story was actually true.

Then one of Germaine's brothers went over to visit the priest. Father McGee told him he had a brother who was gay and had committed suicide. This brother was the one who took it the hardest among Germaine's family. He doesn't like that I'm involved with his sister. He went to see the priest to help him understand for himself about homosexuality. He was just curious, I guess.

"These two persons are involved with one another," Father McGee told him point blank.

I got a lot of sexual harassment over this. People actually assume that I have this manhood, that I was actually born with a man's body, that I have the organ that the man has. I have been teased a lot about this.

A lot of people — married men and women, their wives, girlfriends or their common-law spouses — assume that I'm interested in any woman and that I'm going to make a pass at them. Men might make passes at other men's wives, but they see me as more of a threat because I was born a woman. I have a woman's body. They assume that, because I came out, I'm going to go out with any woman or man in the community. I'm a threat to both sexes.

A lot of men will make a pass at Germaine. They try to get me jealous. They do the same thing with me and try to get her jealous. They are testing us. They say sexual things and we answer back. These are the things I experience in my own community with my own people.

♠ ♠ ♠

I always liked Germaine from the time she was really young. She used to chum around with my sister Julianna and she would always drop by the house. That's when I started liking her. I had these fantasies in my head where I would be talking to Germaine.

"When I finish my education, I'm going to go after you," I would tell her in my mind. "I'm going to make you like me. I'll do anything to get you." But I never said anything to her. I just had my eye on her. I never shared these secrets with anyone. I bottled them up.

At one point when I had come back from a stay in St. John's, I ran into Germaine in a club. I chummed around with her for a year just as a friend. I took her to movies, I took her to restaurants, I took her everywhere. I really courted her. This was the beginning of our friendship. During that year, never did I make a pass at her and I didn't say anything either. I would do these things just to keep her company, to get to know her. But finally I had to do something. I went over to her house. She had no food. She had nothing.

"I can't take this anymore. I have to tell her how I feel," I said to myself on the way.

"I hate people in the community when they assume we're lovers," I told her. "I wish I could get away for a week. I'm sick and tired of people spreading rumours, false accusations."

Then Enen (Helen Hart), who was with the women's group, came knocking on the door to tell me she wanted me to go to a conference in P.E.I. This was just what I was hoping for. I wanted to get away from the community. Helen gave me $500 expense money along with a plane ticket. That's when I told Germaine that I loved her, over the phone from P.E.I. I told myself I wouldn't be able to tell her in person. I had given her $100 before I left to buy herself some food, cigarettes and all that. I phoned her from Summerside.

"How are you? How have you been?" I asked her over the phone.

"I've got a hangover," she said.

She had spent the $100 I gave her on a big party. I told her that I loved her and she accidentally dropped the phone.

"What? Are you crazy? Are you drunk?" she said when she picked it up again.

"No," I told her.

When I came back a week later, she was really scared. I knew she was doing this training in a guiding program, so I went looking for her. I dropped my bags at my sister's place and looked around the community to check out where Germaine was. I heard she was up Grand Lake Road, about 65 kilometres outside Goose Bay, so I couldn't sleep and couldn't sleep.

"Where is she, what is she doing? I'd like to see her. Is she involved with someone else?" All these questions about Germaine were going around my mind.

I managed to get a ride up the Grand Lake Road. When I got to the camp, I saw my sister Theresa and went over to ask her where I would find Germaine's tent. She pointed it out. My sister never knew what was going on. I had never shared with anyone that I liked Germaine, that I was falling in love with this person. I walked over to Germaine's tent and went inside.

"Hi, how are you?" I asked. There were three other women with Germaine and they wanted to know when I had gotten back from P.E.I. Germaine was standing there. She wouldn't look at me. She was kind of nervous. She was assuming I was drunk and afraid I was going to tell her that I loved her right there, that I would embarrass her.

"Germaine, how are you?" I said. "What are you doing?"

She never said a word. She was really shy. She didn't know what to say. The only thing that I was feeling in my heart was that I was happy to see her. When that was over, I told the other girls and Germaine I would see them later. Germaine told me later what a relief it was to see me go.

She stayed at the camp for another week. While I was back at the community, I just slept, watched television and waited for her to come back. Then I heard she got drunk. She and the other students had gone on a tear with their pay cheques. When she sobered up, we got together and we talked seriously from nine in the evening until five in the morning.

"I can't take it anymore," I said to her. "I need you to tell me what you feel. I'm not going to force you or anything. I just want to let you know how I feel toward you."

Germaine never said anything. She just listened, kind of nervous, because this was the first time I had shared my true feelings with her. I wanted to kiss her, but I told her to think about it for three months and to let me know what she wanted after that.

"I'm not going to drop by, I'm not going to phone you, I'm not going to do anything. I'm just going to wait for your answer," I told her. "You've got a lot of other friends that you can chum around with. I've got other things that I want to do too."

"No," she said again. "I don't want to be with anybody else."

Around three or four in the morning, I think she knew. She knew that I really cared for her. That's when the relationship began to develop. I tried to kiss her.

"Please, spare me," she said, and she turned her face away. I had to laugh. We trusted each other enough to do that. Ever since then, we've been together. It's been six years.

☨ ☨ ☨

"Hi, Cecilia, you lesbian!" kids call out to me on the road. What do they know, for God's sake? They think it's a bad word. But now, I don't care. I'm happy that I came out and that I'm with Germaine.

I've had a lot of lovers in my life. Whenever I went to conferences, I always went out to gay clubs and I would pick up somebody of the same sex. I would come back to the community, pretending that I was interested in people of the opposite sex. This was hard, but I did have relationships with men. I wanted the community and my family to think that I wasn't what they thought.

I think we have made a difference in our community for other gays and lesbians. We are the first ones in a Labrador Innu community to come out. I don't know about Quebec Innu. About 15 people have approached me just from Sheshatshu. Some are men, some are women. A lot of them are married and others are single. They all ask me how come I'm not afraid. They ask me what I did to come out. A lot of them tell me that we are accepted by the community now because we've been out for quite a while. The men are more afraid of how the community would take it if they came out because they're men. I think they're scared of being intimidated or sexually harassed, or of getting threats.

I think my approach of going public has been positive. A lot of people still come up to me looking for my help, whether I'm an Innu lesbian or not. They want to know what made me be like this. They're curious. Some people blame it on the White society, because I've been away travelling a lot outside the community.

"This is me. What you see is what you get," I simply say to people.

Where did I find the courage? I guess the more people want to know about us living together, the more they want to find out who I am, the more strength they give me. Before I actually came out, I would get the courage to tell everyone that I loved Germaine at my drinking parties. I was more bold when I was drinking, and then rumours got around. Then when I came out in 1991, people were more or less shocked. What has become of Cecilia who used to help out with these forms, or who used to do these things to help out? Can a lesbian still do this? These same people still come to me for help. It's amazing that they still have this trust in me. More and more people are accepting me, so I feel like I did the right thing.

Our families took it really hard. The one who took it the hardest was my oldest sister, Theresa. She never said anything directly to me, but I heard from other people that she was thinking, "This is my own little sister that I raised. What has become of her?" I used to tease her a lot about it. Every time she talked to Germaine, I would say, "Don't make a pass at Germaine, please." And she would crack up. I would do the same with my brother Paul and he would call Germaine his sister-in-law. So my family look at me more as a man, because they call Germaine their sister-in-law.

Germaine's parents ask me if they should call me their daughter-in-law or son-in-law. At first Germaine's mother used to say, "There comes that crazy woman. You're crazy in the head." She really thought I was nuts. Now she is really very open. I have tremendous respect for her. When Germaine's father found out, he said, "Never mind the two of them. They won't have kids anyway." He has 32 grandkids. But I think it was hard on her parents. They had to try and make sense of this. We had to show them and they taught us how.

My daughter, Seraphine, is 18 years old. She had a son in February two years ago. Not only am I a lesbian now, but I'm an Innu lesbian grandmother. I love my kids very much, but they had a hard time with my coming out. Seraphine has never spoken to Germaine. I tried to get her to talk to her, but she won't. The funny part is with Germaine's son, Greg, who is 16. He will talk to me about anything. He'll ask me to buy him a tape. If he wants money, I'll give him money. Her son is more accepting toward me than my daughter is of Germaine.

My son, Raphanel George, who is eight, is also affected by this because a lot of kids tease him that his mother is a lesbian. I guess it hurts him. But every time I see him, I try to explain to him, and tell him not to listen to all that and just ignore it. He's probably hurt the most by all this.

"When you grow up, I'll tell you everything," I say to my son.

I tried to explain to my daughter why I came out, why I want to be this way, but she never really gave me a direct answer. I think she still holds that anger part inside her. Our children get the harassment as well and it's really unfair, although now our kids are not bothered by others so much anymore. It wore off after a while. People get tired of the same old story over and over again.

For other gays and lesbians in the community, I think it's really up to them to decide when they are able and ready to come out. Nobody can force them to do this unless they're ready. But I would encourage the single closet cases to come out. The married people — those who don't want others to find out who they really are, that they are attracted to the same sex — they are the ones who have to face the really difficult turmoils. A lot of them have kids. If they come out, what will happen to their kids? Their families will be torn apart.

I've talked about this on an open night-line radio show in the community. My brother-in-law Sylvester, Germaine's brother, would tease me on the radio. We were co-hosting these shows together.

"Okay, brother-in-law," he would say on the radio. People would laugh. People phoned in and asked about it, so I talked about it openly. It was just to let people laugh about it, instead of being all tensed up. At the end of our programs, we wanted to make the tone lighter, to make people laugh, so we tried to make it like a comedy. When we did these shows, there was a lot of anger and people had concerns about the Innu Nation, the band council, the different Innu organizations, the church. So at the end of the show before we closed, we wanted to lighten things up. That's when we joked about this and people enjoyed what we did. Sometimes the leaders would get really angry with us and threaten to cut the power off so we couldn't be on the air. But mostly people enjoyed what we did. I'm very comfortable talking with people. I'm not afraid to say whatever is on my mind. I'm not afraid of what people think of me.

I think Germaine and I have shown that we are strong. We can overcome anything that comes our way. We are pretty decent people even if people think we're crazy. Alcohol still plays a part in all of this, because of where I grew up in a dysfunctional family. I've seen alcohol since I was quite small. I guess it's still a part of me. I still drink, but not as much as I used to. I enjoy being a lesbian. I enjoy helping people. I enjoy being frank and open-minded to new people, to let them find out who I am and what I am. I'm not scared any more.

My hope for the future with Germaine is for us to get our old-age pension plan together, to have a healthy relationship, for people to really understand where we're coming from. I don't want them to look at lesbians in a bad or unhealthy way. I want them to look at us like we're human beings. I am not some freak person. There's nothing wrong with us. But, being a lesbian in an Innu community is like living on a roller coaster.

Sorrow

Christine Poker

All night she cries, tears run down her cheeks.
Her friends, her friends are not there to comfort her ...
She thinks they betrayed her, are against her ...
He was gone, the one she always depended on.
The one who loved her!

Thinking that maybe God made her suffer for her sins.
She has nothing to do with God now ... there is no God!
Her mind is completely blank. Maybe she is just dreaming.
But why is her mother crying?
And why is it that her eyes are wet and hurting?
And is that her mother screaming, "Killers!"?

Oh God, why can't she wake up now?
Her mother is still crying.
She wants to hold her, kiss her,
to tell her, "Everything is all right."
Yes, she could feel her anger.
"I am alone," she thinks.
He is gone forever, but where?

Is there a God? How can he do this to me?
She cries to the Lord for mercy.
"Is he laughing?" she thinks.

She groans and hides her face in shame,
no one is there to comfort her.
Please understand her pain, kiss her,
make her pain go away.
Her eyes are painful, overflowing with tears.

She stretches out her hands,
no one is there.
Oh, why don't you hold her,
tell her that you are there for her?
Hold her in your arms,
put her to sleep, look at her?
Her heart is broken in sorrow.
Her eyes are worn out from weeping.

She cries for her mother, sisters, brothers ...
But how can she comfort them
when there is no one there to comfort her?
She cries for help, even God refuses to listen!
She blames God, her hope in him is gone.
Nothing left for her to be proud of.
He is gone forever, she thinks.

Looking back now,
it happened many years ago.
But still she remembers her dad's loving face.
Always remembering, she can't hold back her tears.
She thinks now, the Lord is all I have ...
And so in Him I put all my hope!
The Lord is very merciful!
He brings us Sorrow
but his Love is strong!
He takes no pleasure in causing us grief and sorrow!
She cries, her eyes hurting, her head pounding.
Looks at her children and smiles.

I Am My Father's Daughter

Nympha Byrne

In the vast open spaces of the barrens, life when Nympha was a small child was safe and secure. But when her family moved into a house in the new village of Utshimassits (Davis Inlet), her life became filled with peril. In nutshimit (the country), the Innu were connected to each other, to the land, to the water and to the animals. This connectedness contrasts sharply with the turmoil of community life. Alcohol became a way of life. Suicides began to happen and continue today in both Sheshatshu and Utshimassits at a rate unparalleled in the world. The suicides are connected to the booze: to feelings of shame, fear, abandonment and feeling trapped. Everyone in the village knows each other so well, yet they don't know what devastation each carries within the heart. It happens over and over, so that suicide has become eerily normal. When someone dies, people will grieve for him and try to be there for the family, but then they carry on with their lives. Nympha believes the Innu have lost touch with their spirits, with the animal spirits and with the Creator. They remain in a black hole. They need to use their grief to show them the way out. She herself has found healing by returning to the land to reconnect with herself and with the spirits. She looks to the elders as her teachers to show her the way.

When we were living in the country, I was only small. I remember we were always doing things together with our parents, Shishin and Tami (Cecile and Tommy Rich), and my grandmother Matinueskueu (Monique Rich). My grandmother was like our mom. She would make things for us, like moccasins. She adopted and took care of my younger sister, Shutit (Judith). I remember my grandmother and mother made me a parka out of caribou one time. The hair was on the inside. At first I was afraid to put it on, because I was worried I would suffocate when I tried to get it off again. But after a while, it was my favourite special coat. I was the first one in the family who had one and I didn't see many other children wearing a parka like mine.

When my father came back from hunting, we all used to sit around in the tent to rummage through his game bag to see what animals we might find. My parents used to clean the animals together. As we children got older, we would help pluck the feathers off the birds, like geese and partridge. Sometimes my father would not catch too many animals, maybe only a few partridges. My mother would cook gravy. We would get just one small piece of meat, like one leg of partridge for each child. When he got rabbit, my mother would make lots of gravy. There were always leftovers.

When we travelled in the barrens, I remember it would be really cold. The wind would blow. I remember I could feel the frost on my cheeks, and my breath would freeze on my scarf. Sometimes my parents would go on ahead, and we would walk behind, pulling my grandmother on our komatik when she was really tired. We travelled by dog team with eight or nine dogs. After we had set up camp and we were all settled in, my father would make a really big pot of food for those dogs. I would watch him make the fire and fill the pot with water. He would mix in some grains, seal fat, the guts of the caribou and stir it all up. I remember watching those hungry dogs. They would scramble around the pot, and I was told to keep an eye on them to see that each one got to eat. There was always one dog who was the leader. My father wanted to make sure that he had enough food to eat. Sometimes during our travels to the country, the dogs would have puppies. When it was really cold, we would carry one of those puppies close to us to help keep us warm. We would walk a long ways, stop for tea and keep on going.

In the night-time, my father used to tell us legends until we fell asleep. My sisters Kistiniss (Christine) and Akat (Agathe) and I would cuddle into each other. My brother, Antane (Andre), would be curled into my dad. We would fill the stove with wood and leave the candle burning. I remember one time my brother said to my father, "You are too tired now. Don't tell any more stories." He would get on our nerves, because he knew we wanted to hear more stories. He was the spoilt one. But I was the girl my father liked to spoil.

When the weather was really bad, there was one story that helped to turn the weather around the next day. It was about a boy called Aiasheu who was left on an island. At the end of the story, he turned his mother into a *pipitsheu* (robin) and his little sister into a *shashakuatipeshish* (sparrow). He himself became a *metshu* (eagle). This boy told his mother and sister that they would always be around the people, but they would not see the eagle very often because he would be off in the mountains. When the robin sings, it announces the rain, while the sparrow's song brings the good weather.

When my father told legends, the stories were so real, I felt like I was in the legend. I would imagine myself in the story. I could picture the trees, rivers and lakes. I could see how beautiful they all were. Kuekuatsheu, the wolverine or the trickster, was another story. This one had no ending. This story has many parts and keeps on going all the time. For example, the geese have long necks because Kuekuatsheu tricked them and stretched their necks. He also killed and ate them.

When the weather was bad, we used to play string games, or my grandmother would tell us stories about her life. Sometimes when my mother and grandmother made moccasins or mitts, they would give us the scraps to make things too. We used to play with a file for sharpening. We would throw it into the boughs. If it landed standing, the thrower would get another turn. Sometimes we would go off hiking and hunting by ourselves or with my mother or with another adult in the camp.

When my father got back from his hunting trips, I would help him take off his moccasins and hang them to dry by the stove. My grandmother and mother would take turns cooking. They would always have a hot meal ready for him when he returned. My sisters and I watched and learned how to cook this way. We all got along so well. It was a happy time in the country.

♟ ♟ ♟

When we came to live in Utshimassits, my parents started drinking. It was really bad. It hurt everybody in the family. My sisters and I started drinking too. There was a lot of violence. When we were in the country, we used to listen to our parents all the time when they wanted us to do something. But in the community, we didn't want to listen to them.

My parents started drinking because there was nothing to do. There were no jobs. But when I was really young, we would be out in the country and come back to the community. My father had a job with the priest working on the houses. Those days were good even if we were in the community. A lot of people were always helping one another. Men would be out hunting together. They would be playing checkers or cards all night. Women used to do things together too to help one another. Instead of turning to homebrew, people were always visiting and sharing meals together. The women would make a big pot of food and people would help themselves. There would be a big pot of tea. This would happen on the weekends, rather than when we were in school.

As I got older, I didn't see this happening much. There was more drinking. Now, women are fighting one another. Women used to tell their girls not to do stuff, but now they just let things go. A lot of women are drinking with their husbands too. When I was young, my dad would drink but my mother was always with us. When she started drinking, it got really bad. We were left to look after ourselves. In the mornings when it was time for school, we would sleep in. There would be no meals on for us. My parents would be drinking very early.

My parents' drinking really hurt me. I always felt like my parents didn't want me. I felt like they didn't love us when they turned to booze. It still hurts.

When they were in the country when we were getting older, they used to drink in the country too. When we knew we were getting ready to go, we would run away. We didn't want to go because of the booze. We would walk back to the community. We would have to do all the work they would tell us. I didn't want to be around them when they were drinking. They would stay up all night.

We always had to try to make them happy and we thought they would stop drinking if we listened. But even when we listened to them, they wouldn't stop drinking. We would have to cook the meals. They would get us up in the middle of the night telling us to cook meals. When my parents were out drinking, my older sister looked after us. She was like a mother. She would cook meals and do the laundry. My dad used to hit us when he got really mad. My other sister was the hard case and she would fight with my parents.

They would want us to get water to make their homebrew. We used to help them. They would show us how and we used to make it for them. It's like enabling, that's what my sisters and I were doing. To make them happy, we had to do it. When my parents were drinking, we didn't want to stay home. We would go to my aunt Nushin's (Lucy Rich's) house and spend time there. Then we started to act up. We were drinking and we missed a lot of school. It seemed the homebrew bucket was more important to my parents than the children.

One time I tried sniffing gas. There was nothing for us to do in the community. When my father heard about the gas sniffing, he was really upset. I was really afraid of him. He told me not to do that again, that it wasn't good for me. He told me he would go and get five gallons of gas, bring it inside and watch me sniff. That was the end of it. I never sniffed gas again.

♣   ♣   ♣

I remember when I first went out with my husband, Lou, before we got married. A nun sent for my father in the country to let him know that I had done something wrong going out with a non-Native guy. She sent the chief to the country to find my father's camp and to bring him back to the community. The chief went on his ski-doo to pick up my father. I felt that the nun wanted to see how my father would react about me going out with Lou. My father didn't say anything when he saw me, but he went around the community and started drinking.

"What did you do wrong that I have to be picked up in the country?" he asked me later. He already knew that I was seeing a non-Native guy.

"I am seeing Lou," I told him.

"Is that all you did?" he asked.

"Yes."

My father was upset with me, but I knew he was more upset with the nun. I was mad at the nun too. I didn't like the way she was treating people in the community, like everything was her business. The nuns and the priest were telling people what to do all the time. They judged our parents and tried to make us be like them. They thought that they owned our lives.

When I was pregnant, another nun, who was the public health nurse, asked me if I wanted to think about adoption for my baby. I said no. I asked one of the girls what the word "adoption" meant. In those days, when I didn't know English, I would just say no. I didn't want to give my child away to the White world or to another Innu family. There was a lot of drinking in the community, even with my parents. I did not want my child in the arms of someone who was not capable of looking after a baby. Nobody could have talked me into doing this. I guess the nun thought that I would not know how to take care of my baby. I already had experience in caring for a baby. I had learned when I was young how to clean a baby or make a bottle. I used to watch my mother when she nursed my brothers and sisters. I wanted to be just like my mother and breast-feed my baby. I also used to take care of my sister's baby.

I remember how nosy that nun was. She wanted to know if this was an Indian baby or a White baby. I gave her my boyfriend's name, as if she don't know who the father was. That shut her up. I told her that I would nurse my baby when it was born. She tried to talk me into doing the things she thought would be best for me, but I didn't listen to her advice. My parents were my advisers, not the nuns or the priests. One of the nuns told me that my boyfriend wouldn't stay with me, and that he would leave me when I had the baby. But I knew I would take care of my baby even if he abandoned us. I didn't think he would do that to me and the baby.

I gave birth to my baby in the Goose Bay hospital. My mother had me in a tent with the help of Innu midwives. I wish I had had Innu midwives too, elderly women like my mother had to help her. I was alone in the hospital room. I remember I was always ringing the bell to call for the nurses and doctor. I was afraid of the labour. I was 18 years old. I was afraid that something would go wrong and there were no other Innu around to help me. The window was open and I could hear a sparrow singing outside my window. I should have named my child Shashakua-tipeshish, after this sparrow. It was like this sparrow was looking after me. I was in labour for six hours. I thought she was the most beautiful baby when I saw her. I held her and put her to my breast. I can't describe how beautiful that feeling was. I couldn't stop holding her.

It's been 17 years since my husband and I were married. We are now raising four beautiful children and they mean a lot to both of us. Our oldest child is 18 years old. We have our ups and downs. Nobody is perfect. We are like other married couples. I know we love each other and we did what was best for our children.

When we decided to get married, I was pregnant with my second child. I remember when the priest asked me if I was going to have any more children. I said that I wanted four children, two boys and two girls. He told me that wouldn't happen, but I now have two girls and two boys.

I also remember when the priest said that people who did not want to have children would not be allowed in church. I didn't worry about that, because I was about to have two. I used to be shy and didn't say much at all. When we told my father that we were getting married, he agreed. He said we should get married, because we had to raise our children together. I agree that children need both parents. The missionaries were the ones who made us Catholics. Two of my aunts don't have children, and they still go to church and consider themselves Catholics.

We were married on June 11, 1982. The ice was just breaking in the harbour. We were living in a tent back then. Our oldest child was staying overnight with her grandparents. We had our wedding cake made by the teachers and the store manager's wife. We had a lot of people helping us get ready, even the nuns, those penguins.

♟ ♟ ♟

I sometimes disagree with what the priests used to say. I remember my sister and I used to go to church every day. We were good Christians, saints even. I was afraid if I didn't go to church that the devil would come after me. When we prayed and made the sign of the cross, the priest would tell us we had to use our right hands. He said the left hand was the devil's. I used to watch my friend, who was left-handed, to see how she would manage with her right hand. I was afraid that the priest would hit her or yell at her.

The priest was also involved with the government. After the houses were built in the community, the government would send his agent to check the houses to make sure they were clean. When the women knew this guy was coming, I remember my

mother would start cleaning the whole house. She had to haul
water and heat it up on the stove. She never had cleaning
supplies and the women would often share what they had with
each other. When we first moved into the house, it was empty.
There was no furniture and we could hear an echo when we
walked around. I remember we slept on the floor.

I remember how the priest would have the women go off berry
picking for him. My mother would go off in the boat to Shankus
(Sango Bay) and leave us behind. They would leave in the
morning and be gone all day. When the men went hunting, they
were also expected to share their food with him.

When the school was built, everyone in the community was
put to work. It was like a labour camp and the priest had everyone
working — mothers and fathers and children. My mother made
me a bag to carry sand over my shoulder to the spot where the
school building was erected. I was only small then, maybe seven
or eight years old.

When we were in school, the priest and the nuns taught us.
I remember one time, my friend had just come in from the
country, and she was behind in her schoolwork. All the students'
marks used to be posted on the blackboard. I was doing well with
my English. My friend was having so much trouble with hers that
I had to teach her. When the nun saw me helping my friend, she
walked over to the blackboard and erased all my marks and put
in a zero instead. It was like I didn't know anything. These things
that happened could easily make you feel low self-esteem.

Another time, the priest wrote something on the board and
asked me to read it. I didn't know how. He stormed across the
room and tipped my desk over.

"If you don't want to learn, we might as well leave your desk
this way,' he yelled at me. His face was so red and scary. All the
students were looking at me. I didn't want to be in school. I was
afraid to learn. I felt so humiliated. I could feel his anger, like he
would hit me. He would hit the students with a ruler back then.
I wanted my father to take us back into the country.

"Be good to your neighbour and help them if they need it.

Don't be mean to each other," I remember the priest used to say. The priests used to show movies in the church. One time I heard a lot of commotion outside when I was watching the movie. A lot of people were standing around when I ran out. The priest was beating up on my father. One of my uncles went and stopped the priest. I felt so mixed up about what the priest was saying. I was standing by the fence and I was really afraid. That was the first time I saw a priest beating someone, although later I remember there were other beatings by another priest.

The next morning, my father went to speak to the priest. The priest told him to forget about it and gave him a crucifix. The church left me so mixed up. I think the church made my father feel very ashamed. I talked to him about it one time. He told me he was drinking so much because the church had taken everything away from him, his culture, his life. His life was so messed up. But in the end, my dad died a Catholic.

Before my father passed away, he told us that when he died he did not want us to dress him formally in a suit. When he died, I remember the doctors wanted to do an autopsy. I had a big problem with this. The doctor told me, "We have to know why your father died." I did not agree with him. The nurse and the doctor finally convinced me after a long discussion. I didn't know what to say. I didn't know what to do because I found it really difficult when the doctor kept saying the same thing over and over again.

In the end, they took away my father's body. After they brought it back, my father was very, very different. It didn't look like him any more. I said to myself, "Why did the doctor do this?" I couldn't believe it was my father's body. But I gave him what he wanted. I gave him moccasins and his own jacket. He didn't want a beautiful casket. My husband built a casket for him. In our culture, we don't take things out of people's bodies when they die. Years ago, the elders would just bury the bodies with respect.

I miss my father now, although I feel like he is always around me. He comes to me in my dreams. He tells me he loves me and I can talk to him in my dreams. I still hang on to the things he taught me before he died.

♣ ♣ ♣

As the priest rang the church bell in the early afternoon, I saw many people walking down the road, headed toward the church. Once inside, I looked into each face as they walked up the aisle to see the young man's body in the coffin. I hurt terribly. It was very hard to hold back my tears. I felt a big lump in my throat. That usually tells me it is time to let go. The young man was everybody's family. Our community of 500 is one family. We loved the young man deep in our hearts. He will never be forgotten. I wish this had never happened.

The church group started to sing the same songs I had heard a month or so ago. It had happened again so soon. We had to face yet another burden in our community. It was like one after the other. The rate was too high for a small community. It was a scary situation.

I felt a terrible pain inside when I saw the grandmother stand with her cane to see her grandson's face once more. I saw the deepest pain in her eyes as she looked at the body and kissed it goodbye. After she sat back in her seat, the grandfather stood up to say his goodbyes. Both grandparents were in poor health and they had to face this. He was raised by his grandparents, my aunt and uncle, who loved him very much.

I looked around and there were no dry eyes in the room. I felt a painful energy all around. Each one of us went to the body to say goodbye. I walked up and looked at his face. It was hard to believe he was gone. I felt a cold shiver go through my body. I leaned over to touch my lips to his face. His skin was cold. I walked back to my seat. I started to think about the kind of person he was when he was still alive. He was a happy child growing up. My brother and he were the same age.

I strongly believe that we can save someone's life if we take our time to listen. Sometimes all they need is someone to talk to. They need guidance from someone they trust. We have to be available to them. Maybe the young man thought that death was the only way out. I often hear elders talk about the suicides. They are new to them. They never used to experience these tragedies in the past. Now another death had shaken our community again.

♣   ♣   ♣

One night when we were camping, I went outside to look at the stars. The wind blew my hair softly off my shoulders and whistled in my ear. The wood crackled inside the stove. The smell of split wood outside the tent was so purifying. The air was so clean. I felt as if I were not alone at all standing there. Every part of nature was watching me. Our ancestors before us were present standing next to me. I looked around and the tree branches were covered with snow. The mountains looked as if they were covered with white satin sheets from the moon's light shining on them. Inside the tent, I cuddled into the blankets. I blew out the candle. The moon was so bright and I could see the shadows on the canvas walls of the tent. I could see the shape of every twig from the tree branches. I feel so rich whenever I'm in the country, because the land is my survival. Nature takes care of me.

Set My People Free

Mary Adele Andrew

*Mani-Aten (Mary Adele Andrew) died at age 63 in
1996. She was born and raised in nutshmit, married
at 17 and raised 15 children. She always encouraged
her children and grandchildren to fight for their land.*

My name is Mary Adele Andrew, Mani-Aten in our language,
Innu-aimun. I am 57 years old. I was born and raised in the
country. My parent's names were Stakeaskushimun (Shimun or
Simon Gregoire) and Marie Gregoire. They were both in their
70s when they passed away. I deeply respect the way they brought
me up, a lifestyle of surviving in the country 11 months of the
year and spending the other month at either Uashat (Sept Isles)
or Sheshatshu.

When I was 17, I married Matshieu (Matthew Ben Andrew).
We had 15 children and they are all here today, sitting and
listening for the outcome they face. Six of my children have been
in jail for two weeks. They are here facing you, the judge, to
answer to charges of causing mischief, simply for trying to set up
camp at or near the runway of Takutauat (Goose Bay). Takutauat is the proper name for Happy Valley-Goose Bay. The name
means "plateau" and it describes the area. This Innu name has
been used for thousands of years.

There are thousands of Innu names for the lakes, rivers,
mountains, peninsulas and other geographical features of our

land. These names have been here and are still used by us, the Innu, after thousands of years. Today, the maps drawn by the Europeans carry the names of these geographical features in English, for example: Churchill Falls for Mista-paustuk, Churchill River for Mista-shipu and Mealy Mountains for Akami-uapishk^u. These are only a few, and the names I give you in Innu are the proper ones.

In my lifetime I have travelled many thousands of miles on our land on foot and by canoe, first with my parents and later with my husband. When I was six, I started to walk behind my parents on the long, hard portages along the way to our hunting area, either to Minaik (Menihek Lake) or Mishikamau (Mitshi-kamau Lake).

I could give you just roughly an idea of how extensively I travelled this land with my parents and sisters and brothers. We travelled from Uashat to Kantshekakamat, a lake in between Schefferville, Schefferville and Uaskaikan (Fort Chimo, or Kuu-jjuaq). From there, we went to Utshimassits (Davis Inlet), where we spent the summer. And from Utshimassits, we travelled back to Mishikamau, where we spent the whole winter with minimum supplies. Our parents provided everything else we needed with what they killed and harvested.

The government's intrusions and exploitation of our lands started over 40 years ago. First the government had to settle us. The officials promised us warm houses with running water. Mind you, I have only had running water in my house for the last two years. The government schooled my children, trained them to learn another culture and society. While they took our children to put them in school, the government's people promised us family allowances, welfare assistance and old-age pensions for elders.

We, the parents, were told our children would live well once they became doctors, lawyers, police officer, teachers and nurses. We believed them, but none of my children became any of these. The reason is that my children say they much prefer the life I had with my parents. Ten years ago, I began taking them back into the country and passing down the skills I have to them. Now they also take their families with them. I have been a widow for 10 years now, so my boys missed their chance to learn the skills from their father. But today many other Innu hunters teach them while they are out on the land.

My children are determined to keep their culture and their land from further destruction. I feel proud of them today, because they are fighting along with me for what they truly believe is ours, the land, Nitassinan.

While we were being settled by the government, that's when its people began their onslaught of our lands. They mined Wabush and Schefferville; the runway at Goose Bay was built; and the Great Rapids and Mishta-paustuk (Churchill Falls) were dammed by the Europeans. While they made their riches off our land, the Innu suffered poverty, alcohol abuse, wife beating and wildlife laws. The government's people were trying, I guess, to make us live in shame. Every time caribou were brought in by the hunters, the RCMP raided our houses. Finally our way of life was made a criminal offence. It is now a crime to hunt caribou. Our main survival in the country for thousands of years has become a crime.

You need not ask me if I feel betrayed, because I do.

I tell you today to set my people and my children free. Over 40 years of forced settlement has been prison enough for me and my family. If you do not set my people and children free, then you will have to incarcerate me and my other children as well when we face you on the 20th of June, because I, too, have protested and been arrested each time.

I have told you about the destruction of our land. This is more criminal than what we are doing, fighting back peacefully. The ultimate crime is that of the government when they flooded our lands, hunting areas, our belongings, canoes, clothing, traps and other essential materials we needed to live in the country. Worst of all the governments, foreigners on our land, flooded over the graves of our ancestors. That is what I call a crime.

So I believe today the court should be the other way around. Your government, the military, the RCMP as enforcers of these foreign laws, should be facing an Innu judge.

I Consider Myself
a Full Native

Natasha Hurley

*Natasha was born of an Innu mother and Newfound-
land father, Melvin Hurley. He came to Labrador in
the late 1970s to work with the Linerboard, a local
forestry project. He moved into Sheshatshu when he
met Natasha's mother, Mani-Mat (Mary Martha),
and is one of the few non-Innu who have learned to
speak Innu-aimun. Natasha is Miste Mani-Aten's
(Mary Adele Andrew's) granddaughter. She is one of
a generation of Innu that has lived in both worlds: the
Innu world of nutshimit (the country) and the White
world of the community; however, these two worlds are
not equally embraced as Natasha talks about her self-
identity. This piece was written in April 1995.*

I attend Peenamin Mackenzie School in Sheshatshu. I'm 12
years old and in level four. I have very nice classmates. Most of
them are my friends and some are really close ones. My mom's
name is Mary Martha Hurley. She works at my school as a
teacher's aide and she teaches from kindergarten to Grade
Three.

I don't find our school interesting at all. It feels like the
school wants Native kids to lose their culture. It also feels like

the White teachers are taking control over us Natives. This problem is not only with teachers but also with racist people.

I go to the country almost every year with my family and some other people that live in our community. I enjoy going in the country and cleaning animals. I like to walk around to look for animals which I like to eat. My grandmother is a very nice person to talk to in the country. She's sometimes comical and sometimes she tells her grandchildren, like me, stories about her childhood. I always help my grandmother in the country. I clean up her cabin and wash her clothes when my aunts are gone for a walk or picking boughs for the floor of the tent. I also like to go on ski-doo rides with my uncles and my dad when they're hunting for animals in the country.

I'm half Native and half White, but I consider myself a full Native. My dad is a Newfie and my mom is Innu. My great-grandparents are dead. Their names were Shimun and Marie Gregoire. My grandmother's name is Mani-Aten. My dad's name is Melvin Bud Joseph Hurley and he lives here with us. I think the reason I consider myself a full Native is because all my friends are Native and you know what teens are like. They want to be exactly the same as their friends. But I'm proud of who I am.

Stories My Grandmother Told Me

Pamela Hurley

Pamela is Natasha's sister, the daughter of Mani-Mat (Mary Martha) and Melvin Hurley. She wrote the following piece in April 1995. It is the story of a teenage girl who learns through conversations with her grandmother Miste Mani-Aten (Mary Adele Andrew) about some important lessons of life — lessons which range from the disappointment of unrequited love and to the need to fight against NATO's destruction of her homeland. With the passing of her grandmother in 1996, Pamela says it feels like part of herself died as well. She looked to her grandmother as a great role model in her life and she misses her every day. She likes to think that her grandmother would have been very proud of her for continuing with her education. She says she owes her grandmother a lot just for having been there for her when she needed her.

I am a 16-year-old Innu teenager who lives in Sheshatshu, Labrador. I attend Grade Eleven at Peenamin Mackenzie School.

My family is really important to me because they are the ones who teach me things throughout my life. For example, my grandmother Mary Adele Andrew tells me stories about all the hardships she endured throughout her life. Through these little conversations, it's like she teaches me the small lessons of life. When I talk to my grandmother, I always try to get all the information out of her that I can. I ask her a lot of questions about what it was like to live before Sheshatshu was settled. Her stories are very entertaining.

When she wants to, my grandmother can be a very funny lady. She tells us many tales, like about how she met her first boyfriend. This story starts off with this guy who really liked my grandmother. One day he asked her out, but at that time she did not like him. She had her eye on someone else, so she said no to him. After a while she thought about it some more and decided to agree to go out with him. However, much to her disappointment when she asked him out, he said that he didn't want to go out with her anymore. Whenever my grandmother tells this story she just laughs a whole lot. She talks about how she regretted her first decision.

I really admire my grandmother because she is a really strong woman. She raised 15 children literally on her own. She is still very active in the fight against low-level flying. I am behind her all the way in this struggle. When I think about how she spent all her life on the land, I understand how these jets are destroying the homeland which she holds very closely to her heart and I hold to mine. I am very proud and happy that she is my grandmother.

Some People Get
the Order of Canada:
Excerpts of Prison Writings

Rose Gregoire

Rose writes about what happened in Sheshatshu when she and a group of women decided to reclaim their place in Innu society in the late 1980s. For too long, the women had been relegated to the margins because of the teachings of the Catholic Church and Euro-Canadian culture. Women would say they could not go to meetings because their husbands forbade it. They had also been silenced by imposed foreign leadership structures such as the band councils. The women were not involved in these structures, and therefore had nothing to lose by their acts of rebellion against the Canadian state and NATO military. The women began to meet in order to support each other in reclaiming power within their personal and family lives. Together the women also mustered the strength to organize subversive acts that would rally their people to reclaim power over their homeland. The following was written in October 1989, while Rose was in jail on charges of public mischief for her role in the protests against NATO on the military runways in Goose Bay. Rose

feels some people would get the Order of Canada for
protecting human rights. She says, "I am not wishing to
get the Order of Canada. I'm just trying to explain our
struggle."

The women's group was formed three years ago to try to help
women in the community with the kind of problems we have.
We have all kinds of problems, like wife abuse, alcoholism among
the Innu women, child neglect. We are also trying to get the
women to speak out for themselves, to stand up and be strong
against the men. We encourage women not to fight among
themselves and to try to find out what the real problem is.

A lot of women in the community think they are not allowed
to speak out at meetings. They think that is the men's job. I
believe strongly that a woman is just as good as any man, or
maybe even sometimes better. One time in our culture, men and
women made decisions together, but ever since the White culture has appeared into our lives, it seems only the men make
decisions.

In our culture, women used to do the hunting with or without
their husbands. I can remember when we were in the country,
my father, Stakeaskushimun (Simon Gregoire), would leave in
the mornings to go hunting and wouldn't come home until dark,
while my mother, Miste Mani (Marie Gregoire), also hunted. She
used to do everything: set traps, shoot animals. My mother was
just as good as any man. I also remember that my father could
not make a decision without my mother's approval. They both
had to make a decision. It was almost like the whole family was
involved in the decision making.

When Innu women try to stand up for our rights, we are
struggling to get our culture back. When we first started our
meetings, there were only a few women involved. It was hard for
women to come out and speak at meetings, because we hadn't
done that for so long. The women were so used to staying home
to do the housework. So that's what we have tried to do: to get
women back on their feet so they won't be run over by men.

It was hard for the men to accept this for a while. It was hard for them to see women organizing a meeting to try to talk about community problems. We had a hard time, but we kept on having meetings. After a while, once they understood what we were trying to do, we worked with the men.

We were the ones who organized that meeting about protesting against the military low-level flying. We got after our leaders in the community. We asked questions and tried to find out what was happening between the government and the Innu. We told the men that if we opposed the military, then we should do something about it. We told them talk was no good. We needed action. Anyway, the leaders of the community were angry with us at first. They probably thought we were trying to take over their leadership, but after a while they supported us. They joined us in our protests against low-level flying, and ever since we have worked together. We haven't been able to do very much on the community problems, because we are very busy on this proposed NATO base in our homeland.

The non-Innu people who live in Labrador often point out that our organizations, which are supposed to defend Innu rights, have received large amounts of money from the Canadian government. This is true, but we know that these organizations were introduced among us in the 1970s to try and control us. They make it impossible for us to fight back except in ways and places where the rules of the game are set by the Euro-Canadians. And if we do something they don't like, they threaten to cut off the money, and sometimes they do. So even here, in our ways of expressing our anger and sadness and resistance, we have been dependent.

These organizations, including the band councils, were imposed on us. They were not Innu structures and they do not work in the way our society works. Even some of our "chiefs" know and understand this very well. Although some of them are in these positions and trying to deal with the problems in our villages, they support very strongly what we are doing. Because the women have not been involved in these foreign organizations, it has been almost easier for us, the Innu women, to fight báck in this new form of resistance against what is being done to our people. We were never really part of the system that was imposed on us, paid for and controlled by our foreign rulers.

Our fight for our people is not a fight just for women but for all our people. It is not a women's issue but an Innu issue. We have welcomed any Innu person who will fight alongside us to create a free and healthy world for our children and grandchildren.

When we gain control over our own lives, then we can start working on our own people. We are working so hard on NATO, because it is almost like a life-and-death issue for us. Our culture will be gone. If the NATO base is approved for Goose Bay, it's just as well that the government build more penitentiaries and leave lots of room for graveyards. They will need them for my people.

One last thing: We are fighting for our land and for our rights. We identify as a distinct hunting people in our land Nitassinan. We are not going to jail and being separated from our children just to get a rich land claims agreement. Our fight is not about land claims, another thing being used against us to force us to surrender what we will never ever give up — our ownership of Nitassinan.

The Government of Mischief

Anne Marie Andrew

Anne Marie describes her experience of feeling under siege as NATO war machines moved in to practise war games in her homeland. For her the issue is clear: the Innu have never signed a treaty to surrender their rights or their land. The Innu have never given their consent for any developments that have occurred on their land. NATO was the last straw. Anne Marie was one of the women arrested for her role in protests against NATO's military flight training in Nitassinan. Other women arrested included Mary Martha Hurley, Tshaukuish Penashue, Janet Pone, Helen Gabriel, Jackie Ashini, Ann Hurley, Rose Gregoire, Francesca Snow, Mary May Osmond and Germaine Rich. Some of these women also took up the challenge of serving as ambassadors for the Innu to bring messages of anger and hope all over Canada and the world. The following are excerpts from a presentation Anne Marie made at an annual general meeting of the Roman Catholic Social Action Commission in St. John's in February 1989.

My name is Anamani Antane and I am an Innu from Sheshatshu, Nitassinan. I am married with six children. My youngest boy is 2 years old and the oldest is a 14-year-old girl. I am expecting another one soon. I was born in the country and delivered by Innu midwives. At an early age, I was adopted by my grandparents, as is the Innu custom. The reason for this custom is that as I grew older, I looked after my grandparents. Both of them were very old when they died, and I learned and experienced life in the country.

⚑ ⚑ ⚑

Today our children are taught in schools that they are Newfoundlanders and Canadians. The school should stop teaching our children this lie, because when a child is young he believes what he is taught. I have told my children they are not Newfoundlanders, they are Innu. I have taught my children what I learned from my grandparents. When my husband, Greg, and I were in the country, our kids learned a lot about our culture and all the names of the places we went to in the last two years.

Our people still go out to the country each fall and spring. As I talk to you, there are Innu families in the country who are living the life of our ancestors. Some of those people are at Minai-nipi, where a bombing range has been set up by the NATO forces. They are camped only a few miles away from where Innu people last year occupied the bombing range and stopped the bombing runs by NATO forces. This bombing range was set up by the Government of Canada without the agreement of the Innu people.

I was one of the 11 Innu women who spent two or more weeks in jail. We have seen from watching television that people in other countries have been arrested by police for demonstrations. We never thought this could happen in "Canada." We, the Innu, have been protesting on the Goose Bay runway and we have been jailed because the Government of Canada is giving our country away to other countries. We will continue to protest. Close to 300 of our people have been charged with mischief by the Government. Our Innu elders have testified in court that the Innu are a people and that our future is threatened by the NATO base and low-level flight training. If we do not stop them, we will be the ones who will suffer and disappear as a people.

Low-level flight training and a NATO base cannot exist together with the Innu. Our choice is clear and has been clear. The NATO base must go. We will fight hard and we will never give up the right to be free. If we don't stop the NATO base and low-level flight training, the Innu nightmares will be real. Our culture will die and be replaced by a different culture, the culture of death for our people. Child neglect will increase, family violence will increase, alcoholism will increase. There will be prostitution of our people, sexual degradation of our daughters. Wives will leave their husband and their kids. There will be unwanted pregnancies, unhappiness, sexual assaults, suicides and other illnesses of a very sick culture.

We, the Innu, have survived in our country for thousands of years despite its harsh climate, because our ancestors passed down their knowledge and skills to us. The threat to our existence comes not from wartime experiences between major powers, but during a time of peace when there is no world war. In our country now, we see military jets flying daily over our camps, frightening our people, dropping their bombs on our country. We will continue to protest. We will walk again on our land together with our children, our husbands and our elders, always singing and praying in our own language, and always in the hope that our prayers will be answered. Together with your help, we can build a better future for our children and the world.

Chickadee

Christine Poker

Early one morning a young man and an elder saw someone looking inside their tent. Neither of them had ever seen that person before. The young man looked at his grandfather and asked who that person was, but his grandfather pretended that he didn't hear him. The young man kept asking his grandfather who this was. Finally his grandfather said he knew the person but he could not tell him.

The young man kept asking his grandfather, but the old man didn't want to tell. The young man was really curious and thought about the ways he could make his grandfather tell him. He remembered that the night before he had made some homebrew, which was his grandfather's favourite drink. They would drink it after hard work. They would drink a little bit, just to make them relax and rested.

When the day was over, the young man took out the homebrew. He knew it was strong. He asked his grandfather if he wanted to taste it and the old man said yes. He knew that his grandfather would ask him for more. He gave him a lot and told him that it was enough. But his grandfather wanted more when he had finished.

"If you tell me who that person was, I will give you a whole bucket," the young man said to his grandfather. His grandfather agreed to tell him.

"That person looking inside our tent is a bird. He changes himself into a person only when he wants to visit people. That person is really a chickadee," said the old man.

I Followed My Heart

Nympha Byrne

No permanent courts exist in any of the coastal communities of Labrador, so a circuit court with a full slate of characters — a judge, a Crown prosecutor, RCMP and legal aid lawyers, along with all their props — travels periodically to these communities, much like a travelling road show. The court is held in English, a language many people speak barely or not at all, and interpreters are difficult to find. When someone agrees to translate, he or she is faced with many legal terms for which there are no Innu words or concepts. The Innu word for "police", for instance, is kamakunuest *or the Man Who Locks People Up. The justice system is a foreign one that clashes deeply with Innu culture, and one that the Innu feel creates even more problems for individuals and their families. In December 1993 a group of women in Utshimassits (Davis Inlet), including Nympha, were fed up with what they saw happening in court and decided to take action. Their decision came from a simple belief that women can do anything when they set their minds to it — but it was an unimaginable act that shocked all of Canada.*

I remember listening to the judge during the court session. The RCMP officers stood by the door. The families of the accused sat around and waited to hear how long their son or brother or husband would be locked up. There were some people in the lock-up in the trailer. They were waiting for their sentencing, waiting to be taken away out of the community. I didn't stay very long. I was too angry to listen to any more charges and sentences. These people don't understand us, I thought to myself. They don't understand our culture.

For years I have watched non-Natives come in and out, and do what they want. They are not sensitive to our culture. Sometimes they would just throw the charges out, because they were too old. The court would often leave town before having heard all the cases, and people would forget about the charges by the time the court came around again.

I remember one time not long, before we threw out the court, a young man had been charged with assault. His girlfriend, who was his victim, was supposed to testify against him but she was very afraid. She couldn't speak English. I watched her and she looked so scared. She sat at the stand with her head down. There was no translator. She was six months pregnant. The judge was really hard on her. He didn't talk very nicely to her. He said he would wait as long as it took her to say something. He said if she didn't testify, he would just release her boyfriend. She still couldn't say anything. She was also afraid of his family. This often happens when a woman is assaulted. She won't press charges because she is afraid that the man's family will be really mad at her. They will harass her and talk behind her back. I tried to encourage her to say something. I was mad at the way the judge was handling the situation. I went to Katie Rich's office. She was the chief at the time. We talked about it and she said she knew this kind of thing was happening in court.

The circuit court came around again. This time I just stuck my head in there. I was still so angry. I didn't want to listen any more. Katie went and sat in while the people went forward with their charges. I was working with Social Services at the time. From my office window, I could see Katie walking back and forth to her office during break time and lunch. I could tell she was really angry. Then she called me on the phone. She was wondering what to do. I went to her office and she showed me a letter she had drafted. The letter was telling the judge to leave the community with his court. I barely read the letter and I signed it. My heart was telling me that something needed to be done. I knew the women had the strength, the heart and the power to take action. There were maybe 15 or 20 other women who also signed the letter. Some of them were pretty nervous, but Katie told them they did not have to come with us to present the letter to the judge. It was their choice. Everyone decided to come along. Katie asked Innu constable Justine Noah Jack to accompany us, so she could keep the peace and so things wouldn't get out of hand.

We marched in while the court was in session. Katie led the way. I followed with Justine Noah Jack, and the rest of the women came behind. It was very exciting. We were not aggressive. We walked in quietly and peacefully. The room froze and everyone turned to look at us. The judge, the lawyers and Crown prosecutor stared in disbelief. Katie just walked up to the judge. I remember looking at his face. Did he look frightened or was he surprised? I don't know how to describe it. The judge took the letter and read it. He didn't know what to say. He told us he had to make a phone call. He left the hall and headed for the RCMP trailer. He never came back. We waited for him. The people were sitting around looking and the men were laughing at us. They told us we were asking for trouble and we would land in jail. One of the women went over to the judge's table and sat in his chair. His papers still lay on the table. The RCMP were around the whole time, but when they saw the judge wasn't returning, they took his papers and recording equipment and left.

Finally, we adjourned the court and everyone walked out. I went back to my office to lock up. A lot of people were gathering outside the RCMP trailer. They started a bonfire to keep warm because it was very cold. People began shouting to the judge to leave town. Later that day, the charter came to fly the judge, the lawyers and the Crown prosecutor back to Goose Bay.

We took this action because, the way I see it, the courts have failed our people. When they throw people in jail, there are no programs to help them with their problems. What purpose does it serve for them to be in jail? When they return to the community after spending time in jail, they do the same thing all over again. Many people told me they couldn't believe we had thrown the judge out of the community. But for me, it was nothing. It was no big deal. When I saw the story on the media, it was such a big thing for the non-Innu society. But for me, it was just that I could see something was wrong and something had to be done about it. I had to do this for my people. Sometimes what I have seen is that my people let things go, instead of standing up for themselves. This time we had to take some action.

They didn't charge us right away. Katie, Justine and I were the only ones who were charged and it was a year and a half later before they came to arrest us and take us into custody. They never charged the other women. I guess because of our jobs, they thought the three of us were the ringleaders. In 1994 my family moved to Goose Bay and even when I was there, the RCMP never came to pick me up. I remember waiting, but they never came knocking on my door. There was talk about our charges. Katie would call me all the time to keep me informed on what was happening. We would wonder why they were taking so long to put us in jail. We would laugh about it. I felt like they could see the mistakes they had made in our community, and they must have been feeling guilty about it. They were realizing how little they knew about our culture with all their papers and their foreign laws. I had always had a lot of difficulty understanding their courts, all the big words they used that we have no translation for in our language.

Finally in the spring of 1995, I was back in Utshimassits to collect stories for this book and it was then the RCMP took us into custody. Camille was very annoyed because we had a very small budget for this book and we hadn't finished the job. But all she could do was take pictures of us being hauled away. Many people from the community followed us to the plane to show their support. For a while, a couple of the men stood face to face between the blades of the propeller to keep the plane from leaving. In the end the plane took off and they brought us to the lock-up in Goose Bay. Many people came to visit us: family members like my sister from Utshimassits, lawyers, leaders from the Innu Nation and the band council. Camille came to give me a hard time for abandoning her and to show her support.

We were given undertakings to sign, but Katie and I refused. Justine decided to sign. Katie and I were shipped to the Women's Correctional Centre in Stephenville, Newfoundland, until our court date. In all, we spent 10 days in jail. We were always having fun and laughing in there. We stayed up late in the night, talking and sharing stories. I felt like a caged animal. I knew why animals in zoos look so sad. I didn't feel like I belonged in that jail. I worried about my children — what were they thinking?

While we were still in the lock-up in Goose Bay, my youngest cried and said she wanted me home. She kept telling me that I hadn't done anything wrong and I shouldn't be in jail. They came to visit me to bring me fruit because the food they gave us was so greasy. My sister Judith and her husband also came. She looked so sad when I saw her face. "How could they lock you up?" she asked me. I described to her what our cell was like. We had two benches for beds, and Justine had a mat on the floor. The toilet was right out in the open in front of us in this small room. Those two kept smoking cigarettes. I didn't smoke and it was hard on my lungs. Then we left for Stephenville.

I hated the jail in Stephenville because of the barbed wire around the building. Then I really felt like a caged animal. When we first went in there, they strip-searched us everywhere. I felt invaded. They made us shower and took us to our separate cells. We were in solitary confinement for 24 hours. The next day, they put us in the same room again. We became friends with the other inmates. They couldn't believe we hadn't signed our undertakings. They said if they had been in our shoes, they would have signed right away. They kept asking us about throwing the judge out of the community. They were so amazed. They said they could never have done what we did. I ended up counselling a White woman. She was talking about her drinking problem and we shared our stories. We became friends. She said she really missed me after we left. Katie had her own buddies. I would hear them laughing in the smoking room.

When our trial date arrived, they took us to Deer Lake, where we caught a plane to go back to Goose Bay. A lot of supporters were waiting outside the Supreme Court when we arrived. The weather was down, so my mother and Katie's parents couldn't make it from Utshimassits. Both Katie and I had braided our hair. I remembered how one elder had once told me how my hair was my strength. We walked in to face the judge and he released us. We thought we would be sentenced to jail for sure. This felt like another victory. We went over to my house, drank tea and laughed about it. We were so saucy.

Almighty Woman

Nympha Byrne

dedicated to Katie Rich

Almighty Woman,
you have so much power
trying to gain strength
for your community.

"I am so proud of you."
And I have high hopes from you.
"I will walk with you."
You, Almighty Woman,
you are the strength
for your people.
And your land.

You are still nurturing
your little children,
but you can't wait,
because your elders
and your people
come next.

Almighty Woman
Almighty Woman,
you are a fighter
for your culture.
You have a heavy load.
I see the brightness
in your face,
because you believe
in yourself.

Almighty Woman
Almighty Woman,
you've been crying for so long,
you've washed your face
with your tears,
letting your hair grow
for your strength,
braiding your hair
for your proudness,
sharing your spirit
for kindness.

Almighty Woman
Almighty Woman,
you've touched the hearts
in your community,
you make your elders so proud.
The Great Spirit will thank you
for all your strength,
you will be a legend
to your people.
You will empower your community
and your elders,
your people and children,
you free your spirit
for your beliefs ...

In Our Culture,
We Don't Sign Papers

Justine Noah Jack, Katie Rich & Nympha Byrne

The following are excerpts of the court testimony of three mischievous women in the Supreme Court of Newfoundland, April 20, 1995. Justine Noah Jack, Katie Rich and Nympha Byrne were arrested and charged with mischief for their role in evicting the judge from Utshimassits (Davis Inlet) in December 1993. At the time Justine worked as a peacekeeper, Katie was the elected chief and Nympha had just completed 10 years of work with Social Services. Although all three worked at jobs where they pushed a lot of paper, their testimony reveals the internal conflict they and their people experience when the papers of the White culture are thrust upon them. The line of questioning from the Crown prosecutor forced them to think and see clearly how their lives had become tied to foreign bureaucracies and their papers and documents. Ironically, when papers matter the most, like the signing of a treaty or land-rights agreement before governments seize Innu land, these papers do not yet exist for the Innu of Labrador.

Justine Noah Jack

When I was young I didn't know what the real Innu life was. I was confused. I didn't learn much about my culture. But as I grew up, I began to understand who I was. It was about three or four years ago that I came to believe that this was our Innu homeland, and that this homeland was under the traditional values, customs and laws of the Innu people.

I was trained as a peacekeeper for nine months in 1993. I learned about the Canadian criminal law in my training. I also learned about the lives of people, about what abuse is. I learned how to arrest people, and I have done that in my job.

The Innu people have not come from somewhere else. They are from this land. I don't consider myself a Canadian citizen. I don't live in Canada. I feel like our land has been taken, that we are being controlled on everything. But we don't want to be.

It is true that I have a Social Insurance Number. I applied for it because I had to. I have received Unemployment Insurance. I feel like I'm begging for everything. When I file income tax returns, I am not thinking about Canadian or Newfoundland jurisdiction. In my mind, I need to feed my children. It's like I'm begging for money. I do it for my kids.

In December 1993 when we evicted the judge, I intended to stay in court until the judge left. I was there when the petition for him to leave was presented to him. I wanted him to leave. There was no violence in the courtroom. No threats were made. I was there to keep the peace. I take my orders from the chief. The authority for me to arrest and release people in my community comes from the Mushuau Innu, from the chief. Sometimes my orders are to hand them over to the RCMP.

On December 1993, I did not feel like I was treating the court with contempt. I just felt they needed to understand what my people are going through and what they need. I did my best according to what I believe.

Katie Rich

When I was growing up, I was taught that this was Innu land, that the Innu have always lived according to their own values, traditions and laws. My parents taught me this. We have been looking after our own affairs for centuries. I have not considered myself a Canadian citizen for many years. As for the Queen, I believe she is in Britain, not in Canada.

Yes, I hold a Canadian passport; I signed the application. I have a Social Insurance Number, I have filed income tax returns, I receive child tax credits, I have applied for Unemployment Insurance and I swore allegiance to the Queen to get work with the Newfoundland government. I feel all these things are crumbs offered to the Innu people.

All the agencies in my community are controlled from the outside. When I was growing up, I listened to the elders. They told stories about threats made to them that if they didn't send their children to school, their family allowances would be cut. At that time, only a handful of Innu spoke any English. Outside officials worked with the priest to instil fear. But we have always known that these crumbs came from the revenues from the resources on our land. We only see the crumbs of this. This is why you see the social problems that exist in our community. What choice do we have? These policies are made for us. There is a policy, which has existed since 1954, that Innu people should be wiped out.

When you look at the people in Utshimassits, you see how your agencies have been involved in the destruction of our nation. Over the years we have said the same thing over and over, but it seems to go in one ear and out the other. I felt I had to take the action I took when I asked the judge to leave. I needed to do something.

I receive a child tax credit, but I pay taxes like anyone else in this country, except for people on reserves. The way the system is designed, it is like we don't exist. I took this action because you need to recognize that my children have the right to exist as human beings. The children in Utshimassits have the same dreams as any other children across this country. As parents, what if we decided that we would get all the revenue that have been taken out of our land? But I don't think the governments would be prepared to turn them over because basically we don't exist for them.

Only a few years ago, the outside world heard about Utshimassits, how children were living, why there were so many social problems. We as parents don't have a choice but to apply for these benefits. My income tax returns are only crumbs from the government. I take what is coming to me, and this is not even half of what I am owed. I have much more coming to me.

We have never known boundaries on our land. We never issued passports to any of the other Native bands who would sometimes visit this area many years ago. I don't think the government would recognize Innu Nation or Mushuau Innu Band Council passports. Nothing of what we have shown of how the agencies have downgraded the Innu has been heard. If we used our own passports, they would probably be thrown in the garbage. That is what you do to everything we try to do.

When we try to stand up for ourselves, to correct the wrongs, we end up in court. We are branded as criminals. I don't see myself as a criminal. I did what I had to do. Ever since I was born, I have seen these things happen. My mother never understood English. The only person who could speak English was the priest. He would explain to my mother what forms he was sending out — family-allowance forms, birth certificates. In our language, there is no word for "birth certificate." When you are bombarded with these things, when it is implanted in your head that you must live differently from what you have known, you end up with chaos. And this is what has happened to the Innu.

I left my community to attend high school when I was 13. I hated being an Innu because I was the only one in my class who was different. I had brown skin, black hair. I was weird, I dressed weird. All the time I was there — for three years — I never spoke a single word in class. But I listened well and I learned a way of life different from mine. I was so involved being out there, seeing the big city of St. John's, that I hated myself as an Innu person. And I found it difficult to fight back.

No matter how much mascara, blush or lipstick I put on my face, I didn't look right. I just couldn't play the part. Realizing that I couldn't be a White person, I had to accept the way I was. Being an Innu then meant being drunk all the time. That's the way our people lived. I came back to the same routine as anybody in Utshimassits. I didn't have a care in the world. Believe it or not, I once had a Canadian flag in my room. Then I started to think, "These are the same people who are treating my people like this." I swore I would do everything in my power to change this. I'm not ashamed of what I did.

My people have been crying for a long time. No one has listened. Only when we took this action, we stopped everybody in their tracks. By the time our children grow up, I want them to recognize their dreams. When I talked to my children, I told them if the court decided to place me in the correctional centre I was willing to make that sacrifice because I felt that we were once a defeated people. But we are not anymore.

I have also found out after being a leader of my community how much hatred exists for my people because we would do anything simply to be recognized as human beings. If I had another opportunity, I would do it all over again. You haven't heard the last of me.

♣ ♣ ♣

On December 16, 1993, the circuit court was in Utshimassits. At this point I didn't know Judge Hyslop existed. For two days, I listened and watched. I didn't like the way the court was being held. At one point, an Innu woman was asked a question. She was asked to tell the court the ages of her two children. She said, "The oldest is 1, the youngest is 6 months." I don't think she realized what she said, that she couldn't have one child that was one year old and another that was six months old. It was then I saw the judge laugh at this witness. In your language, when a person is 35, you don't answer you are 35 and some months old. But when you ask for a child who is one year and six months old, you don't just say one year, you say 18 months. That's how complicated your language is. Most of my people are school dropouts. What I saw in this courtroom was the judge making fun of people because they weren't answering right, or else threatening them if they didn't answer. The court that comes to Utshimassits is not respected because the court's people don't respect our people.

There were a lot of other things that played into why I took this action. A young man was sentenced to three and a half years for a break and enter. Three years ago here in Goose Bay, a man was driving drunk and killed a girl on the road. He served only nine months, even though he had a criminal record. I guess it's good to have friends in high places.

When I left the courtroom that day, I was told another person had been sent to jail. I had had enough. I called together some people to ask their advice. "These things are happening. What should I do?" I asked them and they give me a few options. One option was to assault the judge. I had nothing against this judge personally. Why should I assault him? We talked about it some more. That's when we came up with this letter. That's how it all started. The RCMP had 12 Innu in custody at the time. Six of them were children.

It was my conclusion after sitting in the court that week, that there was no justice here. The defence lawyer had only a few minutes to talk with clients. That's what they usually do when they travel with the circuit. The judge allows the defence lawyer to see his client before court starts, but this is the only time the person sees his lawyer. There are times, even for myself, that we don't understand the legal terms. How can a person who doesn't speak English understand how a court session is supposed to work? If people don't know how it works, they just go in and out of the recreation hall without knowing what is happening to them. I see a lot of things with this system that simply don't work.

I didn't think anyone would listen if I wrote a letter about the conditions and conduct of the circuit court. It's the same thing as always. What I did was what I believed in. After the letter was done, I called some women together. They called other women. Before we went to court, I had about 25 signatures for the letter. I explained my plans to the women. I told them that if any of them didn't want to join us, they didn't have to. Someone asked what would happen if we got arrested. I replied that I was prepared to take the risk.

The other person I called was Constable Justine Noah Jack. I told her we needed to keep order in the courtroom, in case anything went wrong. She has been trained to restore order. I believe I made the right choice to ask Justine to come with us. I took the letter and the women followed me. I was the first person to enter. I went directly to the judge and handed him the letter. The women stood with me around the table. After the judge read the letter, I said, "We're not leaving until you do." He said he needed to make a phone call. We expected him to return because he hadn't adjourned the court. During this whole time, there was no sign of violence or threats.

After Judge Hyslop left, we waited. More people joined us. I left the building to make a phone call. By the time I returned, the Crown prosecutor, the court recorder and the defence lawyer had all left, but their documents were still on the table. We sat around and waited. An RCMP officer arrived and took the documents and recording equipment from the table. The crowd cheered because I think these people, who have seen themselves defeated so often, saw they had the power to do something. The power was brought out by the women and children, and other people in the room. That was the end of it.

I believe that what I did needed to be done because the justice system has failed the people of Utshimassits. We had plans to correct this. We sent letters and faxes, but the action we took finally made them see what was happening. It took a year for the former band council to negotiate a policing agreement. This would not have happened if we had not done what we did.

I believe our people governed themselves before any White people came to this land. We had our own laws. Our elders and parents are the ones who taught the children how to survive on the land. We already had the things that make a people a nation — our traditions, rituals and religion — but then the missionaries came into our midst and told Innu people that practices like the sacred Innu drum were evil. When you are told that the beliefs you were taught by your mother and father as you grew up are wrong, I believe this creates a collision of two cultures. We are caught between being White people or being Innu people.

Because both my parents were drinking, I was ashamed of them. They were drunks. As one elder told me a few weeks ago, I was only looking at the bad things. I didn't look at the good things. That's what I'm doing now, overlooking the bad things like drinking or leaving the children. In my family, I was the oldest and I was left alone with my brothers and sisters. I'm overlooking this. I believe that since the Innu have begun standing up for themselves, we are seeing the hatred coming out of the non-Innu people who live around us.

We have a right to exist as a people. My grandfather never signed any treaty or agreement with anyone, yet we were pushed aside. We were too busy getting drunk as our land was being taken around us. But if you come to the community today, you'll see people are standing up, taking the risk of being sent to jail. What the Whites have taught us is how to become beggars in our own territory, but if we try to pick up the pieces, we will realize the power that we have. We will see more of this power.

Nympha Byrne

Yes, I have a beginner's driving permit and a Social Insurance Number. I am receiving Unemployment Insurance, and I have been a Justice of the Peace. I became a JP because the people in my community needed someone to sign papers, so I agreed. I never thought of the Queen when I signed the papers. We need to sign papers for everything, for the RCMP, Social Services, to get any kind of money. Our people have always been pushed around. I myself don't believe in that anymore. Our people have been pushed around too much. We are like puppets to the government people. Everything has to be on paper. They have to have a name or a signature.

I want to talk about one time when I was really sick. I was taken out to St. John's. The nurse in Utshimassits went to my father to get him to sign a paper to authorize any surgery. They wanted to do some tests on my brain. I think if my father had signed that paper, I wouldn't have been the same person. I'm really glad my father never signed. The nurse was really mad. People have been pushed and told all the time to sign all these documents. In our culture, we don't need signatures. It's just the White man that needs papers.

I am really fed up with what's been happening in my community with the Innu just being the puppets of the governments. I did what I did because I wanted to be there for my people. I was taught not to hate other people no matter what colour they are. I learned that from my grandma, never to put anybody down.

I have four kids. It's like when you're there for somebody, they're your family. The people in my community are like my brothers and sisters. When I hold my baby close in my arms, I feel good. That feeling was there too when I was there for my people this time. I felt really good when I did what I had to do. I was always afraid to stand up and say what I really thought.

My father was always hunting. I grew up in the country. That's where we spent most of our time. But the land is hurting right now. To me the land is like my grandmother. We have to take care of it because we live on the land. When my child is hurting, I need to run to my child and just hold my baby. That's the way I see it when the land is all broken. We have to go back and be there for it. Also when people are hurting, I like to be able to be there to help them.

In your culture, everything has to be signed. In the church, too, like when you get married. In our culture, we don't sign anything. I learned a lot of things when we were in the country. I respect our people and our elders. But I don't understand you people, your system, your government policies. I was told to sign those papers. I don't know the Queen. I didn't feel like I had a choice. I just signed those papers.

Whose Law
Am I Breaking Anyway?

Christine Poker

Long before European contact, the Innu used the rich mineral resources of their land for tools and trade. They quarried a material called Ramah chert for pottery and other things and traded it with nations who lived as far south as what is now known as Mississippi. In 1949 a railway was built from Uashat (Sept Iles) to Schefferville to allow the mining of a rich iron ore deposit in the area. Many Innu were hired to work in this mine, but they were given menial jobs and paid less than White workers. The Innu were prevented from joining the unions, and although housing and a reserve were built for them, when the mine shut down, there was nothing left but huge open pits, abandoned buildings and no jobs. The Innu of Labrador are loath to repeat this experience. Most believe that the Inco subsidiary company, which plans to build a mine in choice Innu territory at Emish (Voisey's Bay), is like the atshen. Once human, the atshen became cannibals and their hearts turned to ice. Pretending to be cold and hungry, they would come into Innu camps and, once they were in the tents, they would try to kill and eat everyone. Although the Innu have participated in the federal

*government's environmental-assessment process to re-
view the impacts of a mine at Emish, and although they
have tried to negotiate an impact benefit agreement with
Inco regarding Emish, they have done so because they
feel stuck between a rock and a hard place. Only when
they have organized protests at the site, like the one
Christine describes below, have they been united and
following the call of their spirits.*

When the people talked about another protest at Emish in
August 1997, I was glad that it would finally happen. We all sat
around the big table, talking for a long time, wondering what we
would do. I looked at all the excited faces. Nobody was scared
and nobody asked, "What if something bad happens?" They just
said, "We will do anything to protect our land." I am a person
with negative thoughts, wondering about all the what-ifs?, but
listening to everyone I too got very excited.

The elders were taken to Antenak (Anaktalak Bay) by float
plane. My family went by boat. As we travelled, we saw a bear
and my husband shot it. We saw two more, and I wondered,
"What if this land is all destroyed? Will there be bears running
free like this?" I looked at the mountain when we got to Emish
and I had this overwhelming feeling of how it was as peaceful as
always. There was also a great sadness inside me. I looked at the
miners' camp. It seemed so big. "Surely there will be another
community here," I thought.

I glanced over to the other side of the mountain, where the
Innu were setting up camp. Smoke was rising from the tents'
stovepipes. It was a beautiful sight, but I didn't know what the
miners thought. It would really make my day if I did. Anyway, I
kept thinking about what my mom was cooking. I knew she was
fine. My brothers and sisters were already there so she had a lot
of help. I wanted to go to her camp but we had a lot of gear, so
we decided to set up our tent with the Sheshatshu people.

Some Utshimassiu (Davis Inlet) Innu had set up camp with
the Inuit protesters from Nent (Nain) at the foot of the hill and

the Sheshatshu Innu had their camps on the shore. The miners' camp was in the middle. The police were already there to protect the miners' camp. I was wishing they would protect the land instead. I knew nothing would happen to the miners, but surely the worse possible things would happen to the land. And they will also happen to the Innu, because whatever happens to the animals will also happen to the Innu, and whatever happens to the land will happen to the animals.

People came to help us set up the tent. I felt really cozy and warm when it was finished. I was glad to see my friends from Sheshatshu. The next day we went to the other camp for a meeting. There were a lot of us and we decided to walk slowly toward the miners' camp. Many police were standing around. Somebody said, "Let's go this way where we're not allowed!" Someone else said, "Let's go! Nobody owns it!" Some decided to follow the trail and I went with my husband and others into the woods towards the camp.

I felt really scared, but I kept saying to myself, "You are not alone. Whose law am I breaking anyway in the middle of my own country?" Every time I thought positive thoughts, it made me stronger. I held my little daughter's hand. I saw police with cameras and kids trying to cover up their lenses. My two sons were running ahead and I called out to them, "Don't touch anything, not yet anyway." They didn't hear me. My son said something bad to a photographer and tried to block his camera with a protest sign. "Don't do that. He is on our side," I called out.

The kids were running in all directions while the adults walked slowly together. We didn't plan to touch anything. "They are everywhere," I heard on a police radio. Everyone was wearing the same tee-shirts with INCO signs, but if you looked closely they said, "Undermining the Innu, INCO at Voisey's Bay."

I was holding my little daughter's and son's hands. I kept thinking, "What is going to happen? Will police grab me and will my kids be hurt?" But I followed my mom, who was way ahead of me. The police were standing looking at us. My mom and her friend Munik (Monique Rich) were holding their signs. Munik pointed her sign at a policeman and said in English, "Read!" The policeman was not smiling as he looked away. She pointed at the sign again, and this time with an angrier voice, she said, "Read, read, read!" I started laughing. The policeman just stared at the sign. Everyone in the crowd was laughing.

My mom and Munik then walked over to the policeman taking pictures and started posing for him. I could hear the elders like my mom and her friend talking with angry voices. We were all looking at some White people gathered around a trailer window laughing. I wished I could know what they were thinking. "What are they laughing about anyway? It's just starting," I thought. I was really angry. "They will not be laughing soon," I called out to my friend. One woman walked toward the window with her sign. When they saw her coming, they all disappeared.

Later, after I took my kids home and I was cooking and waiting for my husband to return, my friend came to our tent. She told me that the protestors had gone into a trailer that had collapsed on them and that someone had cut the telephone lines. She also told me that my son had got hit by a policeman and had a big cut on his mouth. I was so upset. "I will see this policeman and he is going to get the same treatment," I thought. Horrible thoughts of what I would do came into my mind. It wasn't long before my husband and son came home and his cut wasn't as bad as I expected. I felt better.

We could hear laughter at night when people talked about their days during the protest. When I think about it now, I wonder if the White people would do the same if they knew they were being destroyed. When I visited the elders during the protest, I could see sadness in their eyes because their grandchildren were having to fight for their land.

My Dad's Moccasin

Rose Gregoire

Many scary nights — for a little girl
hoping to sleep well and be safe —
and someone to hold her words
of prayers repeated over and over again,
asking for protection only from the
Creator.

The Creator gave me my dad's moccasin
for safety.
That's how I survived,
I loved my dad's moccasin.
When something bad happens
to me in the night time,
I pretend I am in my dad's moccasin
and I feel safe,
while I watch those ugly hands
hurting the little girl — and yet
I feel safe
in my dad's moccasin.

Thank you dad for your moccasins.
I thank the Creator for answering
my prayers,
with a pair of moccasins.

Thank you, Mother, for making those moccasins
for Dad.

For a long time
I thought the Creator
didn't answer the child's prayer.
I thought my mom never cared.
I thought my dad couldn't care less
about me,
but he had hung up
his moccasin so I could use it.
My mom and dad didn't realize how
much they helped me.
The Creator knows and understands
because he gave me a pair of moccasins,
an answer to my prayers
so I could feel safe.

Contributors

Angela Andrew was one of eight children born to Tshetshepateu, or Early Riser, and Kukumanesh, or Oldest Girl (Edward and Adeline Rich). She married Etienne Andrew and they raised eight children: Paul, Gordon, Jeannie, Nancy, Ruby, Virginia, Archie and Elizabeth. Angela and her family live in Sheshatshu, where she worked for many years as a literacy instructor in adult education before returning to university to study for her education diploma. She has taught Innu history and traditional skills in a band council education program. In 1989, she took her last drink, and she has been involved in a number of healing programs since. Most of her children have followed suit. She is also well known for her craft work. She revived the art of making tea dolls, an art form that many other Innu women have since taken up to help provide more income for their families.

Peter Armitage

Anne Marie Andrew is the daughter of Mani-Matini and Tshutauish (Mary Madeline and Joseph Nuna). She was adopted and raised by her grandparents Shushepiss and Eskueshish (Joseph and Mary Nuna). She spent much of her childhood living in *nutshimit*

Camille Fouillard

with her grandparents. This was unusual for someone of her generation. Most of her peers were in school. She also attended school periodically, but eventually dropped out at the age of 13 to look after her grandparents and because she had fallen so far behind in her studies. Anne Marie married Greg Andrew, the son of Miste Mani-Aten (Mary Adele Andrew). She has eight children: Pauline (Wendy), Eskueshish (Clem), Napeu (Greg Jr.), Olivia, Janet, Neil, Kirk and Marie. She has 10 grandchildren. Anne Marie and Greg have often taken their children out to *nutshimit* in the spring and fall. Anne Marie was arrested for her role in the Innu protests against NATO's military flight training over Innu land. While pregnant with her youngest, she spent time in jail at the Women's Correctional Centre in Stephenville, Newfoundland.

Alphonse Ancrew

Caroline Andrew, with her granddaughter, Whitney.

Caroline Andrew's Innu name is Kanani. She is the daughter of Miste Nuk and Munik (Luke and Monique Nui). She married Etuet (Edward Andrew) and had four children: Josie, Jack, Brenda and Stella. She also adopted her oldest grandchild, Alphonse. She has 18 other grandchildren and one great-grandchild. Caroline was one of the first Innu to attend school in Labrador and she is one of the few bilingual Innu of her generation. She worked as a teacher at Peenamin Mackenzie School for 24 years. She taught Innu-aimun, English and Catholic hymn songs to children mostly in the younger grades. She also taught in Utshimassits for six months in 1998. She used to do a lot of things with her hands, such as sewing moccasins and knitting, but now arthritis in her hands has made these pastimes impossible. For many years, she was active in the church. She read the word of the gospel, sang hymns and attended church when there was a priest stationed in the community. Now, she likes to spend her time with her grandchildren. She has a cabin on Kakatshu-utshistun, where she likes to take her grandchildren to teach them what she learned from her parents.

Mary Adele Andrew, or Miste Mani-Aten, was 63 years old when she died in 1996. She was born and raised in *nutshimit*. Her parents were Stakeaskushimun and Mani (Simon and Marie Gregoire). Miste Mani-Aten married Matshieu (Matthew Ben Andrew) when she was 17, and they had 15 children: Germaine, Charlie, Greg, Ben, Paula, Alex, Mary Martha, Elizabeth, Patrick, Justine, Clem, Guy, Anastasia, Eric and Max. She

Camille Fouillard

had 50 grandchildren and 13 great-grandchildren. She spent her early married life in *nutshimit* for 10 months of the year, with visits in the summer to Uashat or Sheshatshu. She had her first five children in *nutshimit*. In the early 1960s, her life changed dramatically when her family, along with many others, was settled permanently to village life in Sheshatshu. Matshieu died in 1977. In the late 1970s, now a widow, she began to take her children and their families back to *nutshimit* regularly in the spring and fall. She was a great cook. She was very active in the Innu campaign against military flight-training in the late 1980s. She always encouraged her children to fight for their land.

Nympha Byrne

Maggie Antuan is 79 years old and her Innu name is Tapatapinukueu She is the daughter of Uitsheuake (Abraham) and Mani (Mary Abraham). Her Innu name was given to her by Miste Mani-Shan (Mary Jane Pasteen), who was her grandmother's cousin. She married Shinipest (Sylvester Antuan) and had four children. Two died, and the surviving children are Penote and Nishkuess (Vivian). Her parents were Mushuau Innu from Uaskaikan. After her father died, she moved with her mother and brother Nuk (Luke Nui) to Sheshatshu. The part of her life that she likes to remember is when she lived in *nutshimit* and walked great distances. She says they did not need ski-doos or even dogs back then. They ate only wild meat and she learned how to survive from her mother: how to sew, clean caribou, take care of the animals and make snowshoes. She learned to put up a tent, pick boughs for the floor and get wood for the fire. Now Maggie lives in Sheshatshu with her sister Annie Michel.

Nympha Byrne worked for over 10 years with the Department of Social Services in a variety of capacities, including as a child-care worker. She has been trained in addictions counselling and has been active in the healing movement in her community of Utshimassits. In 1992 she served as commissioner for the People's Inquiry, a community self-examination organized by leaders and elders after six children died in a house fire. Nympha has also been an activist fighting for Innu land rights and self-determination. She was one of the women who threw the judge out of the community in 1993 to force the provincial government to provide more cultur-ally appropriate justice services to her people. In recent years, Nympha returned to school to complete a high-school and college diploma. Recently she was employed as a probation officer, and she now works as a community liaison, working at the new solvent-abuse centre in Sheshatshu. Nympha married Lou Byrne and is the mother of Shunee, Roy, Shane and Kimberley. She is also the sister of Christine Poker and the daughter of Cecile Rich.

Camille Fouillard has been work-ing with the Innu for the last 15 years in the areas of community development, activism and advo-cacy. Through her work, she has helped create many forums for the Innu to tell their stories. She served as coordinator of the 1992 Davis Inlet People's Inquiry. The Inquiry report, *Gathering Voices: Finding the Strength to Help Our Children* (Douglas & McIntyre, 1995), has attracted a great deal of attention  for its innovative methodology, and the candidness of the voices gathered. She worked on a number of other community consult-ations in Davis Inlet and Sheshatshui, including one on the pro-posed Voisey's Bay mine and on land claims negotiations. Camille is also a freelance researcher, writer and photographer. Last but not least, she is the mom of Esmée.

Charlotte Gregoire is the sister of Mary Jane Nui and the sister-in-law of Miste Mani-Aten, Tshaukuish and Rose Gregoire. She is the

Tom Green

daughter of Mineshkuesh (Theresa) and Tshenish (Charles James Pasteen), and the granddaughter of Miste Mani-Shan (Mary Jane Pasteen). As a young woman she worked in the hospital in North West River, where she met and married Shuash (George Gregoire). They raised their seven children — Jerry, Jacqueline, Elizabeth, Peter, George, Jonah and adopted son, Jerry — in Utshimassits. She travels to *nutshimit* with her family whenever she can. She is very skilled in *nutshimit*, not only in the women's work, but she can do any kind of men's work as well. She likes to do beadwork and to sew. She makes items such as moccasins and mitts for her family or to sell. In the community, she occasionally works as a home-care worker or janitor.

Camille Fouillard

Rose Gregoire is the daughter of Shimun and Mani (Simon and Mary Gregoire). She is the younger sister of Miste Mani-Aten (Mary Adele Andrew) and Tshaukuish (Elizabeth Penashue), and the sister-in-law of Shanut (Charlotte) Gregoire. She lives with Richard Adams and their four children — Janet, Christopher, Moosy (Richard) and Theresa — and her two grand-children, Nikisha and Nigel. She completed Grade Nine in school and went on to graduate from a nursing assistant course in St. John's in 1969. She worked at different jobs: in the hospital in North West River, as a counsellor for the alcohol program in

Sheshatshu, and with Social Services for 14 years. She was part of the group of women who spearheaded the Innu protests against NATO's military flight training over Labrador. She has also been central to the healing work in her community, particularly in helping women and children who have survived sexual abuse. She now works in a shelter for women and families who are escaping violence in their homes.

Mary Martha Hurley is the daugh-ter of Miste Mani-Aten and Mat-shieu (Mary Adele and Matthew Ben Andrew). She is one of 15 children. Her Innu name is Mani-Mat. She married Melvin Hurley, from whom she is now separated. They had two children, Pamela and Natasha, and adopted a son, Trevor, from her sister Justine. She completed Grade Nine in school, but returned to university to obtain an education diploma. She has taught at Peenamin Mackenzie School for 10 years. In the early 1980s, Mary Martha started to return to *nutshimit* regularly with her young family in the spring and fall. She was one of the key women organizers of a series of protests against NATO military flight training over Innu land. She spent the longest time in jail of all Innu arrested for these direct actions. She has travelled all over Canada, as far away as Yellowknife, to share stories of the Innu struggle.

Camille Fouillard

Natasha Hurley is the daughter of Mary Martha and Melvin Hurley. She was born in 1982. She now attends high school in Sheshatshu and hopes to graduate in 2001. She likes to write and play volleyball on her school team. In 1997, Natasha and a group of her friends organized a youth theatre group. They produced an

original play, which was a candid and disturbing portrayal of the social problems of their community. She used to like to spend time in *nutshimit* with her grandmother Miste Mani-Aten (Mary Adele Andrew). She learned to do many things from her. She could even clean a caribou skin by herself. As a young girl, Natasha was involved in the anti-NATO protests on the military runways in Goose Bay. This was part of her education in land rights. She wrote many letters to her mother while Mani-Mat was in jail.

Pamela Hurley is the daughter of Mary Martha and Melvin Hurley. She is 20 years old and grew up in Sheshatshu. She graduated from Peenamin Mackenzie School in 1997 and is now studying for her Bachelor of Science degree at Dalhousie University in Halifax. Pamela walked with her grandmother Miste Mani-Aten (Mary Adele Andrew), her mother and others on the military airport runways in protest of NATO low-level flying. She remembers this time as one when she was very proud of her family for fighting for their beliefs. She is an avid volleyball player, and in her spare time she likes to read. She is still undecided about what she wants to do when she finishes university but is leaning toward something in the field of sciences.

Justine Noah Jack was born to Manian and Shimunish (Mary Ann and Simon Noah). Her grandparents were Ueuete-miskueu and Tumish (Alice and Thomas Noah). She married Michael Jack and they have three children: Nelly, Virginia and Denise. For many years she worked as an office clerk for the Innu Nation and as a court interpreter. In 1993, she graduated from the First Nations' Tribal Justice Institute in Mission,

B.C., then returned to Utshimassits, where she has worked as a peacekeeper ever since. She was the first of three Innu to become peacekeepers, and the only woman so far. She would like to see other Innu women follow in her footsteps. She believes that would make her job easier. She would like to see more Innu trained to work in all the different positions in the justice system. In June 1999, Justine also graduated with a high-school diploma.

Madeline Katshinak is 73 years old. She is the daughter of Shinipest and Mani-Shan (Sylvester and Mary Jane). She married Shushep (Joseph Katshinak) and they adopted two children — Tanien (Daniel Poker) and Mani-Akat (Mary Agathe Rich) — when they were very small. She is from Utshimassits, but now lives in Goose Bay, ever since her husband had a stroke and was placed in a seniors' care home. Her health is also failing and her eyesight is poor, although she still

Nympha Byrne

manages to make moccasins to sell. She said these days are a far cry from those when their health was good and their bodies strong enough to walk from as far as Kauishatukuants to Sheshatshu. Those were the days when the only supplies they needed that did not come from the land were flour and tea.

Tom Green

Mary Georgette Mistenapeo's Innu name is Manteskueu. She was born in a place called Kauashauet-inats in 1941. She married Edward Mistenapeo and they raised eight children in Utshimassits: Mary Theresa, Sarah, Sam, Yvonne, William, Anne Stella, Eric and Nora. She also adopted Alberta Tuma. She says she has too many grandchildren to count. In 1992 she served as commissioner for the People's Inquiry, a community self-examination organized by leaders and elders after six children died in a house fire. In 1997, she was a member of a community research project that produced a video to document socio-economic realities of the Innu as part of the environmental-assessment process for the proposed Inco nickel mine at Emish. She also sat on the Mushuau Innu Renewal Committee, which is overseeing the construction of a new community in Natuashish for the Mushuau Innu of Utshi-massits. She has been a church leader at different times, but is no longer as active with the church. Since this story was told, Manteskueu has lost a second daughter and a grandson to suicide. She continues to practise Innu traditional medicines, and makes crafts such as moccasins and gloves for her family or to sell.

Mary Jane Nui's Innu name is Ketshastipineu. She was born in Ashuapun and is 63 years old. She married Shuashim (Joachim Nui) and had eight children: Marcel, Elizabeth, David, Jimmy, Mark, John, Clarence and Mary Ann. She says she has stopped having babies! She has many grandchildren to look after — 22 in all. Mary Jane has long been active as a Catholic Church leader. She has also been involved in many community groups, including the Northern Innu Health Council and the women's group Innu Iskueut. She also sits on the Mushuau Innu Re-

Tom Green

newal Committee, which was set up to oversee the relocation of the Utshimassiu Innu to Natuashish. She has been involved in a number of protests, including protests at Emish and a protest against the Cabot 500 celebrations in Bonavista, Newfoundland. She likes to make moccasins, snowshoes and mitts for her family or to sell. She has also been active in healing work with her community, including circles and sweats.

Mary Madeline Nuna's Innu name is Mani-Matini. She married Tshutauish (Joseph Nuna) and had nine children: Pien, Theresa, Basil, Daniel, Anne Marie, Justine, Emmett, Edward and Greg. She now has 35 grandchil-

Nympha Byrne

dren and 19 great-grandchildren. She always enjoyed spending time in *nutshimit*, although she never had a chance to go often because her husband worked on the military base in Goose Bay. She also likes to spend time with her family. She dislikes community life because of all the social problems faced by the Innu today. She was widowed three years ago and now lives with her grandchildren Alex and Anshenik. For many years, she worked as the janitor at the band council, but she is now retired.

Edward O'Brien

Mary Jane Pasteen's Innu name was Miste Mani-Shan. She was Ketshastipineu's (Mary Jane Nui) and Shanut (Charlotte) Gregoire's grandmother. She was born around 1875 somewhere along the Ashuapun-shipu, which empties into Emish. Her father was Netuapeu and her mother was Nenitshitau. Miste Mani-Shan was married twice. With her first husband, Pashin (Basil Katshinak), she had five children. With her second husband, Miste Ueapeu (John Pasteen), she had two sons: Tshenish and Nastamkapu or Unborn Child. She lived to be over 100 years old and passed on to her children a legacy of knowledge about the Innu culture and ways that still lives on.

Elizabeth Penashue's Innu name is Tshaukuish. She is from Sheshatshu. She married Francis Penashue, with whom she had nine children: Peter, Max, Jack, Gervais, Angela, Kanani, Bart, Frederic and Robert. She also now has 25 grandchildren. She continues to spend time in *nutshimit* in the spring and fall. The rest of the time, she sets up her tent along the road between Sheshatshu and Goose Bay, a spot where she goes to relax and get away from the stresses of the community. Tshaukuish was a leader in the protests against NATO's low-level military flight training, for which she spent time in jail. She continues to fight to protect the land on many different fronts and is an articulate ambassador, speaking out for Innu rights across Canada and Europe. In the last couple of years, she has begun to organize trips along traditional Innu travel routes. In August 1999, she organized a canoe trip down Mishta-shipu and in April 1999 she pulled together a group for a 100-mile trek through the bush from Sheshat-shu to Minai-nipi.

Catherine Poker's Innu name is Katinin. She is the daughter of Kani-uekutat and Mata (John and Martha Poker). She lost her mother at a very young age. She lived with her father until he died. She spent a lot of time with him in *nut-shimit* during the summer and springtime, well into her adult life.  She also attended school in both Kauishatukuants and Sheshatshu. She remembers fishing and drying cod on the rocks with her father in Kauishatukuants. She has two children: Tuma (Thomas) and Tshemish (James). She likes to do crafts, to tan caribou skin and to make moccasins and other craft items. She is well versed in *nutshimit* skills, for example, she knows how to clean the caribou after the kill.

Camille Fouillard

Christine Poker is the daughter of Miste Shishin and Tami (Cecile and Tommy Rich). She is the sister of Nympha and Aldea. Christine married Prote Poker and has six children: Aaron, Simeon, Tommy, Timmy, Joyce Marie and Tony. She has also taken in and cared for

other children at different times. Christine is a gifted artist and poet. In 1997, she was a member of a community research project that produced a video to document socio-economic realities of the Innu as part of the environmental-assessment process for the proposed Inco nickel mine at Emish. The group produced a video called Ntapueu (I Tell You the Truth). She has also received funding to produce another video. She works with the Innu Health Commission as a counsellor. She is one of the organizers of the mobile treatment programs in *nutshimit*. She also still likes to bring her family to *nutshimit* whenever she can in the spring or fall.

Marie Pokue is from Utshimassits, the daughter of Shimun and Shaet (Simon and Janet Poker). In 1977 when Marie was only 12 years old, she lost her parents and most of her siblings in an alcohol-related boating accident. In 1995 Marie shared this story in a BBC television documentary called *Between Two Worlds* of the Innu. Marie married Simon Pokue and has five children: Dorothy, Darren, Donna, Damien and Desiree. Marie trained as an addictions counsellor and has worked with a family-violence project in Utshimassits as well as with Social Services for six years. She has served three terms on the Innu Nation board of directors. She now lives in Goose Bay and has returned to school to obtain her high school diploma. She plans to go on to university to study social work.

Aldea Rich is the daughter of Miste Shishin and Tami (Cecile and Tommy Rich), and the sister of Nympha Byrne and Christine Poker. Aldea's boyfriend, Mathias, died of a heart attack as a young man and left her to raise their three children — Robbie, Cheryl and Jessica — on her own. She returned to school to get her high-school diploma and is now working as the assistant to the public health nurse. She has also worked at the  store and with the Mushuau Band Council. She likes to take her children out hunting in *nutshimit*.

Cecile Rich is the daughter of Shinipest and Mani-Shan (Sylvester and Mary Jane Rich). Cecile's parents died young, leaving Cecile and her brothers and sisters — Matinin (Madeline), Pinamen (Philomena),  Anatusk (Frances) and Nissikutshash or Squirrel (Raphael) — to find new families to care for them. Cecile married Tami (Tommy Rich) and has eight children: Akat, Christine, Nympha, Judith, Andre, Aldea, Ben and Garry. She also has 31 grandchildren and three great-grand-children. Her Innu name is Miste Shishin. Cecile has been a widow for 14 years, but she still tries to spend as much time in

Joel Rich

nutshimit as possible with her children's families. Her sons hunt for her. She is active making crafts and periodically is hired by the Mushuau Band Council to teach traditional skills, such as tanning hides and making moccasins, to young people. Recently she has become more active in public meetings, where she participates in decision making with other elders concerned with issues that affect the land and the community. She has also been active in recent protests against the mining development at Emish and the proposed hydro development of the Lower Churchill.

Camille Fouillard

Cecilia Rich was born to Katie and George Rich, one of seven children. She grew up in Sheshatshu and was orphaned at the age of eight. She completed high school and attended Memorial University for two years in St. John's. She has two children: Seraphine and Raphanel George. In 1990 she participated in a six-month treatment program in St. John's for sexual-abuse survivors. She has been involved in a couple of research programs with the Innu Nation, for example, a study on social assistance and the Innu, and a study on the differences between life in the community and life in *nutshimit*. For a number of years she was the manager of a local musical group called Meshikamau. She has worked as interpreter in a number of capacities. Over the years she has represented her community at many women's conferences across Canada.

Charlotte Rich's Innu name is Utshimaskueu, or Boss Woman. She says she is 67 years old, or maybe she is 41? She was born in *nutshimit* at a time when birthdays meant nothing to Innu people, and church documents are often not accurate. There may be a record of her birth at the Catholic mission office in the community. Her parents were Etamanisheshish and Shenapeu (Ann and Ponas Rich). After Charlotte married Masku-tiskum (David Rich), they had three children: Justine, Mary Ann and Damien. Her son died at birth and was buried in the Emish area. Her favourite animal is the porcu-pine. She has cleaned many porcu-pines in her day. Her eyesight is very poor now, so she is unable to

Camille Fouillard

do many of the things she used to like, but she still likes to tell stories about the old days. She is a member of the Mushuau Innu Renewal Committee, responsible for overseeing the move of the community from Utshimassits to Natuashish.

Elizabeth Rich was born in 1937 and is 63 years old. Her Innu name is Miste Nishapet. She was one of 13 children born to Akat and Shushepiss Rich. She was born in *nutshimit* with the help of an Innu midwife called Utshimaskuess, or Boss Girl. Nishapet never married but, as is common in Innu tradi-tion, was given a son to raise by her brother and his wife. She lives with her son, Rocky, his girlfriend and their two children. She began do-

Camille Fouillard

ing beadwork and making moccasins in her early teens and still practises many of the traditional skills she learned from her mother. Today, her beadwork articles stand out from many for their colour-ful, traditional, as well as original, designs.

Camille Fouillard

Katie Rich is the daughter of Munik and Miste Pinip (Monique and Philip Rich). Nympha Byrne's and Katie's grandfathers, Joseph and Sylvester, were brothers. Katie is the mother of six: Nachelle, Dawn Marie, Hillary, Nigel, Philip and Petapeu (Jonathan). She is also the grandmother of three. In 1992 she was the first woman to be elected chief of Utshimassits. She spearheaded the People's Inquiry, a community self-examination after a house fire killed six children. In December 1993, Katie led a group of women to evict Judge Robert Hyslop and his court from the community. Her list of accomplishments also includes extracting a commitment from the federal government to fund the relocation of the people of Utshimassits to Natuashish on the Labrador mainland. In 1995, Rich's militancy and determination earned her the Woman of Courage Award from the National Action Committee on the Status of Women. She was also the first woman elected president of the Innu Nation. In 1998, she left politics to look after her family, including her grandchildren. She also worked for a time as a homemaker, tending to an elderly aunt. She now also does a lot of sewing, trying to learn from the elders to do things for herself.

The late **Shanut Rich** (Charlotte) was the daughter of Mani-Upisiskuik and Apinam Uitshimakan. She married Etienne Rich and they had 14 children, 8 of whom died as children from illnesses. The six who survived are Maggie, Lionel, Theresa, Leona, Louis and Louisa. After she began to live in Sheshatshu, Shanut attended mass regularly. She liked to sing gospel songs in Innu-aimun. She also liked to return to *nutshimit* every summer with her family, often at Kenemu, from June until September. Shanut was skilled at crafts. She made snowshoes and moccasins, and knit socks and sweaters.

José Mailhot

She also made winter coats, which she sold to women in the village. She liked to help people out whenever she could. She would go to people's houses when someone had died, and help the family prepare the body for burial. She would also visit elders every Sunday. She died in 1971 at the age of 36, leaving a young family to fend for itself. Her daughter Theresa remembers how her mother would often tell legends to her children at bedtime before they dozed off to sleep, an Innu tradition that lives on today. The legend "Mishtapeu" was originally collected on tape in 1967 from Shanut by student anthropologists Madeleine Lefebvre and Robert Lanari. Her cousin Uinipapeu (Shushep Mak Rich) served as an interpreter.

Glossary

Standardized spellings are listed in square brackets after the spellings used in this text.

akaneshau = Sheshatshu word for "anglophone" now used to refer to all White persons

Anik-napeu = the Toadman

assiminiapi = kind of babiche

atipish = kind of babiche

atshen = cannibal beings

eshun [eshkan] = ice pick

esiutshiuap [aissiutshuap] = moss house

espeshetshimeuean [ashpishatshimeuian] = canopy

espikun [ashpikun] = caribou shawls

eissimeskueu = Eskimo woman

Innu-aimu = the name of the Innu language, literally "Innu words"

kakeshau (sing.), *kakeshauts* (pl.) = Davis Inlet word for "anglophone," now used to refer to all White persons

kakuskuesh = porcupine girl

kamakunuest = police; literally the Man Who Locks People Up *kamanitushit* = shaman who performs the shaking tent ceremony

kamituatshet [kaiamituatshet] = bishop

kauapishissits = smelts

kautashapits = Indians with bows and arrows

Kuekuatsheu = the wolverine, the trickster

kukumesh [kukamess] = lake trout

kushapatshikan = shaking tent ceremony

manteuts [maniteu (sing.), *maniteuat* (pl.)] = visitors

mekanepakan [makanipakan (sing.) makanipakana (pl.)] = shovels

metshu [mitshishu] = eagle

mikuta = Labrador tea

Mishtapeu (sing.), *Mishtapeuats* (pl.) = Giant Spirit(s)

mitishantshuap [matishenitshuap] = sweat lodge

mitshikun = scraper for cleaning caribou hides

makushan = Feast of the Caribou

namesh = my sister, also fish

natesh = my brother

nikau = my mother

ntapueu = I tell you the truth

nukum = my grandmother

numushum = my grandfather

nutau = my father

nutshimit = the country

pimin [pimi] = caribou grease

pipitsheu = robin

shashakuatipeshish = sparrow

Tshementun [Tshishemanitu] = the Creator

tshenut = the elders

Uapishtan-napeu = Marten spirit

Uhuapeu = Owl spirit

uiskatshai [uishkatshan] = whisky-jack

utatshinakeaskut [utatshinakanashk^u (sing.),
utatshinakanashkuts (pl.)] = komatik, or sled

Utinimatsheshu = Spirit Who Gives the Animals to the
People, Master of All the Animals

utshimau (sing.), *utshimauats* (pl.) = leader(s)

List of Place Names

Akamiuapishk^u = Mealy Mountains

Antenak = Anaktalak Bay

Ashuapun = Border Beacon

Ashuapun-shipu = Kogaluk River

Atatshuinipek^u = Lake Melville

Emish = Voisey's Bay

Estinekamuk [Ashtunekamik^u] = Snegamook

Kakatshu-utshistun or Raven's Nest = Grand Lake

Kakesekauts [Kakissekaut] = Fast Rapids

Kamishtashtin = Mestastin Lake

Kamikuakamiu-shipu = Red Wine River

Kamisteueshekat = a place near Miste-shantish (Daniel Rattle)

Kamitishanikants = a lake where Matshieu Ben Andrew used to hunt

Kamashkushiut = a camping place near Kauishatukuants

Kaniapishkau = Caniapiscau River

Kanishutakushtasht = Flower's Bay

Kantshekakamat = a lake between Schefferville and
Uaskaikan (Kuujjuaq)

Kanutemuantsh = a place west of Sango Bay

Kapapist = Big Bay

Kapukuanipant = Jack's Brook

Kashakaskueiats = a camping place

Kashatshipet-ashinin = The Rock that Sticks Out of
Water

Kashupaset-unipim = a lake

Kauashauetinats = near Border Beacon, where Maneskuen
was born

Kauinipishit-namesh = Black Fish

Kauishatukuants = Old Davis Inlet

Kaushetinatshi = a place in the Border Beacon area

Kawawashikamach = a Mushuau Innu community next to
Schefferville

*Kutshinapesh-minishtik*ᵘ = Edmund's Place

Metshituaunapeu kashuaku = the place where
Nisikutshash (Raphael Rich) went sliding

Minaik = Menihek Lake

Minai-nipi = Burbot Lake

Mishikamau = Mishikamau Lake, now part of the
Smallwood Reservoir

Mishta-natuashu = Sango Lake

Mishta-paustuk [originally *Patshetshuna*] = Churchill
Falls

Mishta-shipu = Churchill River

Mishta-minishtik[u] = Big Island

Mishta-nipi = Mistinippi Lake

Mishta-shanipass = Daniel Rattle

Mushuau-shipu = George River

Natuashish = Sango Pond, where the community of Davis Inlet will be relocated

Nent = Nain, a community north of Kauishatukuants

Nitassinan = Our Homeland

Nutak = a community north of Nain

Pakutapin = Tasialuk Lake

Petshishkapishkau = the place where the Toadman lives

Knob La = previously called Schefferville

Shankus = Sango Bay

Shanti = Sandy Brook

Shanut = a camping place

Shapiass = a place near Shapio Lake

Sheshatshu = a community across the river from North West River

Takutauat = Goose Bay

Uashat = Sept Iles

Uaskaikan = Fort Chimo or Kuujjuaq

Utshimassits = Davis Inlet

Best of gynergy books

Pat Lowther's Continent: Her Life and Work, Toby Brooks. Pat Lowther was a down-to- earth woman of considerable talent whose life ended tragically at age 40 at the hands of a jealous and violent husband. Toby Brooks has seamlessly woven together the many threads of Pat Lowther's life — her poetry, her activism, her children, her marriages, her love of nature, her struggles and her triumphs — into a colourful and intimate tapestry.

ISBN 0-921881-54-1 $24.95 Can. $19.95 U.S.

Sweeping the Earth: Women Taking Action for a Healthy Planet, **Miriam Wyman** (ed.). "… a large and long overdue contribution to our knowledge of how human-generated pollutants are affecting our health, our bodies and ourselves. We should feel the rising tide of anger at losing so many of our mothers and sisters and daughters to the 'downside' of the Industrial Revolution. We must launch our new revolution to detoxify the planet. *Sweeping the Earth* provides the spark." Elizabeth May, Executive Director, Sierra Club

ISBN 0-921881-48-7 $26.95 Can. $21.95 U.S.

gynerby books titles are available in quality bookstores everywhere. Ask for our books at your favourite local bookstore. **gynergy books** are distributed by University of Toronto Press, 1-800-565-9523, utpbooks@utpress.utoronto.ca